COURT & COUNTRY

Also by A. L. Rowse

The Elizabethan Age:
The England of Elizabeth I
The Expansion of Elizabethan England
The Elizabethan Renaissance: (1) The Life of the Society;
  (2) The Cultural Achievement

Tudor Cornwall
Sir Richard Grenville of the *Revenge*
Ralegh and the Throckmortons
Shakespeare's Southampton: Patron of Virginia
The Elizabethans and America

Shakespeare the Man
Christopher Marlowe
Simon Forman: Sex and Society in Shakespeare's Age
Milton the Puritan: Portrait of a Mind
Reflections on the Puritan Revolution

The Early Churchills
The Later Churchills
Jonathan Swift: Major Prophet
The Use of History

The Cornish in America
A Life: Collected Poems

Court & Country

Studies in Tudor Social History

A L Rowse

The University of Georgia Press
Athens

Published in the United States of America
in 1987 by the University of Georgia Press,
Athens, Georgia 30602

First published in Great Britain in 1987 by
The Harvester Press Limited

ISBN 0–8203–0975–3

Printed in Great Britain

To
David C. Treffry
on his return to Cornwall

Contents

Preface

This is a work of historical research, though I hope not in the unreadable sense of the word. Much of it is based on original manuscript sources, mostly unpublished, and therefore new.

The theme which the book illustrates in detail is given by my title, the rhythm and reaction between government and social life at the centre and those in the localities. These illustrations in various chapters are mainly, though not wholly, from the West Country; in this the book may be regarded as a sequel to my *Tudor Cornwall*, though here the geographical scope is wider.

'Honor Grenville, Lady Lisle, and her Circle' is in part a by-product of my *Sir Richard Grenville of the Revenge*. Since then we have been given a splendid edition of the *Lisle Letters* by Miss St Clair Byrne. But my work, *pari passu* with hers, was based on the originals in the *Letters and Papers of Henry VIII* (with other documents). I am glad that she also chose to modernise the spelling: ye olde Tudor tea-shoppe spelling is mere academic pedantry.

'Edward Courtenay, Last Earl of Devon of the Elder Line' is based on his unpublished Correspondence among the State Papers in the Public Record Office. Many years ago I brought to light the Diary of William Carnsew, from an unlighted source there—SP 46, State Papers Supplementary. Here I have taken the opportunity to make it readable in modern spelling, and fill out the background with information from various sources. Similarly with 'Richard Carew, Antiquary'. His *Survey of Cornwall* is sufficiently well-known for itself; here I have brought out his life and work from less familiar sources.

Richard Topcliffe and Henry Cuffe were controversial characters, but neither has had historical justice done him, nor has there been much information about, let alone a full account of, either of them. Fortunately I possess a unique book, Topcliffe's own copy of Pollini's scandalous *Historia Ecclesiastica della Rivoluzion d'Inghilterra*, based on the lying aspersions of the *émigrés* against Elizabeth I, Henry VIII and Anne Boleyn. Topcliffe's frequent Marginalia, corroborated by external evidence, give us valuable information, much of it new, some of it scandalous on the other side. Henry Cuffe's story is told here for the first time and justice done him, I hope; though his relationship to Essex and his tragic fate are well-known, his originality as a thinker has not hitherto been appreciated.

Sir Peter Carew and Sir Richard Hawkins are familiar characters, but I have been able to add something new to our knowledge of their eventful careers.

A.L.R.

1

Honor Grenville, Lady Lisle, and her Circle

The Grenvilles and the Bassets both belonged to the Norman upper rank of West Country gentry, where in Cornwall the indigenous families are distinguishable by the prefix Tre, Pol, or Pen—as in Trevelyan, Polwhele, Penrose. Both Grenvilles and Bassets went back to the twelfth century, if not to the Norman Conquest as they claimed. The Grenvilles early established themselves on the wild north coast of Cornwall and Devon, with their home at Stowe in the parish of Kilkhampton, on that high but fertile plateau running in from the cliffs, with their town and harbour at Bideford at the mouth of the Torridge in Devon.

The Bassets were established—right up to our time—at Tehidy in the parish of Illogan in West Cornwall, on the no less inhospitable north coast there, their estate running inland across pasture and heath and rabbit warrens, all good sporting country, right up to the spectacular crag of Carn Brea, with its medieval hunting lodge on the crest. All this country proved to be rich in tin and copper, which eventually made the Cornish Bassets rich indeed, though mining destroyed the woodlands. In the fifteenth century a John Basset married the Devon heiress of the Beaumonts, and this brought them the considerable estates of Umberleigh, Sherwill and Heanton Punchardon.

The grandson of this fortunate marriage, Sir John Basset, married as his second wife, Honor Grenville, daughter of Sir Thomas Grenville of Stowe. By his first wife Basset had only a couple of daughters; he was considerably older than his second wife, and she produced a mass of children, sons and daughters, to safeguard the inheritance. By this time, round

about 1500, the Bassets made their principal residence at
Umberleigh in the valley of the Torridge, a large mansion
equipped with chantry chapel to pray for the souls of their
provident ancestors—of all of which nothing remains, only
the bridge by which they crossed the river. High up on the
hill, in this precipitous country, in their parish church of
Atherington are the effigies removed from the chantry chapel
when the old male line came to an end in 1802 and the chapel
was pulled down. Here too is the tomb of Sir John Basset
with his two wives, himself in full armour, the ladies in the
archaic headdress of an earlier generation, wide ermine
sleeves, at foot the arms of Basset and his Grenville wife,
through whom the family was to continue.

Basset had the usual career of a country gentleman, sheriff
of Devon and so on. In 1525 we find him attending the
grand funeral of Catherine, Countess of Devon, who was the
daughter of Edward IV. Yorkist royal blood brought
grievous trouble upon the Courtenays under the Tudors,
heirs of both Lancaster and York. In January 1529 Sir John
died, and shortly his well-dowered widow married Edward
IV's illegitimate son, Arthur Plantagenet, Viscount Lisle.
Born about 1480, he too was considerably older than Honor
Grenville, had been previously married but had only daughters by his first wife. This was the widow of Edmund
Dudley—attainted along with Empson in Henry VIII's first
year as the too efficient financial agents of his father. She
was the daughter of Edward Grey, Viscount Lisle—the name
was pronounced Lisley in Tudor days—and on his death the
title was re-created for Arthur Plantagenet.

This illegitimate uncle was treated with favour by Henry
VIII in his earlier happier days. Made an esquire of the
Body on Henry's accession, he obtained protection from his
creditors by going to sea on the expedition to Brittany in
1513, in Henry's first French war.[1] The ship struck a rock,
and 'when he was in the extreme danger and all hope gone,
he called upon our Lady of Walsingham for help, and offered
unto her a vow that, as it pleased God and her to deliver
him out of that peril, he would never eat flesh nor fish till
he had seen her.' The Lady obliged, and Arthur went on
pilgrimage to Walsingham, revived in our time, which has
reverted to so much else of the sixteenth century.

That summer Plantagenet accompanied Henry across the Channel to cavort on his French campaign, and next year appears as captain in the *Trinity Sovereign*. In 1519 he and his wife succeeded to the lands of her brother and sister, briefly married to the Princess Catherine's son, Henry Earl of Devon, later executed as Marquis of Exeter by his cousin, Henry VIII. However, all was well for the present: in 1522 Plantagenet accompanied his nephew to the Field of the Cloth of Gold and next year was created Viscount Lisle, with remainder to his heirs male, which so far he had not achieved. In 1524 he was elected a Knight of the Garter and got the keepership of the royal park of Clarendon. In 1527 he headed an embassy to present Francis I with the insignia of the Garter, when a new turn in policy necessitated a rapprochement with France against the overmighty Emperor, Charles V.

For some years Lisle was without a wife, his first wife having died in 1523. Sir John Basset's death gave him an opening to another eligible widow, who had already given evidence of ability to produce an heir. Everything shows that the match between him and Lady Basset was a love-match. Lisle had the easy-going attractiveness of his father, Edward IV, though not his ability; Honor had the forceful personality of the Grenvilles and she was the dominant partner.

Her marriage brought her into the immediate Court circle, an exaltation which had its dangers as well as its privileges and charms. Evidence of both comes from the Lisle Correspondence, the most remarkable to survive from the early Tudor period—as unique and rewarding for its time as the famous Paston Letters of the century before. Only the Lisle Letters have not yet won the fame that is their due too, for they long remained sunk in the unwieldy form of the huge tomes of the *Letters and Papers of Henry VIII*.[2]

The Letters are fascinating from every point of view, political and personal, and for the history of the time. Especially for the picture they give of its social life in Court and country, and at Calais, where the Lisles ruled vice-regally, on the border where England and France met, illuminating of both. For the life of the Court the portrayal is as vivid and realistic as the portraits of Holbein—though, where those are static, here we see life in motion, year by year, day

by day. Somewhere in the mass of Holbein's representations
of denizens of the Court may be those of the Lisles, uniden-
tified and unknown to us—as we recognise others who make
their appearance in the Letters: Sir Brian Tuke, Sir Thomas
Wyatt and Sir Francis Bryan, Lord Russell and the Fitzwil-
liam Earl of Southampton, the Lady Mary and the little
Prince Edward; and again and again the mighty, overbearing
figure of Henry VIII himself, in his differing moods, courtly
and affable, impatient and bonhomous, and then—the swift
stroke of the capricious *faux-bonhomme*.

Naturally Lady Lisle's letters are full of the details of early
Tudor dress and its materials—those favourite colours of the
time, tawny and blue—velvets, silks and satins, the furs of
various animals, with the prices. We learn an immense
amount about the housekeeping of the time, provisions of
all kinds, what they ate and what they fancied—quails and
herons from the marshes around Calais, puffins and gulls
from Cornwall; victuals and French wines, furniture and
jewels, horses and ships. Presents are constantly exchanged;
the Lisles were extravagant, and Lady Lisle over-generous.
For economists, we have prices in profusion; for the
religious, the envenomed disputes that eventually caught up
with them and brought about their downfall. For the Letters,
from 1533 to 1540, cover the dangerous period of the breach
with Rome, the dissolution of the monasteries, the Act of
Supremacy, the fall of Anne Boleyn, the marriage of Jane
Seymour and the birth of Prince Edward, the non-marriage
of Anne of Cleves, the consequent fall of Cromwell; then
Lisle's own relegation to the Tower.

The fortunes of the Bassets got a brief recovery under
Queen Mary—for Lady Lisle remained Catholic, and her
clever son James Basset became prominent as gentleman of
the Privy Chamber and confidential attendant of Bishop
Gardiner. But James Basset died even before the Queen,
leaving an infant son, named Philip after the Queen's consort,
to grow up feeble and helpless in the inclement atmosphere of
the Elizabethan age. For this branch of the Bassets continued
Catholic into the next century. The Letters begin blithely
with the Lisles' good fortune, and end under the black clouds
of the crisis of Henry's rule and of the Reformation. Thus
they are not only intimately revealing but historically

representative—so much more authentic than any thesis or any amount of argumentation: life itself, real and raw.

When the Correspondence begins the Lisles are settled at Soberton in Hampshire, near Bishop's Waltham, convenient for Portsmouth and Southampton, for Lisle was Vice-Admiral along that coast. He was active in the county on various commissions, had been sheriff, and served his turn in the House of Lords. In 1527 he was in touch with Robert Thorne, the interesting Seville merchant to whom we owe much of our earliest information about Spain in the New World. In October 1532 the Lisles accompanied the King to Calais, the object of the journey being to present Anne Boleyn, as Marchioness of Pembroke, to the French Court, an official recognition of her position and approaching marriage. On the last Sunday of the month Francis I supped with Henry. Afterwards Anne, the Lady Mary (little can she have liked the occasion), Lady Rochford (Anne's sister-in-law), Lady Lisle, and three more ladies came in masked and danced with the French King and his lords. Henry then took off the ladies' visors and all danced for another hour. The rumour was that Henry intended to marry Anne during the visit. This did not take effect, however; it may be that Francis I persuaded him to wait a little longer. Not until Anne became pregnant in January were they privately married, in hope of an heir.

Cromwell made the Lisles a supper there on All Hallows day (November 1st). Arrived at Soberton Lady Lisle returned £20 Cromwell had lent Lisle and sent him two cheeses 'and such wildfowl as I can get.' She wished to know of his safe return, for they themselves had been in great peril for lack of a good pilot. (Her balinger, the *Sunday*, had to be repaired.) Her steward at Umberleigh, John Davy, wrote 'Thanks be to God for the safe coming home of my lord and your ladyship, for here was great discomfort. The mill is in decay and must be repaired, or it will hurt your fishing.' He sent on the accounts of Umberleigh and Tehidy. That summer he had put into boxes the deeds of her jointure, and reported the heriots that fell due on the death of two tenants at Whitechapel—two oxen, for which the widows had paid in 32s. Among those who had had the deer at Umberleigh

last summer were her nephew, Sir Richard Grenville, Sir
William Courtenay, and the Chancellor of Exeter. The prior
of neighbouring Southwick apologised for having no duties
to send the Lisles towards their heavy charges at the King's
visit to Calais.

There had been trouble with Lord Daubeney (later to
become Earl of Bridgwater) who had sold timber from the
manor of Beaford. This was the harbinger of prolonged
dispute over a complicated land settlement. The Basset heir
was to succeed to certain lands in case of the failure of male
heirs to Bridgwater—which was at it turned out. In February
the King was writing to Lisle that the deer in his park at
Clarendon were much decayed: if Lisle did not take better
care he would commit the keepership to others. Next month,
a sign of favour, he gave the wardship and marriage of the
Basset heir, who was a minor, to Lisle.

The family figured at the sumptuous coronation of Anne
Boleyn, intended as a demonstration by Henry of his
potency. At the grand banquet in Westminster Hall Lisle
figured as chief pantler, in charge of the provision of bread
for the multitude; Sir Richard Grenville, who had a Court
office as sewer of the Chamber, was among the servitors at
the Queen's board.

The visit to Calais was the prelude to Lisle's appointment
as Lord Deputy, in succession to Lord Berners, the famous
translator of Froissart. This vice-regal post was one of both
eminence and strategic importance as the key to the control
of the Channel, the last outpost of English possessions on
the Continent from which to keep an eye on France. ('Spial-
money', forming the largest element in the Lord Deputy's
emoluments, makes the effective point.) Lisle wished to have
Lord Berners' lodging there; the gardener was retained to
keep the house and garden sweet till he came. The King sent
for all the pheasants Berners had kept—who had also kept a
retinue of forty servants. Lisle would keep ten or a dozen
places for men recommended; at once Henry's sister, Mary,
formerly 'the French Queen', wrote in her shaky hand for a
place for a soldier. This kind of thing was usual, and later
gave trouble.

At once the letters begin, which we are so fortunate to
have, impounded with all the Lisles' papers when he was

sent to the Tower. They flow to and fro across the Channel
in ever-increasing numbers until they become a flood in their
last years at Calais, 1539–40. Here is Thomas St Aubyn, who
had married Honor's sister Mary, writing on All Hallows'
eve 1533, from Clowance the neighbouring estate to Tehidy,
where he acted as steward for his sister-in-law during her
son's minority. He has attended all her manor-courts, though
the casualties and profits are not as good this year as last;
and has been out at the 'washes' early and late to see that
she loses nothing of her tolls. This refers to the tin-streams,
for the area was rich in minerals, which—in the immense
development of mining there in the 18th and 19th centuries—
made a great fortune for the lucky Bassets, utterly wasted in
our time.

Thomas thanks her for her gift of conies from the warrens
at Tehidy—open to the north shore, the sand dunes and the
Atlantic winds blowing. He sends her a dozen puffins from
that coast—more to come for Lent—which Boswarthogga
and John Keigwin (good Cornish names) of Mount's Bay
will take up-Channel. His wife thanks her for her beads:
there is none such in Cornwall, as far as he knows. No
one will take the barton place at Tehidy, where hedges and
outhouses are in decay. 'As for the hedges that Harry Nance
made, it is now abroad like the feathers of a goose new-
polled with a hungry fox.' He will send her some fat conger
against Lent. Will she provide James Tehidy with a new coat,
his old one being threadbare? Writing on St Blaise's day, he
subscribes himself 'your old kanaffe', i.e. knave, which
shows that the 'k' was then pronounced (as in knife, derived
from *canif*). St Aubyn comes across to us as an amusing
personality; his wife later subscribes herself 'your loving and
lowly sister'—part-recognition of Honor's vice-regal exaltation, perhaps partly Tudor humour.

In her exposed post Lady Lisle was bombarded with
requests, particularly from impecunious churchmen—and she
was vulnerably devout. The curate of Bishop's Waltham asks
for a gown cloth she had promised, and for a chantry or
other benefice. 'You have so many whelps pertaining to you
that poor Thomas Gilbert shall be forgotten.' The prior of
Southwick was always begging for something. A priest at St
Thomas', Exeter, does not mind whether she provides for

him in these parts or elsewhere, except that he has a special
mind to pray for his master where he lies, i.e. Sir John Basset
at Umberleigh—'an it must be, an it will not be, God is in
every place.'

From Umberleigh her chantry priest, Sir John Bond,
thanks her for his gowns, but reports as to her fishing that
the water has been very little all summer. Mistress Jane, the
eldest daughter, has arrived and lies in her corner chamber.
From Soberton her steward reports that he has put 24lb of
fine yarn to weaving for her flannel; please to send for the
swans and peahens, for 'the fox hath killed your crane.' From
Bruton she hears that the buck she struck in Canford Park
was never recovered.

As for the family, the 'whelps', Anne has been placed with
Mme de Riou at Pont de Rémy—evidently to be 'finished'
or polished, for she was to have a career at Court, constantly
noticed if not favoured by the King. She has received shoes
and hose, too small for her, and wants an everyday robe.
John, the eldest boy, has been put out to board at home, the
parson of Colemore near Alton to teach him every day. Her
sister-in-law Margaret writes: 'I would I were one day with
you. I trust to see you yet before I die.'

Then all the grandees: the Archbishop of York asks for
them from Southwell, 'every one asks after them.' Lord
DelaWarr thanks her for three dozen and ten quails from the
Calais marshes, the residue were lost in the carriage. The
bishop of Chichester shall have half the sturgeon. Bishop
Gardiner, Sir Francis Bryan and Sir John Wallop were on
embassy at Marseilles—evidently recruiting support for
Henry's marriage to Anne Boleyn—when the Pope arrived
there. The formidable Gardiner sent an open missive: 'My
good Lord and Lady, I recommend me unto you even in the
sight of the world. Ste. Winton.' Friendly letters arrive from
the Marquis of Exeter and Sir John Russell, who was to
replace him in the West. The Marquis' Yorkist cousin, Lord
Montagu, perceives that Calais is somewhat chargeable, as
he always reckoned it would be 'to such a free stomach as
my Lord hath.' He advises Lady Lisle to look well upon it
at the beginning, for everything is harder now than at her
parting. He sends commendations to his kinsman. Their
kinship to the Yorkist house was to bring them all into grave

trouble. At the time of the Duke of Buckingham's fall Lisle had been questioned concerning Arthur Pole, of Yorkist royal stock, who spent a lifetime in the Tower.[3] The Keeper of the Tower, Sir William Kingston, writes that the King hawks every day; himself had received her token which came to him in the church of Blackfriars. From Court she heard that Henry was merry, hunting the good red deer, but it was difficult to get any venison for her, 'he is very dangerous of that flesh.' King and Queen were in good health, and to come by water from Windsor to Westminster, thence to Greenwich where Anne intends to take her chamber. There Elizabeth was born in September.

Next year, in time for Lent, Lord Montague thanks Lady Lisle for two barrels of herring, and one for Lord Burgavenny (Abergavenny). Queen Anne was much pleased with her present of dottrels (a kind of plover), and had appointed six for her supper, six for Monday's dinner and six for supper— her brother, Lord Rochford, had conveyed them, and presumably 'the linnet that hung in your chamber. Her Grace is good lady to you.' In April the news from Greenwich is that 'the Queen hath a goodly belly, praying our Lord to send us a prince.' This urgent necessity had been behind Henry's separation from Queen Catherine; once again his hopes were to be defrauded.

Mrs Staynings writes about her troubles, her husband in prison and herself with child; 'for I am in the taking that I was in the last year—if it had pleased God he might have sent it to your ladyship, the which would have been more gladder than I am.' She sent a coat cloth of fine green for John Basset, so much crimson satin to stock him a doublet— one sees the picture as in a Holbein—and so much black satin for another.

Sir Richard Grenville, her nephew, is in hand to buy the post of High Marshal at Calais from Sir Edward Ringley. The King has so far refused to sanction it and rebuked Cromwell for speaking up for Grenville, declaring that there should be no rooms (offices) bought or sold hereafter in Calais. Next thing, Henry declares that if rooms may be sold, he will have the advantage himself. Grenville was pressing Lord Chancellor Audley for Lisle to have the government of Guisnes added to him, but Lord Rochford already had that grant. By the end of the year Grenville's bargain with Ringley had got through; we find him thanking Cromwell for his help with a present of 18,000 Western slates for covering his houses.

In June 1534 Bishop Gardiner addressed to Lady Lisle the only letter of his that survives to a lady.[4] Recognisably it begins, 'knowing how effectually your ladyship is accustomed to solicit your friends' cause, and nothing doubting of your special love and friendship towards me', he recommends to her the case of a widow requiring justice at the Marshal's hand. This may have been a factor in the growing disaccord between aunt and nephew. He was Cromwell's man, the Lisles friends of the conservative bishop.

Henry used the able Bishop Gardiner as his principal envoy on diplomatic missions abroad, so that it fell to the Lisles to entertain him on his way to and from Calais. In September Gardiner was asking them to entertain a French gentleman, whose family had given him hospitality in Provence.

A young member of this numerous family, John Grenville, was also on his way up. He sent news in March of various Acts of Parliament and of its prorogation. 'My old master, Sir Thomas More, is clearly discharged of his trouble'—but this proved only temporary. John Grenville was a lawyer, and an energetic man of business. He brought in the Book of the Subsidy and Loan of that year for Cornwall. He was now in service with More's successor, Audley, as Lord Chancellor, who commented that he might do the Lisles some pleasure, since they trusted in Grenville's diligence, suit and labour, 'as is the part of a natural kinsman.' He had promised that he 'would warrant the Lord Chancellor'; however,

> his warrant is but very slender, for he has many suits to his master for other matters. He would promise for his own father more than he could perform, that he might get benefit by his purse: but his labour does not last longer than he has his request. He regards no friend so well as money. Lady Lisle is not to have overmuch confidence in him: she will lack no fair promises so long as he has from Lord Lisle what he labours for, whereby he is a gainer and has ready money.

The Henrician world was a hard one, a struggle for survival

in which the reptiles ate each other up. One can see the hardness, and the insecurity, in the faces depicted by Holbein. Of course there were kindly, generous people among them; this is what made, and makes, the Lisles so attractive. Hence they became victims. Before the end of the year Cromwell was writing to Lisle that he 'should not bind himself at any man's request to promise what he cannot perform; or by his excess of living make himself so needy as to have more estimation of money than regard to the tale it bringeth.' Nevertheless Cromwell was to drive a hard bargain with Lady Lisle for her manor of Painswick, when they needed money. Then, upon his attainder the manor was disgorged and came to the Crown. Cromwell was a practical man of business—but his advice went unheeded.

Still the presents and exchanges went on, and the expenses piled up. Katherine, Duchess of Suffolk, sends thanks for good wine, and a dog; the Secretary to the Queen of Hungary—ruling for Charles V in the Netherlands—has been well entertained on passing through Calais. Such entertainment was a major burden accruing to the job of Lord Deputy. And Calais became a target for all the Grenvilles. In April another nephew, Digory, brought with him nine silver cramp rings and one of gold. These sacred objects, having been blessed by the sovereign on Good Friday, were sovereign for cramp or epilepsy. They figure frequently in the Correspondence, which has its anthropological interest too.

Fascinating evidences of the New World occur, with its exotic creatures. The Admiral of France, declaring that no king or queen should be served before Lady Lisle, sends her three small animals brought from Brazil. Two small ones are marmosets and eat only apples, small nuts and almonds, and must not be given anything to drink but a little milk warmed up. The large animal must be kept near the fire; the little ones hung up at night near the chimney in their *boîte de nuit*. (One occasionally sees such pets portrayed in the pictures of the time.) Sir Richard has arrived in London: he had presented a couple of fine bloodhounds to the Admiral, who has given him a little marmoset for his wife, of which he is very proud.

In London their faithful agent, John Hussey, has not yet delivered to Mr Skut (Scot?) the twelve yards of satin he has

bought, for the quails for him are not yet come. He can find
no cloth of silver he likes at the price, but sends the 'muster'
of three pieces: the plain at 40s 10d the yard, the violet with
knots of silver, 46s 8d, the branched (i.e. figured) 40s. He
likes the plain best; he sends her ribbons, pins and frontlets.
Mr Skut will make up the satin after the most used fashion
now, large and long with double placards (i.e. under-panels),
and when the fur comes he will see it trimmed. Mr Skut was
a person to be cosseted with quails; for he was the Queen's
tailor, as he had been to Catherine of Aragon. Queens might
come, and queens might go, under the bulk of Henry VIII;
but Mr Skut went on for years.

A harness-maker wants to know if her ladyship will have
her saddle and harness fringed with silk and gold, and
whether of Lucca or Genoa velvet. Other lords' wives have
theirs of Lucca velvet fringed with silk and gold, 'with
buttons of the pear fashion and tassels quarter deep of silk
and gold.' Will she have the stirrup parcel-gilt, with a leather
covered with velvet, or else to have a foot-stool according
unto her saddle? And what device is to go in the saddle's
head of copper and gilt?

From Umberleigh Sir John, the priest, writes: 'I wot not
what to say of Mistress Jane Basset. She has been away since
Candlemas [2 February], but has kept a woman servant—I
know not to what intent—who troubles me much. Her
servant put up the back door that lies into the park by some
subtle means, which put me in great fear to what intent it is
done.' From Hampshire a priest is recommended: 'he writes
a very fair secretary hand, and text hand, and Roman; and
singeth surely and playeth very cunningly on the organs. He
is very cunning in drawing of knots in gardens, and well seen
in grafting and keeping of cucumbers and other herbs.' If all
true, evidently a treasure.

At Pont de Rémy Madame du Bours now receives Mary
Basset, in addition to Anne; thanking Lady Lisle for the pins
and sleeves, she sends preserves and cherries. At home James
was put to school with the abbot of Reading: 'my lord of
Reading makes much of him and plieth him to his learning,
both to Latin and French. He is as tender of him as if he
were the King's son.' Alas, the King was not tender of the
abbot, who supported his cause all the way along in the

Divorce and its sequel, until the end, in 1539, when he went into opposition and was executed. This was Hugh Faringdon—a thousand pities that the splendid Norman abbey did not become one of the new cathedrals, as was intended, but for the expense of Henry's extravagant third French war.

The year 1535 was dominated by the question whether Sir Richard Grenville would be allowed to join the Lisles at Calais as Marshal. He had paid Sir Edward Ringley £400 for the reversion to the office, and the patent was made out in March. At the last moment Ringley did not want to give up, in spite of a meeting between him and Sir Richard at Canterbury arranged by the indispensable John Grenville, to whom the King handed the patent at Court. Sir Richard meant 'to prove himself in the right and Master Ringley false, or it shall cost £500.' Secretary Cromwell was displeased; from Calais, 'when Mr Marshal cometh, he shall have his part; for surely he loveth him not.' So it went on—a ding-dong tug-of-war for place and profit as characteristic of Henrician politics as of Elizabethan, and indeed of the next two centuries.

On Michaelmas eve Sir Richard came to Court to take leave of the King, but 'he told me that Ringley desired to continue in office. I told him that I had paid £400 and had his bond in 800 marks to surrender his patent by Bartholomew day.' Secretary Cromwell spoke up in his favour, but Grenville dared not press the matter further until he knew the King's pleasure. In the end agreement was reached. Grenville to Lisle:

Ringley is a very hard man, and if Master Secretary had not made an agreement between us, we should never have agreed. The fishing of the moats is clearly mine. I pray God send us good store of eels. Your part shall be in it. Let your servant receive of Ringley his great bay horse on St Lawrence's day. If the Commissioners propose to diminish the office let me have your favour.

The ladies were on better terms. Lady Ringley thanked Lady Lisle for many kindnesses. 'Your beads of coral with a heart of gold were a great comfort to me, knowing that you loved them so well that you were wont to wear them about your arm.' She sent her a token 'by him called Master

Marshal that I love best and your ladyship next. I beg you
to cherish him in my absence.' Ringley was occupying the
place at Grenville's wish until he could arrive to take over.

The King received appropriate recognition of his part in
the affair. The Keeper of the Tower thanked Lisle for the
jennets (ponies), 'which made the King merry in Waltham
forest'; and reported, 'her Grace has as fair belly as I have
seen.' The Queen, we learn in December, sets much store
by a pretty dog, and 'her Grace delighteth so much in little
Purkoy ['Pourquoi'?—Anne had been brought up at the
French Court] that, after he was dead of a fall, there durst
nobody tell her Grace of it. But she values a dog more than
a bitch.' On the other hand, Hussey wrote, 'touching your
monkey, the Queen loveth no such beasts, nor can scant
abide the sight of them.' Perhaps, too, in her condition she
feared the effect on the child she was carrying; when the
hoped-for son appeared still-born, that was to seal her fate.

Clouds were indeed gathering. Hussey reported from
London, 'no news but of certain that were put to death, and
your ladyship is so pitiful I would not write unpleasant
things.' That summer died More and Fisher, and the Carthu-
sian monks who would not accept the new deal in Church
and state. The crisis of Henry's reign was approaching, when
much of the North rose against the revolution that he and
Cromwell, with Parliament's support, were carrying
through. The crisis was dangerous, prolonged and complex,
not only religious and political, but economic and even inter-
national. For Henry's chief fear was of a conjunction of
Charles V and Francis I—of the Empire and France (with
Scotland)—against him: to meet this he was using the wealth
of the monasteries to build a fleet and fortify the whole
Channel coast—

Majestic lord, that broke the bonds of Rome.

For him the crisis was personal too: he *had* to provide the
country with a son to safeguard the succession—and he had
left it dangerously late. Only someone with a Stalin-like
nerve of steel could have steered the country through such a
revolution.

Lady Lisle had received her regular New Year's Gift from

the Queen in her last year of precarious exaltation. And Hussey had done his best to get his mistress a waiting gentle-woman: 'there is one, an Aragonese, who dwelt with my Lady Mary, daughter to the Princess Dowager [the title to which Queen Catherine had been relegated], who speaks good English. Great suit is made to have her. She is the best cradlewoman in the land, well brought up and a good cook. I can yet get no grant of her.' Later: 'she will marry and serve no more.' Lady Lisle also was in hope of providing her lord with a son and heir. From Court came another word of warning to the Lord Deputy from John Grenville: 'the Lord Chancellor prays you not to be so liberal in granting these petitions'—easy-going Lisle! And the rumour around Cromwell was that Lisle's wife meddled too much with his business.

Like many ladies of that age her ladyship fancied her skill in concocting medicines: Lord Edmund Howard had taken hers, it caused the stone to break and he had voided much gravel; but 'it made him piss the bed, for which he was beaten by his wife.'

An order had gone forth to pluck down all weirs in Devon-shire. That at Umberleigh had been broken up by Sir William Courtenay, at the instance of neighbour Giffard (presumably of Weare Giffard on the Torridge—a conflict of interest). Now Sir William Courtenay was dead at Powderham: 'some be sorry and the most part make little moan.' Digory Gren-ville wrote from Stowe that he had hoped to see his aunt again at Easter, 'but I took a misfortune of my horses that I was in the case that I was never able to leap upon my horses never since, and had great pain ever since. I had liever £20 that I were with you, for I lack company to play with me, and I can do no other service because of my hurt.'

From remote St Keverne near the Lizard the vicar gives thanks for the good cheer that he too had received when last with the Lisles. He sent a kilderkin containing four Cornish congers, 'upon the token that your lordship laughed heartily upon the great wise answer that I gave unto my lord.' Every-thing shows the Lisles to have been a jolly euphoric couple, given to enjoying life and making it pleasant for others.

Sir John Bond reported that Sir John Basset's obit had been kept on Tuesday before the Purification of our Lady,

but there had not been 'such a winter this twenty years for
wind, rain, thunder and lightning.' He and John Davy had
made Digory good cheer when he was over with them; but
the priest continued at loggerheads with Mistress Jane. She
told her mother tales of the goings on of parson Brimmelcombe: 'Thomasine, Thomas Seler's harlot, is now his. And
here the said Thomasine is covered underneath Joan Brimmelcombe, the which men think her well near as unthrifty
as the other.' Would Lady Lisle 'send word of your pleasure
as to your lamp in the chapel: he burneth never day in the
week and scant holy days, except that I do light himself. Am
I to maintain your taper in the chapel of our Lady at Alston?'
The time would come when the dissolution of the chantries
would extinguish these lights, superfluous expenses.

Sir John came back with the charge that Mistress Basset
was vexed that he would not let her have the keys of all the
chambers: 'Madam, I will get my fingers unto the elbow
before she or any other have such keys till you command
me.' Then Jane again: 'but now I am taken up with Sir John
Bond, and also with Brimmelcombe, that I cannot tell what
to do. For they had liever that any brothel in this part were
here than I; and so the said woman that I wrote unto you is
here daily.' Marriage of the clergy was to be the remedy for
this kind of thing—but not quite yet.

Comforting news came of John Basset, the eldest son and
heir, whose chamber in Lincoln's Inn was being trimmed up
with yellow and green say (a silky kind of serge). In August
young James arrived in Paris, to be placed in the College of
Calvy, where he was to have his bed alone, and to dine and
sup with the Principal. The Lord President had given him
good welcome, and would do his best to further his learning
and good manners. But James did not prosper at first with
his learning, for all teaching in the college was in Latin, so
that he does not learn French.

Anne writes for red cloth to make a mantle with a satin
hood, and asks her mother to procure her 'une dogue', which
she has promised to a gentleman. Her mother obliges with a
hawk and a greyhound to Madame du Bours; but Mary
should ply her work, her lute and the virginals, and not play
too much.

Meanwhile, the little ships ply up and down the Channel,

and across the Straits to Calais, bringing provisions of fish, beer, timber, salt—along with the visitors. John Davy, the factotum, is master of one ship bringing twelve sugar loaves in a chest, a piece of great raisins, a tapnet (basket) of figs; spices, torches and wax; cinnamon, ginger, cloves, almonds. All very expensive—and the Lisles denied themselves nothing. More and more money is needed to provide for Master John; and 'the pewterer is owed money for making and changing your vessel' (i.e. plate).

New Year finds parson Bond and Jane still bickering: 'I know not what to say about Mistress Jane Basset. Her sisters cannot please her.' He has delivered such things as are necessary, but cannot satisfy her: two feather beds, three sheets; two cows, one horse, also 'a greyhound which lies on one of the beds day and night, except when she holds him in her hands.' Jane has received the stuff—'he says they are as he received them, but some of them are not able to bear handling to be carried into the wind.' And—'your chapel stands unserved.' Too much of that kind of thing all over the country also needed reform. St Aubyn sent thanks for the token and heart of gold sent to his wife, but they had not arrived; for Richard Harris lost it and his money by a subtle companion who left him at Chard; still they hoped to hear of it. He sent a firkin with a dozen puffins, directed to the Red Lion in Southwark.

In March Queen Anne sends Lady Lisle sleeves for a kirtle, and Mr Basset, i.e. John, must have a gelding to ride into the country. About Easter the Lisles were sent for to have gone into England; then difficulties supervened. Sir Richard Grenville was ill, and we hear of bad feeling between him and his aunt. In England all the talk was that 'the abbeys shall down.' Lady Lisle remained irremediably conservative and Catholic; her nephew, of the younger generation, was in favour of moving with the times and making the most of the opportunities opening up with the dissolution of the lesser monasteries. Nor was Lisle averse from taking his chance. All this year is filled with negotiations for the grant to him of the little nunnery of Frithelstoke, with its lands conveniently near Umberleigh.

Meanwhile a monk of Christ Church, Canterbury, desires her ladyship's favour to a singing child he has sent to my lord, her bedfellow. He sends over, too, 'a beast, the creature of God, sometime wild but now tame, to comfort your heart at such time as you be weary of praying.' Brooches are being made for her: one with the Assumption of our Lady, the other with a personage sitting under a cloth of state. And the Lisles borrow a crucifix and candlesticks from Canterbury: subsequently returned, they were annexed to the Crown. Master Skut promises her her gown against Corpus Christi day, but it requires half-a-yard more, fourteen yards in all. Master George Basset, for whom a velvet coat is being made, is with the prior at Winchester; Bridget with the abbess: the curate of Soberton goes to see them. In France Madame de Riou and Anne Basset had returned from their journey, on which they saw the Holy Tear of our Lord. Anne was thought handsome and *de bonne sorte*; Mary was at Abbeville. Their mother sends to Madame d'Azincourt *'du drap bleu* for the child she beareth, and a girdle that has been about the body of Sainte Rose.' Credulous women, evidently.

In May came the thunderclap of the dreadful accusations against the Queen. The blows fell swiftly: on 12 May Hussey wrote that Norris, Weston, Brereton and Marks were condemned to be hanged, drawn and quartered. The Queen and her brother were to be arraigned in the Tower. Next day Hussey wrote at length, taking it for granted that Anne was guilty. On 17 May Lord Rochford and others were put to death on Tower Hill; two days later the Queen was put to death within the Tower 'in the presence of a thousand people.' (Having failed to produce a male heir, Henry wanted to get rid of her: she was framed, and Cromwell had to do the dirty work.) The way was now clear—both Catherine of Aragon and Anne dead—for Henry to make an indubitably legal marriage and assure the succession. His eye had fallen on young Jane Seymour for the purpose.

Before the end of the month Henry and Jane were privately married. In June: 'here is a triumphant Court and many ancient ladies and gentlemen in it.' How they had hated Anne Boleyn!—her execution made for reconciliation within the royal family, between Henry and his daughter Mary, and the marriage with Jane was welcomed by conservatives: old Lady Salisbury, for example, came back to Court. Hussey reported, 'your ladyship hath two nieces with the Queen, daughters to Mr Arundell', i.e. Sir Thomas Arundell, married to the sister of Henry's subsequent queen, Catherine Howard, now a maid of honour.

Was there a place for Anne Basset? Lady Lisle greeted the new Queen with a token, who replied with another in return. Lady Salisbury, who was in charge of the new Queen's ladies (though the mother of Cardinal Pole!) wrote that Queen Jane was glad to hear from Lady Lisle, but her suit for Anne Basset would take time as she is yet young. Lady Lisle should come over for the coronation. But that never took place: Queen Jane, having done her duty by producing a prince at last, died shortly after.

Hussey reported that the new Queen, having appointed all her maidens already, Lady Salisbury would do her best on the next vacancy. Then, with mere male kindliness, 'God have mercy on Mr Norris's soul! for my lord may say he lost a friend.' (Elizabeth I, as Queen, made a point of favouring the families of those who had been victims along with her mother, alike innocent.) However, Hussey hoped, new friends may be gained at length; he suggested that her ladyship might send the Queen her bird and her dog.

In November she was hoping for a son and heir for Lisle: 'I am glad your ladyship is so well sped. Jesu send you a son.' After some disappointment over the Lisles' business: 'I think I was born in an unfortunate hour, yet always trusting your ladyship will be my good lady, or else I have served an ill saint.' Such was the familiar fashion of the time, but Hussey comes across as an individual, trusty, friendly and humorous. 'If I thought it should not be painful I would never cease praying unto God that your ladyship might have two goodly sons, as I have full hope that God will show his handiwork.' By December the news had got about. From Paris Sir John Wallop, a previous Marshal of Calais, sent her two bottles of holy water from Avignon; he was pleased to hear that young James was now speaking French. Richard Lee, Surveyor of Calais, wrote 'that it hath pleased God to visit her with a child, he most heartily thanketh her good ladyship for her marmelado.'

At New Year 1537 Bishop Gardiner was writing from Paris

to Lisle to prepare shipping for him and his horses on his
return from embassy.[5] In October Gardiner—off again in
the whirligig of diplomatic activity that Henry's difficulties
involved him in—wrote to Lisle the news of Europe from
Lyons: 'thus the world wavereth and fortune playeth. I think
they might leave game when they would; for all the poor
folk that look on be weary, and themselves also.'

The early part of the year 1537 was dominated by the
Marshal's anxieties concerning the safety of Calais—evidently
he had no high opinion of Lisle's competence—and still more
worries about the marriages of his daughters. Sending a New
Year's gift of a leash of falcons to Cromwell, now Lord Privy
Seal, Grenville gave his opinion that it was injurious to the
safety of Calais to allow so many aliens to flock into the
town. Though not more than four or five hundred denizens
were numbered in the register, Grenville said that there were
6000 with families. This must have been an exaggeration; but
the situation was not safe. The French were crowding into
Calais, and taking cattle within the Pale. However, it was
for the King to see to as he pleased.

Grenville was to marry his daughter Jane to the son and
heir of Sir Richard Whetill, who had been mayor of Calais,
but the son had sustained much loss by his father's unreasonable will. Grenville now made suit for his prospective son-
in-law to Cromwell. The omni-competent minister sent over
a commission under Lord Sandys to go into the dispute.
Then Surveyor Lee at Calais wishes to have Grenville's
second daughter Margaret as a match for his son. It is fairly
clear that Sir Richard—the Grenvilles were always family-
proud, with their Norman descent—did not regard Surveyor
Lee's son as good enough. But Lee was a confidential servant
of Cromwell's, and Sir Richard had to explain himself.

He did so at some length. He could not deny the Lord
Privy Seal anything upon such promise he has made of friendship in the matter between the Surveyor and himself. He is
in debt by the charges he has sustained these six or seven
years. The marriages of Lady Lisle's sister, his own sister
and his eldest daughter had cost him 700 marks.[6] His attendance in Parliament for five years cost him 500 marks. (This
was the historic Reformation Parliament of 1529–36, which
had ratified every step of the revolution made by the

governing class, under the leadership of Henry VIII and Cromwell.)[7] The high marshalship of Calais, with the cost of attaining it, accounted for another 800 or 900 marks, in addition to 1200 marks for the payment of his father's debts and bequests. Then there were the expenses of housekeeping. He could have had £40 a year jointure by marrying his daughter to Tregian's son and heir—this was the rich merchant of Golden, whose brass we see in the church of Probus. He does not crave that sum of the Surveyor, but will take him for friend for Cromwell's sake. If Cromwell will receive his daughter into his house and marry her from it, he will give him 100 marks when he can do so with ease.

Hussey reported that Cromwell did not like Grenville's letter, and advised Lisle, when he knew the last of the Marshal's mind, to send his answer to the powerful minister. For his part Cromwell hoped that all unkindness between uncle and nephew would be forgotten. Sir Thomas Palmer's opinion in the family quarrel was that he would not have Cromwell make any appointment with Grenville without Lisle's consent, 'for you have lost friends for his sake.'

Now Lady Lisle was admonished by Archbishop Cranmer. Surveyor Lee had defended her by saying that she entertained all the preachers sent over to Calais. Cranmer recognised that, but had heard reports that she was given to be a little 'papish'. He desired the Lisles to favour those who favour the truth. This was a pointer to troubles that lay ahead.

Cromwell promised his thanks to Grenville for eventually coming to terms with the Surveyor: the marriage took place and young Lee thanked the Lord Privy Seal for his mediation with his father-in-law, 'who is now right kind to me.' Hussey gives us what had been the inwardness of the matter: 'Margaret Grenville has well sped, for the Lord Privy Seal thinks the Surveyor's son worthy to have as good as she, notwithstanding her birth; but when they marry he will be able to find her [provide for her] like a gentleman.' But, of course, Thomas Cromwell was not a gentleman himself.

Lady Lisle fancied herself running neck and neck with the now pregnant Queen in her expectations. We learn that Queen Jane is great with child, and will be open-laced with stomacher till Corpus Christi day. The King had written to Lisle for fat quails for her Grace. As soon as they came to hand Hussey rode to Court with them; the King and Queen immediately ordered half to be roasted and the rest kept for supper. While eating them the Queen promised to take one of Lady Lisle's daughters. Would she please send over both for the Queen to choose?

This turned out to be Anne Basset's opening: she was sworn in as one of the Queen's maids. Catherine would meanwhile be entertained by Hussey—she eventually found a berth with Lady Rutland—and Cromwell promised 'to speak and do for them.' It fell to Hussey to make all the preparations for Lady Lisle's expected lying-in, in the state appropriate to a great lady. He was collecting a bed of estate, with satin and ermine coverlet, and carpets to boot, though he had to wait till Lady Beauchamp was churched. Mr Skut laid down that the fashion of nightgowns was 'such as you have already made of damask, velvet or satin.' But now her nightgown and waistcoats were made in every part like Lady Beauchamp's—the very fashion that the Queen and all ladies wear.

Annys Cockerell, a midwife, sends her a box of 'manus Christi'—a commonly known medicine for her case at the time. Hussey thinks that if the Lisles have their son christened in the chapel of the Staple at Calais, a font may be got at Canterbury. But no son eventuated; Lady Lisle thought she had over-reckoned herself. In August she was still in pain, and Hussey heard that she was grieving inordinately: 'I pray you show that confidence with which you were wont to inspire others.' He begs her not to despair. 'Tyldesley has been in hand with me for the carpets and also the Queen's red traverse [screen], for her lying-in.'

At this time we have a kind letter from Margaret Grenville consoling her: 'take no thought for nothing of this transitory world. Ye have the love of the people as much as any woman that ever I heard of. I am sorry that you should have any grief, for I know you of old, for you would no trouble to any living creature.' She sends two pairs of sleeves, 'not so fine as I would, but I cannot get here cloth of the breadth of which you wrote, as it is made in Brittany.'

Her sister Mary St Aubyn writes from Clowance on Midsummer day that her husband often talks of her great goodness: 'though youth has ruled him before this, now he

is well amended.' Next day he thanks her for her gulls—he
had ten, and cousin Digory Grenville of Penheale the other
ten. 'The raven has destroyed the harnsews,[8] above a dozen
'sygys' (i.e. sieges, or sittings). At New Year he thanks her
for a handsome reward to his daughter, her niece, and for
conies, gulls and a ship of wheat. His cousin, Sir William
Godolphin, has taken as much as they could carry away, but
the ship stands as full laden as ever. He would be glad to
come to Calais: 'I would then trust to make you to say that
I am not your pricklouse nor knave, but mercy ever cry to
have.' This sounds like a stave from some song of the time.
He is happy to hear of her recovery now and that Lord Lisle
is 'so gentle and kind at all times and most at her uttermost
grievance.' How agreeable a character Thomas St Aubyn
comes across to us in his letters!—exceptionally so for an
Henrician.

The King sent over a red deer to the Lisles. It was young
Jane Seymour who solved his personal problem for him by
producing a son at last—and thereupon died. In November
Sir John Wallop reports that 'the King is in good health and
merry as a widower may be, the Prince also. The Queen is
to be buried at Windsor at the end of this week.'

Henry had plenty on his hands this summer with the
Pilgrimage of Grace—all Lincolnshire and Yorkshire in rebellion against the suppression of the monasteries, while the
new deal was approved by the progressive South and East.
He did not fail to make the point that his policy was in
step with Parliament, and in his anger pointed out obstinate
Yorkshire as 'the beastliest in the realm.' From Windsor he
directed operations with a masterful combination of force
and guile, leaving Cromwell to raise the necessary cash in
London.

In 1537 Lords Darcy and Hussey were brought to trial for
their connivance with the rebels, the Marquis of Exeter placed
in the invidious position of presiding over it—when his
sympathies were with the opposition too. Exeter's precept
was made out to John Grenville, serjeant-at-arms, who now
comes forward among the younger members of the family.
He was living at Kensington, whence he engaged in the
prolonged negotiations for Lisle's grant of Frithelstoke
priory. For himself he was after the little priory of Tywar-

dreath in Cornwall,[9] and was picking up desirable offices
such as customer of the tin-tolls in the hundreds of Penwith
and Kerrier. That was not much: he wanted the controller-
ship of customs in the ports of Exeter and Dartmouth, which
would bring in more cash.

In September Audley wrote to Cromwell to favour 'a poor
younger brother who has many children and served the King
well at the last rebellion. He had no office but that of serjeant-
at-arms, which had cost him much money. The King had
granted him the lease of a little priory in Cornwall, but he
was so molested by Mr Arundell that he got little profit out
of it.' This was Sir Thomas Arundell who, from his strategic
position in the Court of Augmentations, was building up a
large patrimony from monastic properties for the Catholic
Arundells of Wardour. It was a pity John Grenville did not
hold on to the 'mansion' of Tywardreath, or we might have
had a Grenville house in that pleasant position on St Austell
bay.

Cromwell did what he was asked and Grenville became
controller of those ports; he writes, if he live, he will prepare
some pleasure for the Lord Privy Seal. Next we find him in
hand with Hussey to buy Lisle's property of Kingston Lisle.
The Lisles are now understandably in want of cash and having
to sell property. Grenville offered £100 for immediate
possession—it must have been heavily mortgaged. Hussey
was sure that Lisle would not part with it for less than £160.
Grenville said that he would give no penny more than his
original offer.

In August Lisle got the grant of Frithelstoke, the site,
church, bell-tower and churchyard, the manors of Frithelstoke and Broadwood Widger, with the rectory and
advowson of the parish church. The value was £92.4.8 a
year, the rent £15 9s—a welcome gift. Cromwell deserved
recompense: Sir Thomas Palmer suggested another partridge
pasty, for the last, he said, was the best that ever he ate.
When one goes to Frithelstoke today nothing is there but
the east end of the ruined church, with the beautiful lancet
windows that had looked down upon the nuns' devotions
over the centuries.

Lady Lisle gave the nuns at Dunkirk constant employment
at needlework for her family and retinue. Her pen-friend the

prioress, Antoinette de Saveuses, sends a pair of *coiffes de nuit* for the Lord Deputy, and will send two more of another fashion for her own use. A greater part of what the nuns had received in the last three years has been applied in honour of the holy sacrament. Madame du Bours thanked her ladyship for two salmons and a barrel of herring: 'you make me feel that you never forget me.' But that was what everybody felt about Lady Lisle, generous soul that she was. From Paris James writes that he has made the acquaintance of the sons of the dukes of Vendôme and Guise—what vistas of the future wars of religion that opens up!

At New Year 1538 Hussey describes vividly a pleasant scene at Court, with the King receiving his New Year's gifts and Cromwell saying, 'Here cometh my Lord Lisle's man.' Henry replied merrily, though Hussey could not tell what he said (Henry had a light tenor voice). He asked for them, standing leaning against the cupboard receiving all things, Master Tuke at the end of it penning all things; behind his Grace stood Mr Kingston (Keeper of the Tower, and a favourite) and Sir John Russell; beside him Hertford—Jane Seymour's brother—and Cromwell. In February Hussey writes, 'you have demerited high thanks for the boars' heads of the King, and of the Lord Privy Seal for the pasties of capons.' Hussey was sending over two hundred sweet oranges. Fox, bishop of Hereford, sent Lady Lisle a remembrance in recompense for her cup which was lost on his going on embassy into Germany. Bishop Gardiner, also *en mission*, asked Lisle to forward to England a diplomatic packet from the Emperor.[10]

Preparations were now afoot for the happy marriage of the Basset heir to Lisle's daughter, Frances Plantagenet. Hussey sends the Archbishop's licence for them to be married in Lisle's chapel. In England the suit concerning the Basset inheritance goes on and on, with the usual Tudor complexities. Daubeney had the lands in question on the understanding that, if he had no male heirs, they should come to Basset (there was a family connexion). The suit came up before the King and Council—one sees how Henry gave himself to business—Cromwell and Richard Pollard taking Basset's part. 'Mr Pollard desires to have your house at

Umberleigh this summer for six weeks or two months. I
think you should offer it him with thanks'. Daubeney, now
Earl of Bridgwater, had made over his rights to Hertford;
the law and opinion of the judges were against Basset. No
remedy was to be had except at the King's hands, 'and it had
never been seen that the King should stop the course of his
common laws.'

In all the historical discussions about Henry VIII's
'absolutism', his overriding the law, etc., this is important
direct evidence. His rule was authoritarian and forceful, even
brutal and without much mercy, but it did not run contrary
to law, the precise definition of tyranny. The rumour was
that Bridgwater intended to put away the Basset inheritance;
however, 'the King has been good lord in the matter', with
the help of Cromwell and Pollard, but especially of Russell,
at this time of crisis President of the temporary Council of
the West. Young Basset went over this summer to defend his
case, and stayed with Russell. The family wanted him to
enter Cromwell's service, as a step to the King's. The case
was so important to them that Lady Lisle went across that
autumn to pursue it. We have a charming letter from Frances,
longing to hear from her bedfellow; while a servant writes
that her 'ague would soon be past if Mr Basset might come
to Calais and see her.' He was meanwhile waiting on
Cromwell in hopes: 'Mr Basset is a good waiter and will be
a good courtier.'

Landing at Dover, Lady Lisle writes to Lisle that she is
merry, 'but should have been merrier if I had been coming
towards you.' While supper was dressing she told them all
merry tales. Hussey met her at Canterbury, with the news
that Cromwell was determined to have Painswick: 'I pray
God I lose no more.' Lisle to her: 'Mine own sweetheart, I
never thought so long for you, for I never sleep after two of
the clock . . . I never longed so much for anyone, since I
knew a woman.' The King, who had now given Anne Basset
a finding, regal and courteous as ever, made a grand banquet,
partly for her mother. She describes his gracious treatment:
'we were highly feasted, and after dinner today his Grace
showed us all the commodities of his palace'—'by her that
is more yours than her own, who had much rather die with
you there than live here.'

At Calais Lady Clinton reported the dinner given for all the Council: 'in your absence you were drunk to by my Lord and all your good lovers. My Lord said he thought the time long of your absence.' She took the opportunity to see the Prince, 'the goodliest babe that ever I set mine eye upon'; and also the Lady Mary, who asked heartily for you, and the young Lady Elizabeth. Thus, with all the trouble in the world, Henry had managed to complete a family, though he had not yet given up hope of more. Meanwhile, Lisle was longing for his wife 'as much as a child for his nurse'—and perhaps that described the situation. She replies: 'Mine own sweetheart, even with my whole heart root.' She had spoken plainly to Cromwell about their business, but 'how he handled and shook me up I will not now write, nor is it not to be written. He said plainly your annuity should not be more than £200. [They were hoping for £400.] I can neither eat, sleep, nor drink, my heart is so heavy, and it will never be light till I am with you.' Lisle to her: 'I think so much on you I cannot sleep in the night when I think on you in two hours after.' At the end of December she was home again with him.

In all the hardness of that brutal time the love-letters of that married couple make charming reading—a soft light irradiates them amid the Holbein-like realism.

There was plenty of hard reality in the business Lady Lisle had to transact on her visit. For all their grandeur at Calais, the duties and entertainments, the Lisles were now heavily in debt, and under the necessity of selling property. Hence their suit for an annuity, and for some pickings from monastic property. Other people, closer to power—the source of all good things—were doing much better. A letter from Devon advises Lisle to come over, 'the sooner the better for his profit, for here every man shifts for himself.' The Lord Admiral has four priories and a nunnery; Richard Pollard has Combe Martyn (where was a silver mine) and 'rules all now in Devon.' What Cromwell got in all there is no reckoning— but that would be disgorged on his fall. Sir Richard Grenville would like a friary in Exeter: he does not get it. Lisle would like Plympton priory: he does not get it. The King says he will grant no abbeys. Lisle gets the little White Friars in

Calais—but only after agreeing to Cromwell's terms over the
goodly manor of Painswick.

Lisle's interest in this was only after the demise of his wife,
for it was part of her jointure. We cannot go into all the
complications: the gist of it was that Cromwell got this fine
property in Gloucestershire at a rent of £120 a year. He
insisted on receiving £1000, which was Lisle's interest in it
on his wife's death—this was in return for services, though
Hussey thought it 'a large gift for pleasures and friendships
past.' However, the services were real. The Basset inheritance
was cleared of Bridgwater's claims and his later covenants
with Hertford. Apparently Lisle would receive a loan of £400
for pressing current needs, and the annuity for his office of
£200. John Basset was received into Cromwell's service.

The personal life of the past is more interesting than dead
business. Early that year Archbishop Cranmer was informed
that Grenville's chaplain at Calais had shown the soldiers of
the garrison a book to prove Purgatory and that it was right
to pray for the Pope. Cranmer's informant thought it needful
to send preachers over this Lent, and suggested the Lutheran
Dr Barnes.[11] Lady Lisle became even more devout after her
disappointment of an heir for Lisle. Hussey begged her

> to leave part of such ceremonies as you use, as long prayers and offering
> of candles, and at some time to refrain and not speak though your
> ladyship have cause, when you hear things spoken that you liketh not.
> Your ladyship might do a good deed to conform yourself partly to the
> thing that is used and to the world as it goeth now—which is undoubt-
> edly marked above all other things.

Rumours were circulating about her Catholic devotion,
when—with the movement towards Reform and simplific-
ation of rites and services now in progress—she was dragging
her feet. Hussey felt obliged to warn her again: 'if it might
please your ladyship to leave the most part of your memories
and have only Mass, matins and evensong of the day, I think
they shall have concerning your ladyship nothing to speak
of.'

In the increasing religious dissensions in England Henry
VIII had great difficulty in maintaining unity and uniformity:
only by strenuous exertion of his authority could he keep
order in the nursery. These disputes were reflected at Calais,

where they were highlighted in that post, exposed to all the winds that blew. An agitation was raised there by the preaching of a friar, known as Adam Damplip: his real name was George Bowker, but one sees the reason for the soubriquet given to this nuisance. Cromwell had him sent over for examination.

To these agitations, growing more critical each year, were added disputes within the Council. Lord Edmund Howard, an old friend of the Lisles (and father of Henry VIII's penultimate wife, Catherine Howard), was sent over to investigate: he reported that there was small love between the Deputy and the High Marshal, as also between the Marshal and the Knight Porter. Calais was riven with disputes and jealousies: too many protuberant personalities confined within too small a space.

With John and Frances now provided for, it was time to think of James, and the Lisles naturally thought of the Church. The youth, now at the College of Navarre, did not like sleeping three in a bed; but a robust emissary sent to investigate his complaints said that it was large enough for four men. James, however, demanded a small bed apart. When Lisle asked Cromwell for a licence for James to have a benefice in the family patronage with cure of souls, the minister replied that the matter lay with the Archbishop of Canterbury, 'who has denied the same to the best in the realm, so that farther suit is frustrate. You should write no more of it: it is vehemently taken as unlawful. But if you can spy out a prebend or free chapel, Cromwell will be friendly in it.' James's tutor was directed to obtain the first two orders, prior to priesthood, to qualify him for the prebend obtained. But the archdeacon of Paris would not license his suffragan to give holy orders to an Englishman: he said laughingly that the English smelt of fire. And Hussey's opinion was that the youth was 'meeter to serve the temporal powers than the spiritual dignities.' So James was sent over to England, to serve Bishop Gardiner, in which capacity he was to make his fortune.

From Umberleigh the news was that all were in health, though sickness was general throughout the country, and they die in the parish now and then. 'As to making up your weir, you must take patience, for Master Fortescue of

Philleigh made up his weir again and is brought up for it by
privy seal.' In France the cherries were spoiled by high winds,
but Jacques Robert sends Lady Lisle a great pannier of the
finest to make preserves. A Protestant divine sent her a little
book teaching what is good and evil before God; and later
she orders an English bible from Rouen. Hussey paid a visit
to Calais, but forgot the spoon for Cromwell; he sent her a
box of treacle from her own apothecary's. A French doctor
prescribed a sensible light diet for her disease: evidently, like
Mary Tudor later, she mistook the symptoms for pregnancy.

John Grenville got licence for a deputy-controller to do
his work for him in the West, he had so much more important
work to do in the service of Chancery. Notably at the end
of the year, when the Marquis of Exeter and Lord Montagu
were arraigned of high treason, largely on the evidence of
Montagu's light-weight brother, Sir Geoffrey Pole, who
turned King's evidence to save himself. He ruined his family
by it—though later he received absolution from the Pope,
for what good that was. The Poles and Courtenays were in
conspicuous opposition to Henry VIII's new deal. More
dangerous for them was the fact that both families were of
Yorkist royal blood; Henry VIII told the French ambassador
that he had long intended to extinguish the house of the
White Rose. Their equivocal behaviour at the time of the
Pilgrimage of Grace, and the sentiments dropped among
them, betrayed by Sir Geoffrey, now gave the King his
chance.

Writing the news of this thunderclap—Exeter, Montagu,
Sir Edward Neville in the Tower—Lisle says 'I dare write of
no more as yet.' No wonder he was stricken with fear—his
own turn was yet to come. Sir Brian Tuke, Treasurer of the
Chamber, has been entertained at Calais; 'I think you have
of her ladyship as great a jewel as any nobleman could wish.'
Nevertheless, he reminds Lisle that his debts bring him to the
verge of outlawry: 'do not suppose you cannot be outlawed
because you are a lord of Parliament or in the King's service
beyond sea.' His latest debt is on behalf of Mr Basset's ward.
Law suits are still going on about the leases on his properties,
on which Bridgwater will not relax his hold. Hussey, good
fellow, on the news that he was ill: 'die when he will, he
shall have my good will.'

Both Lisle and Grenville wished to get leave to come over about their affairs this summer of 1538, but both could not be away from their post. In May Sir George Carew reported to Cromwell that 'the whole Council is unwilling that the word of God should prosper amongst us, except Lord Grey, Sir Richard Grenville and himself.' Command had been given by the Deputy that the Bible be no more read at Mass. Surveyor Lee was in favour of God's word—naturally: Cromwell's man. In June Hussey met the Marshal riding to Court. He was not very proud of his welcome by the Lord Privy Seal. The King asked about Calais. 'I replied that all was meetly well', Grenville assured Lisle; 'the King then rode hunting. My cousin Anne is merry, and I brought her to my wife, whose bedfellow she was four or five nights when I was in Court.' The King had allowed him leave on business, so Sir Richard was able to spend the summer at Stowe, on his western cliffs.

From thence he wrote a long letter to Cromwell, most revealing of the mentality of the governing class agape for monastic land to fall into their mouths. He has bethought him that if he has not some piece of this suppressed land, 'I should stand out of the case of few men of worship of this realm.' He is as glad as any man of the suppression of these 'orgulous' persons and devourers of God's word and takers away of the glory of Christ; he reckons they were also takers away of the wealth of the realm (here he had a point), and 'spryes to the devilish bishop of Rome.' He would gladly buy some of the suppressed lands in these parts 'that his heirs may be of the same mind for their own profit.' This is a very tell-tale phrase, and mostly it worked out like that; but not always, for some families that profited largely from Church land continued to be good Catholics. He made an offer for the neighbouring priory of Launceston. However, the King had a mind to annex this to the Duchy of Cornwall for his son.

Grenville found how great a friend Lord Russell was to Lisle; 'he showed me how he might have been Deputy and the advice he gave you when you wished for it. It would have been more to your profit to have remained in England.' No one knew better than Russell how advantageous it was to remain close to the source of power and profit. Wise,

wary, and reliable the King had found him, and awarded him
a grand appanage based on Tavistock abbey from which to
rule in the West. 'The Marquis nor none of his ancestors was
never more esteemed nor better beloved in these parts than
his lordship is.' Russell was a far abler man: his elevation
was a step to more efficient government such as both Henry
and Cromwell had at heart.

Grenville's wife wrote to their aunt that they had been
staying with Lord Russell: 'I have never been so gently entertained in my life as by him. If you were here, my husband
would be better entreated to remain in these parts.' In
October they moved back to Calais. At New Year a leash of
falcons went off to Cromwell. A veteran there wrote to him
'to advise the King to have rulers here who favour the word
of God, and then this malice and grudge would cease.' Lord
Grey, Grenville and Carew 'favour all such as love the word
of God.'

Sir Brian Tuke thanks Lady Lisle for the goodly flowers
sent to his daughters and the best baken partridges that ever
he has eaten. The ship *Spark* went in upon the sands at
Margate and is lost. 'All the men and her taffeta is saved, but
wet. John Tebrowe has small luck at sea, God send him
better fortune a land.' Thus Hussey; then, 'Mr Skut has
promised to make your taffeta gown, which is not much
worse for wetting. I send you a matins book of the best make
and print.' He wishes that Lisle were made governor of
Prince Edward, or some other office in England.

John Grenville continues to make his way forward: he has
the money to make a purchase of lands from the Court
of Augmentations. He is in the Commission of Peace for
Middlesex, and has entertained young James at his London
house. He is still with the Lord Chancellor, who is offended
that Lisle has not sent the wines he promised. But there is
expectation of a Queen. Henry and Cromwell, alarmed at
the reconciliation of the Emperor with France and fearing a
joint move against England, are negotiating a German
marriage alliance which will give Charles V pause. It is
expected that Serjeant Grenville will be promoted to the new
Queen's service; for Lisle's sake he wished Hussey to have
his present preferment, worth 100 marks a year, but the Lord
Chancellor had anticipated him.

John Basset's wife is brought to bed of a daughter, and everyone is disappointed. Hussey: 'God send Mrs Basset joy of her goodly babe. I would it had had his father's mark. By God's grace at the next shot she shall hit the mark.' James— who has his prebend and is now in Bishop Gardiner's household—wished too that sister Frances had had a boy. He asked for his clothes to be sent now to Winchester, a *soyon* of velvet or satin, a doublet of silk and taffeta, *chaussées*, velvet shoes. We have seen that he was a choosy, discriminating boy, evidently intelligent. Bishop Gardiner sends his respects; 'the bishop of Bangor has made me good cheer for love of you, and given me a crown.'

In May the King made a grand banquet, at which most of the great ladies were present, Anne and Catherine Basset among them. Their mother sends a basket of peascods to the King, and receives cinnamon and ginger from Lady Rutland. Catherine is under her wing in her household. Hertford— later to become Protector Somerset—would welcome her to his house. But Catherine does not wish to leave Lady Rutland, and wants money for her journey to Belvoir. Her mother acknowledges Hertford's good will with the gift of a linnet.

But her mother is hard put to it to find cash. We have a letter to her from Mrs Gilbert, grandmother of the famous Elizabethan Gilberts, asking for the residue of her money in Lady Lisle's hands. She has had none for two years, and is now sued to outlawry for a small debt: she can do nothing unless her creditors help her. It is now thirteen years since this matter first began, and Lady Lisle's bailiff, Richard Harris, will pay nothing without special orders. Two months later the lady is making the same complaint, and recounting the charges upon her.

At Calais the extravagant *train de vie* continues. A Bruges goldsmith receives 272oz of plate to be made into silver plate with gold rims; English plate does not correspond with theirs, he will make assay and report the difference. A cloth merchant of Bruges receives an order for five timbers (skins) of ermine, the finest and whitest that could be got, at five florins the timber. In London the drapers and grocers want their money; the faithful Hussey: 'if they be not paid now they will never trust more.' Money is wanted to pay for

plate; and again, 'the grocer is not content, and I know I
have lost his friendship.' Anne Basset is better and wants
money; and they of the Parliament chamber have been in
hand with Hussey for their fees. Sir Brian Tuke thanks Lady
Lisle for baked partridges, baked carp, etc.; but what about
taking order for their debts to the King? 'On my faith I dare
not let it sleep as I should like to do, and have done this ten
years . . . I assure you there is nothing I have so long
respited. There must be an end of it at once, and the longer
the more to your discomfort and my blame.'

Nor were the tangled difficulties over the Basset inheritance and the Painswick bargain yet resolved. Lady Lisle's
agent, Harris, advised her to pay some reasonable sum down
and so take possession of the debatable land. To make assurance by Parliament would be very expensive. But no sum
was it possible for her to put down. And all Tudor folk were
racked with suspicion. Lisle's counsel and Cromwell's met
at the Rolls, and Cromwell drove through his bargain. He
would have Painswick 'for ever.' If Lady Lisle refused, he
expected collateral security. Until Painswick was settled there
would be no grant of the Whitefriars at Calais.

'For ever' for Cromwell would mean just a year, when he
would meet the fate he had arranged for others. In the next
year too, 1540, would die a natural death Henry's favoured
servant, Kingston, Constable of the Tower, who had received
so many victims within its walls. Immediately upon
Cromwell's execution Kingston received the gift of Painswick; that is why, when one goes there today, in the church
lies the Keeper of the Tower in state, under his stone canopy
with clustered shafts, there in St Peter's chapel.

On the side of national defence Henry was taking no chances;
an impressive show of musters was put on, Cromwell leading
a trial attack on the city at the head of 1500 men. On the
diplomatic side he was pressing on Henry an alliance with
the German Protestant states to give the Emperor Charles V
pause. Someone observed Cromwell arguing with Henry in
a window embrasure until sweat poured from his face; he
broke off, and then went back to it hammer and tongs again.
It was extraordinary that people would take liberties with
such a man as Henry.

In September Lisle went over on his urgent affairs, in company with the Palsgrave (the Count Palatine of the Rhine) whose mission it was to conclude the marriage treaty of Henry to Anne of Cleves. Lady Lisle reports that she has paid high for French wine and sent Lisle partridges, followed by a partridge pasty and a baked crane: he is to present one to the Palsgrave. She would rather have two lines in his own hand than a hundred in another man's—not ordinary business, but such secrets as they wish to communicate. 'Trust to yourself'—if redress is not now had, she does not know when it will be. Lisle should have ridden at once to the King—it would have been accepted.

Next day, she hopes he will continue in his resolution not to trust to any other, and is glad to hear of good communication with the Lord Privy Seal. She has sent over his sables. 'I requested a place of 6d a day to one of your own servants, but hear you have given it to Sir Edward Ringley. Remember who first complained of you for giving rooms to little men.' She was glad that he answered Cromwell as he had; 'even so I pray you hold him, for so you shall have the best of him. And whereas he saith you shall be ruled by men, he taketh his pleasure—but, mine own good lord, if I had not both loved you and drad [dreaded, i.e. regarded] you, he should never have had of me that he hath.' Next, 'I send you my tooth-picker, which I thought to have given the Palsgrave while he was here. Please present it to him, because when he was here I did see him wear a pen or call[12] to pick his teeth with. I have had it seven years. I am glad your partridges pleased you, but I care not greatly if my Lord Privy Seal had not had them.'

Lisle receives his sables, and hopes to have his gowns finished by Sunday: they will serve as well as if he had brought them with him, as the fur of bogy (budge) had done, which was laid in his black velvet gown (as we notice in several of Holbein's portraits). The King had welcomed him and asked after Lady Lisle. He would follow his own suits and not trust other men's means, 'for I do well know what that hath already cost me.' The Duke of Suffolk welcomed the Palsgrave beyond Eton bridge, and the King has feasted him. He would write to Lord Russell—i.e. as President of the Council of the West—to deal with the Earl of Bridgwater for destroying my son's woods: 'I would he were in Abraham's bosom.'

Hussey reported that the King had entertained Lisle lovingly; he had followed her instructions to give her lord good counsel. Lisle was riding to see the Prince, and would return to the King, when he would know his fate. His wife returns to the charge: 'declare to the King your full mind and trust not promises.' Defer writing to Lord Russell about Bridgwater, for John Basset will be of age this month and then he can go himself to Russell. 'I know the Earl of Bridgwater's appetite. The more he is spoken to the worse he will be.'

Meanwhile she was entertaining Lord Chamberlain Sandys, who had been sent over to appease dissensions. She gave a grand supper for him and all the Council. Sir Edward Ringley, deputising for Lisle, was having difficulties with the French. Large sums were being spent on the fortifications, no chances taken. The weather was so boisterous that there was no passage across the Channel for a week: the Lord Chamberlain and the French gentlemen were waiting to cross, also the prior of Whitefriars: 'be good Lord to him.'

Anne Basset had taken her opportunity to speak to the King on her step-father's behalf. At Westminster she lay 'in the chief chamber under the gallery, where the chairs are made to turn from one chamber into another.' She had presented the King with her mother's codinac;[13] he tasted it and said that he liked it. 'I told his Grace that your ladyship was glad that ye could make anything that his Grace did like. His Grace made me answer that a' did thank you with all his heart.' In the autumn she fell sick; the King has commanded her to her cousin, Dene (probably Denny), at Westminster where were fair walks and good open air; her physician recommended exercise. 'We trust we shall have a mistress shortly.' Brother George is now in Court with Sir Francis Bryan. The maidens were being appointed to attend upon Anne of Cleves as Queen—Anne Basset among them, her sister Catherine hoped for a posting; one of them was Catherine Howard.

Lisle wound up his affairs to his satisfaction, and in October accompanied the Palsgrave to Dover for the crossing. It had been 'no ill journey' for this German princeling: he had been rewarded with 2000 marks of good English money. Lisle sent ahead venison and twenty oxen in Bartlett's boat, presumably from the West Country. Hussey thought that Cromwell was through with Lisle for Painswick, who had in return his commission for the Whitefriars and the loan of £400. 'I doubt not your jointure will be made sure this term', i.e. what was left of it, or placed on a new footing. Lisle had left money for a bonnet for her; Hussey has got it made, also a kirtle of the newest make, a lettice (grey fur) cap for Mistress Honor and three pairs of hose.

Shortly Hussey assured her of her jointure of £120 a year, evidently the rent-charge on Painswick, and we may resume her more amenable concerns. From the West Country Mrs Carkeet sends her a barrel of quinces, and Lady Garneys sixty quinces and a basket of barberries. Mr Coswarth the draper desires £8 for crimson velvet. In Paris the peltiers will not sell fur under 15 crowns a skin; dames who wear that fur in the 'poniards'[14] wear the same in all the rest of the gown. Many wear white taffeta armozeen[15] in the suit.

Sister Antoinette de Saveuses is very active at Dunkirk. She has had a representation of St George made 'to put in your cabinet'—but this was broken in the carriage—and has received 'two rosenboz [boxes of rose-petals] in payment for half-a-dozen *bonnets de femme* you had.' Next she sends half-a-dozen men's bonnets at 8s each. The nuns of Dunkirk must have made a good thing out of Lady Lisle. Sister Antoinette had stayed with her at Calais, shortly after John Basset's marriage. And Madame de Riou had been anxious to know within a month or two whether his wife was *enceinte*. Now Madame was having trouble with her husband, and Lady Lisle intends to approach the French king to mediate between them. The nun begs her to be discreet, or the King's reprimand will not do Monsieur de Riou much good. She sends a tree of silk for Anne Basset. Lady Lisle returns with three 'rozenboz'; the nun is ashamed to be rewarded so highly for so little a thing as that damaged by the carrier. Evidently her ladyship thought it more blessed to give than to receive: she was too generous.

The priest she was supporting in Paris has received her tokens; John Scryven 'will lack no pies at breakfast while that will serve him.' Both, however, need more help—like everybody else. The Sieur de Riou wants a couple of greyhounds, having lost all his 'during these wars'; he sends a goshawk—a profitable exchange to him. Hussey sends over the greyhounds—one from Mr Manners, 'whose name is Mannikin, and a hound called Hurl: the master has 8d for their meat.' Mme du Bours receives a gift of one of the hounds. From the Rutlands Catherine Basset begs her mother to sue for her to be one of the new Queen's maids; she thanks her for her petticoat and a 'kreppin' (i.e. fringe.) The Lisles' chaplain, Sir Gregory Botolph, has made payment for 3 oz. of popinjay green silk, for a holy water pot 8d, and for alms and minstrels' reward at church 12d.

No sooner was Lisle back in Calais than, with an unwonted access of energy, he dismissed four men-at-arms and their constable. This made for trouble for, though the age was rough and raw, men had their rights and they appealed to the King and Cromwell. Lisle said that they were unmeet for their posts and, if the King did not see the charges against them, they would be back. 'But I care the less, because I trust I shall not remain here long.' In London Hussey has delivered the two brass falcons (small cannon) to Cromwell and set them in his courtyard at Austin Friars; when the great man got down from his mule he inspected them and ordered them to be stowed under the great chamber. He was less pleased when he heard about the dismissed men; he wished that Lisle had done it in a more temperate way, and the charges against the men sent ahead of them. A week later the men had cleared themselves; now they could not be discharged without disgrace to himself. 'He was never before so sudden with me', said Hussey; at last he prevailed on him to say that 'he loved you no less than his son Gregory.'

Hussey heard much more from the Lord Privy Seal, 'nothing pleasant, which is not to be written.' The discharged men were suing for their livings and Cromwell passed the buck to Cranmer—'God knows what will become of them.' Commissioners examined them, and the Archbishop reported that some of them were involved with the preacher, Adam Damplip. The King thought it a pity the discharged men should lose their places before anything was proved against them—so Lisle was not to give their jobs away before proper trial of the matter. Nor were Lisle's private affairs as settled as could be wished. The King had not granted him the fee-simple of the Whitefriars, i.e. the freehold, nor should he have the annuity. He wished Lisle to receive the incoming Anne of Cleves at the waterside, but not to come over with her.

Cromwell desired Lisle not to sell timber from Frithelstoke in a hurry—which he was doing, the readiest way to raise money. His promised loan of £400 had not yet materialised; Hussey to him, 'they are so variable in all their proceedings, I know not what to trust.' Nor was it opportune either to ask Lord Russell for a loan of £200, or Cromwell for a more peaceful living. Lisle thought he should come over in person; Hussey hoped that he would not come to Dover and 'set such an example of license as to leave your trust. They care not a rush for any slander against my Lord for his coming over, provided they have their purpose, nor if he lost all he had. I doubt if they have either conscience or soul, or believe in heaven or hell.'

Bridgwater was not yet dead, convenient as that would be. In May, 'my lord of Bridgwater is here, very pleasant, and as yet well moneyed. I think he will carry small store out of the city at his return home.' But he had no male heir, so there was a fair prospect for the Bassets in that quarter.

In December preparations were complete for Anne of Cleves' reception with all the honour due to a Queen. She had her safe-conduct for her journey through Flanders. A heavy burden of entertaining would fall on the Lisles. Hussey expedited twenty gallons of malmsey; Cranmer thanked them for the French wines for her reception at Canterbury. The governor of Boulogne sent a boar's head and side for Lisle expecting much company: he has had men in the fields two or three days hoping to take something good. He sent a mule ready harnessed for Lady Lisle, who with other ladies was to receive Anne at the town-gates; a nun sent her gloves; banquets and jousts were planned. What added to the burden was the winter weather: Anne was kept waiting an extra ten days with her entourage for a change of wind.

Meanwhile Henry was awaiting his new bride in a mixture of expectation and apprehension. Just before Christmas Anne Basset wrote to her mother that 'the King is aware of the great charge you sustain. He likes so much the conserves you

sent him that he asks for more of the "codynac" of the
clearest making, and of the damsons.' She hears that Queen
Anne is good and gentle—good news for her future servants.
Lady Lisle received a long report describing every stage of
the Queen's reception in England. On New Year's day 1540
Henry paid her a private visit, banqueted her and came away
privily that night. It was ominous that he could not stomach
the unappetising *Fräulein*. On the morning of Twelfth day,
the day of the wedding, he said to Cromwell, 'My lord, if
it were not to satisfy the world and my realm, I would not
do that which I must do this day for none earthly thing.'
This was a bad omen for Cromwell who had pressed it on
him.

Lady Edgecombe was summoned up from the West
Country to be a lady of the Privy Chamber—her late husband
had been a supporter of Cromwell's. Mary Basset went over
to England, hoping for something in the general post; sister
Anne applied to the King for a place for Catherine, 'but he
said he would not grant me nor them as yet, for a' would
have them that should be fair and as he thought meet for the
room.' There follows a revealing postscript: 'and whereas ye
do write to me that I do not write with mine own hand, the
truth is that I can not write nothing myself but mine own
name. And as for that when I had haste to go up to the
Queen's chamber, my man did write it which did write me
[sic] letter.' This was written from York Place, i.e. Wolsey's
palace, which had became the King's Whitehall.

There a great Court was being kept. Hussey advised Lisle
not to trouble Cromwell 'till these banqueting days be past.'
Catherine Basset remains with the Rutlands, who thank her
mother for wine and herrings; Lady Rutland has given
Catherine a gown of 'caffa' (damask) of her own old
wearing—the girl wants buckram to new-line it and velvet
to edge it. What is to be done with young George Basset,
now with Sir Francis Bryan, Master of the Toils? Lisle wants
him to be sent to Paris to learn the language, as he is a youth
of 'wit', i.e. intelligence. But neither Bryan nor George is
willing to part. John Basset has been with the Earl of Bridgwater, who asked 2000 marks to clear the inheritance, when
Basset offered 5 or 600 marks. Bridgwater has taken back his

wife: it is hoped that John Basset 'may have no loss thereby hereafter.' Apparently not: the Earl had no progeny.

Lisle, grown suspicious, charges that Hussey suffers words to be spoken against him without rebutting them. Not so, he replies, 'they hate me like the pestilence.' Lisle thinks of settling the affair of Whitefriars by sending over Lady Lisle to sue to the King. The prior asks for the pension of £5 a year Lisle has granted him, 'and the hangings of green and red say about the high altar for my chamber. Ringley has a vestment and chalice I left with him'. He had left four feather beds in the vestry—none was left on his return. Lady Lisle is sending Madame du Bours a poodle, 'very good at retrieving the head or bolt of a crossbow, both in water and on land, and will fetch a tennis ball or a glove put on the end of a stick, and other tricks.'

News from England continues to be disappointing. The King has allowed the discharged men their places at Calais— under conditions to satisfy the Lord Deputy. 'The King is good lord to you and Lady Lisle'—that may be. . . . But all the same, in regard to Lisle's warrants, his solicitor writes: 'I find my Lord Chancellor as good as any man could wish, but the search from auditor to auditor, and from clerk to clerk of Augmentations, passeth the Bishop of Rome's feigned purgatory; for it lighteth the purse, wearieth the legs, distempereth the body. The suitor is further off when he thinks himself most sure, but hope assuageth a great part of his pains.' It is an authentic *résumé* of how Tudor business was done.

Henry VIII's prime concern internally was the maintenance of unity, and externally national power and independence. He was above all a politician—that was his job—engaged in steering his country through a revolution directed from the top. He had the support of the governing class in general, who stood to profit immensely from the relegation of the Church to a secondary position in the state and the annexation of a considerable portion of its property and wealth. The chief difficulty, as in all revolutions, was to keep people in line and not to allow things to get out of hand, not to go too fast. Henry decided in 1539 that, for the present, reform had gone far enough. Naturally a conservative, he wanted to

stabilise things on the existing basis and enforce a pause.
Once more, as with the Reformation Parliament which had
endorsed the revolutionary changes, he would call a Parliament to reinforce him in imposing his line. To proceed
'through unity and uniformity' was the rumour reported in
the Lisle Correspondence, the watchword given out from on
high.

Parliament was to meet in April. The Lord Chancellor
instructed Lisle to proceed to the election of burgesses for
Parliament, but not to send them over until he had spoken
to the King about it. Parliament supported the King with a
sweeping Act of attainder against his reactionary opponents,
past and present: Exeter, Montagu, Neville, Darcy, Hussey
and several abbots who had supported or connived at the
Northern rebellion. 'All traitors are attainted according to
their deserts—the great traitor, Pole, Cardinal', the report
went over to Calais. For good measure the Cardinal's
mother, Lady Salisbury, was included. An incriminating
document was said to have been found in her coffer
proposing the marriage of the Lady Mary to her son the
Cardinal (not yet in priest's orders). Anything that touched
the succession raised alarm in Henry, it had all given him
such worry and trouble. Lady Salisbury was sent to the
Tower, but for the present Henry held his hand, the sentence
not executed.

At the same time the Act of Six Articles was passed
enforcing Catholic beliefs. Cranmer and the reformers
opposed it in vain. 'There is great hold among the bishops
for the establishment of the blessed sacrament of the altar.'
The lords and bishops were in daily council; the King wants
the matter decided and intervenes to impose the majority
opinion. 'It will be the wholesome Act ever passed'—such
was the information the Lisles received. Clerical celibacy was
enforced by the religious King—to whom matrimony had
given such trouble, and was to give more. The Archbishop
had to send his wife packing, back to Germany, whence
he should never have brought her. Bonner, a conservative
Henrician like Gardiner—both acquaintances of the Lisles—
was made bishop of London. The reforming bishops, Latimer
and Shaxton, had to resign their bishoprics and were held in
confinement. Thus was the middle way enforced. A corre-

spondent of Lady Lisle wrote the news, which she would not be sorry to hear: 'they be not of the wisest sort methinks, for few nowadays will leave and give over such promotions for keeping of opinion.' That is what most people sensibly thought—and think, at most times.

It was Henry's business to show himself to the people, always merry and in full command, to encourage morale and religiosity, if not religion. On the even of Holy Thursday he took his barge at Whitehall and was rowed up to Lambeth, drums and fifes playing, and thus rowed up and down for an hour after evensong. On Holy Thursday he went in procession about the Court at Westminster, the high altar in the chapel garnished with images of all the apostles, Mass sung by note, i.e. plain-chant, and organs playing. On Good Friday the King crept devoutly in all his bulk from the chapel door to the cross, and served the priest at Mass on his knees. One man was hanged for eating meat on Friday against the King's command. The King receives holy bread and holy water every Sunday—no man dares speak against ceremonies on pain of death.

During the session the King made a grand banquet, with most of the great ladies present—Anne and Catherine Basset lay there all night. Their mother had sent him two hampers of peascods; he has no need of more, for he has just had some that grew in a Frenchman's garden in Southwark. Poor widowed Lady Hussey has a daughter to place—she hopes that Lady Lisle will take her, giving her wages and livery. Kind Lady Rutland suggests this, with whom Catherine is happy, and does not wish to leave her for Lady Hertford: she is afraid she should be taken 'but as her woman, for so Lady Rutland does not use her.' The Rutlands are sent eight dozen quails, two dozen brews (snipe) and one dozen heron-shaws.[16] Lord Hertford has been sent a bird, but the ship leaked and there was all a-do to save the contents. When the bird arrived at Billingsgate 'there the cat made her testament, which my lord of Hertford took right grievously.' So Lady Lisle replaces the bird with her very own: she would not do as much for anyone, except the King.

Hussey reports that Hertford went over to Calais prospecting to become Lord Deputy: if the King resolves so, Hussey wishes Lisle might become governor to Prince

Edward, or some other in England. 'Calais is like the frogs; it can be long contented with no deputy, but is always desiring change . . . I trust that day shall never shine that your lordship shall be his deputy.' Hertford was well out of it. Cromwell tells Hussey that the Council at Calais is divided: 'this is the reason why your letters are not answered.'

Lady Lisle wants a matins book, bound with the epistles and gospels; Hussey sends one of the best printing. She has the daily prayers of the *religieuses* at Dunkirk, who are employed in making numerous bonnets and caps for her and her household. Lady Hertford is sent a stole, and Catherine receives 12 yards of white damask, 2½ yards of carnation velvet, one roll of buckram, and half a yard of velvet for a partlet (neck-wear). George Basset is merry and a good penman; Bishop Gardiner will no doubt furnish James with all things necessary, 'if not all things to his pleasure'—we see again that this youth was rather particular. Mr Skut—the Norman Hartnell of his day—wants two dozen quails by the last of May; he has finished Lady Lisle's black satin gown furred with sables. Coswarth, a less demanding character, has been paid £20, but has 'no cloth of gold as you wish.' Hussey sends receipts for rents, though little comes in.

The year 1540 was decisive, well-nigh fatal, for the Lisles, and it was the religious dissensions at Calais that precipitated their troubles. It was a critical year for others too, and marked another swerve in Henry VIII's policy, until it settled into the last phase of the reign. While the Emperor was journeying through France to his personal interview with Francis I, England was kept on the alert in case of a hostile conjunction of these major powers. Care was taken to stock Calais with provisions and equipment. At one point Lisle reported forces gathering in Picardy. Then came the news from Antwerp: 'the conjunction between the Emperor and the French king is not so great as was pretended.' This was ominous for Cromwell: Henry could now dispense with his German alliance, return to traditional friendship with the Netherlands and Charles V, and at the same time solve his personal problem by relegating Anne of Cleves, 'the Flanders mare', as he called her. He could not bring himself to consummate the marriage, he said; it was declared a non-marriage, and the lady was paid off with a magnificent dowry to enjoy her freedom for the rest of her life in England.

On whom would Henry's alert eye alight? Catherine Howard, daughter of Lisle's old acquaintance, Lord Edmund Howard, was already there, all too available; and Bishop Gardiner pushed all in his power to put her in Henry's way. As soon as he was free of his encumbrance he privately married Catherine, buxom, cheerful, light-headed—and experienced enough to give him contentment in bed. The contest between Gardiner and Cromwell for power waxed so fierce, a witness said, that one or the other must succumb. Circumstances, political and personal, combined to favour Gardiner and he had majority opinion with him, in both Council and country. Cromwell was Henry's creature; he had little support, his unpopularity always a liability, and he could be thrown to the wolves. In the end he was.

Once and again Henry made an urgent plea for people to pipe down in these nonsense disputes. He was determined that they should toe the line; what would happen when his strong hand was removed we see from the turmoil and anarchy during the minority of his son Edward VI—Henry had indeed delayed too long over the divorce of Catherine of Aragon. In March a commission was sent over to Calais to investigate the dissensions. (At home in Lady Lisle's Cornwall Thomas Treffry was supervising the building of beautiful St Mawes castle, to guard the entrance to Falmouth harbour.) The report went back that the disputes had been caused by the preaching of Adam Damplip against the Real Presence in the sacrament of the altar. He was to be examined by Cranmer—himself wavering on that subject in his own mind. One of the retinue was an aggressive sacramentary, and twenty more were touched by it. Sir George Carew was not to be proceeded against: he wished to give up on account of health. The Lord Chamberlain assured Lisle that the King had provided for the security of Calais and for the punishment of sacramentaries.

It was the Lisles' chaplain, Sir Gregory Botolph, an adherent of the old faith, who was to incriminate them. In March Sir John Wallop wrote that he was sorry to lose Lisle from Calais, 'but if Wyatt should supply you in your place, that I would much mislike.' A few days later Botolph made

a hurried departure, aided by the Lisles. Selling raiment,
bedding, books, he asked for his gear to be sent after him to
the Chequer at Gravelines, 'and all my little books in my
study, my gowns and cloak of my Lord's livery.' He begged
for licence to go to the university of Louvain to study. If he
were suspected, Lisle should take Lady Lisle's advice:
'without feigning, I will never have any other master and
mistress during their lives.' In fact, he was to bring them in
question. Kindly as usual, the Lord Deputy assured the chaplain that he might keep his study as a non-resident while at
Louvain.

In April the King recalled Lisle, politely through the Duke
of Norfolk; Sussex was to take over 'till your return'. No
suspicion as yet: at the chapel of the Order of the Garter on
St George's day at Westminster Lisle sat with Cromwell—
just made Earl of Essex in the struggle for power—on the
left of the King. Next day he was prevented from going to
Windsor for the installation. In Calais Lady Lisle gave it out
bravely that he was ill.

In fact the commissioners uncovered something incrimi-
nating concerning Botolph. He had been to Rome colloguing
with the King's great enemy, Cardinal Pole, and with the
Pope, who had provided him with a supply of gold crowns.
To what purpose? The surprise of Calais was the answer.
Prolonged probing revealed plans for entry by the Lantern
Gate, and others were incriminated: Brindlehome, the parish
priest of our Lady, and Clement Philpot, gentleman. They
were duly attainted of treason along with the noxious
Botolph. But the Lisles had given him money and a passport,
recommending him to the care of the nunnery outside
Gravelines, and the Deputy had written a letter to the
Emperor, without permission. The commissioners marvelled
that Calais was not surprised, so little order was kept and so
many foreigners allowed in the town. The whole Council
there was discharged, except for the Vice-Treasurer and the
Porter.

Marillac, the French ambassador, reported to Francis I that
on the 19th of May, at ten o'clock at night, Lisle—'uncle of
this King'—was led prisoner to the Tower, whither three of
his servants had been previously sent, and two days later a
chaplain of his who came in a ship from Flanders. The Lord

Deputy is accused of secret intelligence with Pole, his near relation, to deliver Calais to him; Lisle 'is in a very narrow place, from which no-one escapes unless by a miracle. All accusations here are called treason.' With Lisle shut up within the Tower, and Lady Lisle committed to the charge of friendly Francis Hall at Calais, the illuminating correspondence which has thrown such a light upon these Henrician characters and their way of life comes to an end. The lights go out: we are thrown back upon what remains in official documents and depositions, *disjecta membra*. Even from these not all the life has departed: we can still trace something of what happened to the family.

At Calais, Lady Lisle and her daughter Mary were examined for further evidence. She could speak no French, so her daughter had to interpret for her when the Constable of France wrote to her husband, who had indeed received a letter from the Emperor. She declared all to the Council and asked Anne at Court to explain to the King. A letter from her servant Corbet, in communication with Botolph, had been discovered in her hair-brushes; the letters recovered from the jakes were love letters belonging to her daughter, Mary. The girl deposed that she had been some four years with Madame du Bours, whose son fell in love with her, and sent her sleeves of yellow velvet, then ruffs of gold, at length a primer. He then moved marriage with her, and she contracted marriage with him privily on Palm Sunday eve. She had told her sisters and her mother, who wrote to Lisle and to Anne to inform the King what M. du Bours was and that Mary had been brought up with his mother.

This private contract of marriage with a foreigner was evidently not recognised, for later Mary was married safely to a small Devon gentleman, a Woolacombe.

We can reconstruct the Lisles' interior at Calais from the inventories taken, as in a Holbein. Lady Lisle's chamber with the Turkey carpets and tapestries, her field bedstead with tester and ceiler of tawny velvet and blue satin, curtains and quilt of blue and tawny sarcenet—those favourite colours; red carpets with blue crewel-work, a Flanders chair, and so on. Next to her, her gentlewoman's chamber. Her lord's room had four new Turkey carpets, tapestries, and bed furniture of the same tawny and blue sarcenet. Next was the grooms' chamber. We know the furnishings of the great chamber, great parlour, kitchen, butlery, pantry, ewry; the chapel had a table with a crucifix, before which we may imagine their devotions.

Next their plate and jewels, several chains, girdles, gold rings, a gold rose with diamonds and pearls; and gowns— Lisle's Parliament robe he would need no more, ten lizard (lynx) furs. Lady Lisle's gowns of blue satin lined with buckram, of tawny velvet and black velvet lined with white taffeta turned up with powdered ermines, of tawny caffa damask faced with black cony, of black velvet furred with budge, turned up with pampilion (a kind of fur). Good Master Skut's handiwork over the years.

Outside were stables, and farmhouse with their cattle; and, along with the poultry, a great cage of quails and herons. Much of their possessions came into the hands of their successors: the plate to Lord Maltravers who became Deputy, except for two flagons which went to Lord Sussex, along with most of the horses and the furnishings of the chapel. Thus Henricians ate each other up. The Lisles had been well at ease in their Calais home, but the good days were over.

We owe to Miss St Clair Byrne the probable explanation of the catastrophic about-turn in the Lisles' fortunes—as a frame-up on the part of Cromwell. In the hectic struggle for power between him and the conservatives headed by Gardiner, who were much in the majority, Cromwell was reaching out for any straw to save himself from drowning. The critical situation in Calais offered him a chance. If he could represent to the King that there was a conspiracy on the part of those with Catholic sympathies to surrender Calais to the enemy, then he could represent himself once again as saving Henry from his enemies.

The contact of the Lisles' foolish chaplain with the 'great enemy', Cardinal Pole, was suspicious and provided the straw for Cromwell, gave some colour to his case. Hence the arrest of Lisle and his committal to the Tower. But Henry was not taken in: he came to see that there was no malice in Lisle, let alone any attempt at treason. Cromwell's position with the King was fatally undermined by his pressing the Cleves marriage upon him and the alliance with German Protestants. The moment that Henry was free of any danger of an alliance between the Emperor Charles V and France against him, he was ready to throw over German Protestants, Anne of Cleves, and Cromwell for the respectability of friendly relations with the Emperor and a return to a more conservative course once more.

And this was in keeping with majority opinion in the country. Cromwell had few friends, and throwing him to the wolves was positively popular—as the wicked treatment of Anne Boleyn had been, in whose fate he had been criminally involved. With his execution the evidence on that was now extinguished.

All this was politics, as we see—in which personal sympathies, inclinations, passions were of course intermeshed, notably Henry's in regard to Anne Boleyn and Anne of Cleves. The Lisles were caught in the intermeshing of the machine.

Scraps and pieces remain in the documents to tell us how they fared. They had left many debts, including 'a good round sum' to a goldsmith at Paris, their servants unpaid. In March 1541 the King's tailor, Malt, is ordered to make Lisle 'a large gown of damask furred with black cony' with several other items. For his fellow-prisoner and cousin, Lady Salisbury, the Queen's tailor has to provide plainer apparel. An idiotic insurrection by Sir John Neville in Yorkshire settled her fate: in May the poor old lady was executed, an inexperienced executioner terribly hacking her about. In June the rumour was that Lisle would shortly follow on her heels.

But in July it was Cromwell's turn instead: he knew too much—particularly about Anne Boleyn's fate—for Henry to keep him alive. Later, the ogre was to confess his want of his ablest servant's ability. Marillac informed Francis I that Cromwell had been 'reckoned the sole deviser of the deaths of so many people, but it appears since that he was not altogether author of that piteous tragedy, but rather played his part as it was rehearsed to him.' Meanwhile, Lisle was not led to judgment: it is said that 'he will remain prisoner for life in the Tower, where he is a little more at large than he was. Some lords of this Court have heard their master say that the Deputy offended more through simplicity and ignorance than malice.' So that was what Henry thought of his old uncle.

We have detailed accounts of Lisle's lands, many of them sold to pay for the extravagant *train de vie* of which we have seen plenty of evidence. It appears that his wealth was more apparent than real: a net income of £650 a year, compared with the former Marquis of Exeter's £2000, or the former Duke of Buckingham's £6000. Now Kingston's successor at the Tower receives payment for Lisle's board; as does Francis Hall at Calais for Lady Lisle and her daughters, with three servants and a priest to attend them.

Foxe, the Protestant martyrologist, was able to throw light, in Elizabeth I's reign, upon the dissensions that had troubled the Lisles and darkened their days at Calais.[17] We learn that the fool of a Damplip was formerly 'a great papist' and chaplain of Bishop Fisher's; but that a visit to Renaissance Rome had converted him—like Luther—to the stance of protest, i.e. Protestantism. At Calais, though well received by the Lisles, he preached against transubstantion and against a picture of the Resurrection in St Nicholas church. Three Hosts besprinkled with blood upon a marble altar were discovered to be three white counters painted. Thereupon Botolph informed against him; he was sent for to be examined by Cranmer, who warned him to retire, and he went secretly to the West Country.

Upon this the priest of Our Lady parish took up the tale and preached against the favourers of God's word. Lisle, 'albeit he were himself of a most gentle nature and of a right noble blood, being fiercely set on and incessantly enticed by the wicked Lady Honor his wife, who was an utter enemy to God's honour—and in idolatry, hypocrisy, and pride incomparably evil—she, being daily and hourly thereunto provoked and incited by Sir Thomas Palmer and John Rookwood', informed the Privy Council against the Protestants in Calais. This set going a persecution of them—we see what a pretty kettle of fish religion made there.

A new commission under Sussex exculpated the Protestants and reversed engines. Not long after, Lisle was sent for and put into the Tower. Foxe continued,

and when the King minded to have been gracious unto him and to have let him come forth, God took him out of this world, whose body resteth in the Tower and his soul with God, I trust in heaven, for he died very repentant. But the wicked Lady his wife, immediately upon his apprehension, fell distraught of mind and so continued many years after. God for his mercy, if she yet live, give her his grace to repent.

For all its Protestants prejudice this bears the stamp of truth. Lady Lisle lived on for many years, for as late as 1563 she presented to the living of Camborne, in right of her grandson, a minor.[18] For John Basset, the heir, died young in April of this year 1541, leaving Lisle's daughter Frances a widow. At some time a division was achieved, John's son, Arthur—named for Lord Lisle—succeeding to the Devon estate; Lady Lisle's second son, George, to Tehidy, the Cornish estate. Henceforth there were two lines. It is unlikely that she 'repented' and conformed, for the Devon Bassets continued to be Catholic into the next century. The shock of Lisle's imprisonment was enough to distract his wife's reason, at least for a time, for Henricians knew what to expect—and she and her husband were, exceptionally, much in love. We have seen her to be a forceful character, emotional and impulsive, generous to extravagance, kind and vulnerable, with many troubles and worries on her mind. We hear little more of her: let us hope that, in retirement from the world, she achieved some peace of mind.

Queen Catherine Howard's days were numbered: she had come to Henry doubtfully virgin and, with incredible insouciance, continued contact with her paramours after marriage. On the King's tour to recalcitrant York in the summer of 1541, Lady Rochford watched the back entrances for the Queen to receive them. On All Saints day Henry, all unaware, ordered his confessor to give public 'thanks to God with him for the good life he led and hoped to lead, after sundry troubles of mind which had happened to him by marriages.' Cranmer was no match for Gardiner as a politician, but on All Souls day the Archbishop trumped the Bishop by putting a paper into the King's hand at Mass with charges of the Queen's infidelities. The ageing egoist was dumbfounded, could not at first believe it, and was much downcast at his luck—when he had been happy with the minx—complaining what ill-conditioned women had been his lot and (with masculine egoism) that none of them had put themselves out to make him comfortable.

Catherine was relegated to Sion House 'and lodged moderately as her life hath deserved' while it was decided what to do with her; her household was broken up, her maids of honour returned to their friends, 'save Mistress Basset, whom the King, in consideration of the calamity of her friends will at his charges specially provide for.' He was as good as his word. In January 1542 Marillac reports that Lisle is to be pardoned and his Order of the Garter sent back to him; already he has liberty within the Tower where he used to have but one narrow chamber. Charles V's ambassador relates that Henry, for months downcast, recovered his spirits upon the condemnation of the Queen—no doubt with new expectations. He gave a grand supper with twenty-six ladies at table and thirty-five at another close by, showing much favour to a lady whom Wyatt had repudiated for adultery. Henry, the ambassador goes on, is also said to have a fancy for a daughter of Lisle's wife—a surmise which rests partly on the fact that after his close confinement in the Tower, Lisle has been given liberty and his arms ordered to be replaced in the chapel of the Order of the Garter.

However, Lisle did not emerge: he died a few days after, some said of joy at his rehabilitation. We have the modest account for wax candles and other stuff employed at his funeral in the Tower. At the same time his widow and her daughters were released from confinement at Calais, their apparel and jewels restored, and the large sum of £100 provided for payment of debts and their transport to England. After Henry's matrimonial misfortune he did not marry again for some months, and the lot did not fall upon Anne Basset, but on the kindly, intelligent widow, Catherine Parr. Henry continued to provide for Anne, along with the royal ladies, apparel, silks etc., for several years. And he continued to be kind: Lisle's daughter Elizabeth was to have the first room of a sister that shall fall vacant, meanwhile she was to be maintained 'partly at the King's cost by way of charity.' Money due to Frances, John's widow, was paid; she made another Devon marriage, to Thomas Monk, and thus became an ancestor of the historic General Monk of the Restoration. It is nice to think—though nobody knows it, he would have done—that the restorer of the monarchy had Plantagenet royal blood.

Immediately upon Lisle's death without a male heir the title was re-created for John Dudley—in right of his mother, Elizabeth Grey, coheiress of a previous Viscount Lisle, Arthur Plantagenet's first wife—on his way to his spectacular career as Duke of Northumberland. The Grenvilles continued to prosper, though their leading lady had withdrawn from the limelight. Sir Richard, no longer High Marshal of Calais, was able to concentrate his attention upon his West Country interests and building up the monastic property he bought in South Devon, Buckland near Plymouth. In Henry's third French war we find Grenville leading two hundred men from Cornwall to Dover, to serve along with Sir William Godolphin's 'pioners' (sappers), who played their part in undermining the walls of Boulogne, which led to its capture.

It was Henry's desired rapprochement with the Emperor that led him into his last, most extravagant and least defensible venture; for the Emperor reneged on him, and left England to confront alone a France three times the size in resources and population. It was now that Henry's use of the wealth of the monasteries, the lead from roofs and bells, came into play to strengthen the country's defences, militarily and navally; but the effort was a tremendous strain and diminished the Crown's resources from which so much had been hoped. In the course of the war the King's big ship, the *Mary Rose*, capsized at Portsmouth with the loss of all her men: another calamity for the family, for serving in her was Roger Grenville, father of its most famous member, the hero of the *Revenge*.

George Grenville, evidently a sportsman, remained Serjeant of the King's hunts for many years, and went no further. John Grenville provided for himself bit by bit: receiver of Crown lands in Devon and Cornwall, usefully employed on commissions of the peace there, lessor of toll tin on the manor of Tywarnhaile, purchaser of Tywardreath priory, in receipt of a small annuity on giving up office as serjeant-at-arms. A young kinsman of Lady Lisle, a clerical John, held the family living at Kilkhampton through all the chops and changes of Henry VIII, Edward VI, Mary and Elizabeth—sensible man—from 1542 to 1580. When one goes

there one sees his memorial in the inscription on the porch,
'Porta Coeli, 1567.'

It remains only to follow what happened to Lady Lisle's
courtier children.[19] Herself we find selling off small properties at Frithelstoke in 1547, so by then we may presume that
she had regained her senses, if indeed she had ever lost them.
Anne remained on as maid-of-honour to Catherine Parr, as
she had been to Henry's previous Queens. James's fortunes
were bound up with Bishop Gardiner; so that, when he
became Queen Mary's leading minister, Basset's star was
briefly in the ascendant. This reflected itself brightly on
Anne. As a lady of the Queen's Privy Chamber, she was
granted an annuity of 40 marks for life, and in 1554 a Catholic
marriage was found for her to the heir of Lord Hungerford,
a kinsman of Cardinal Pole. Generous as ever to personal
attendants, Queen Mary provided Anne with a dowry, and
granted her the reversion to the Hungerford lands in
Cornwall. This did not take effect, for by 1558 Anne was
dead. Her marriage can hardly have been happy, for Walter
Hungerford was a light-headed fool—his father had been
executed for sodomy—and she was childless.

Basset acted as proctor at Gardiner's trial in 1550, and was
sent to the Tower with him, for next year, in October we
have a note of his release.[20] It is already an indication of his
return to activity that he was returned to Edward VI's last
Parliament, 1 to 31 March 1553, as member for Taunton.
With Mary's accession that summer Gardiner became her
principal minister, and Basset moved into the inner circle
around him. He was indispensably a member of every one
of Mary's Parliaments: for Downton, Wiltshire, in the first
in April 1554. His new status is registered by his return as
knight of the shire for Devon for each successive Parliament
in November 1554, October 1555, January 1558.[21]

He had married Mary, daughter of William Roper, son-
in-law of Sir Thomas More and author of the famous
biography.[22] Gaining the wardship of his nephew, Arthur,
head of the line, with an annuity out of the lands, James
began to build up an estate of his own in his native Devon.
In London he acquired the house next the Savoy which had
been Sir Thomas Palmer's, attainted along with Lord Lisle.

His main acquisition was the manor of Torrington. Next he got the lease of the Devon properties of Sir Peter Carew, in revolt against Mary's Spanish marriage to Philip. Shortly a further bunch of properties or leases of them were acquired in Devon, Somerset and Wiltshire. Down at Atherington the family living was filled by Gregory Basset in 1556, no doubt a reliable Catholic, upon the 'free resignation' of his predecessor.

By 1555 James was a gentleman of the Queen's Privy Chamber, a confidential servant of her and Philip, after whom his infant son was named, with the Count Feria standing as godfather. Thus, when the young Earl of Devon incriminated himself over the Queen's marriage and after a patch of imprisonment went abroad, Basset took care of his affairs at home, remitting him money and good advice, along with communications from the Queen and Philip.[23] The conspicuous Earl regarded Basset as a personal friend, on whom he principally relied, along with Sir Francis Englefield, and in 1555 James paid him a brief visit in Flanders.

In 1557, for a large sum of money—over £2000—James purchased the reversion to yet more properties in Devon. Monastic land—of Launceston priory, for example—chantry land, manors formerly of the attainted Duke of Suffolk and Marquis of Exeter, though one of the latter, Columb John, had been granted by Edward VI to the Marchioness for her life:[24] all was grist that came to James Basset's mill. But he had opened his mouth too wide and was overspending his resources. In recognition of his status he was to maintain a retinue of twenty persons. He was picking up yet more scraps of land, when he died in September 1558, yet young, only a month before the deaths of the Queen and Cardinal Pole brought the end of their Catholic régime.

James Basset made his will on 6 September 1558, 'sick and weak in body, and yet in good and perfect remembrance and understanding.' From it we have an intimate glimpse into his circumstances and family connexions, which were all with the faithful Catholic circle of Sir Thomas More's family, who mostly went into exile in Elizabeth's reign. What would have happened to James had he lived? His wife was 'ensent' (*enceinte*)—he uses the word twice: we have before noticed James's fondness for French words from his upbringing. He

left her all her jewels and one half of his household stuff; he
hoped that she and his son would succeed to his offices as
keeper of house and park at Esher (Wolsey's former establishment), and Hunsdon. (This royal estate Elizabeth was shortly
to confer upon her Boleyn cousin, who took his title from
it, the later Lord Chamberlain.[25] She was also to have the
rents from Torrington and their house and gardens in
Chelsea.

To Dr John Clement, James bequeathed the great gilt cup
which Count Feria gave at the christening of his son Philip.
Clement, President of the Royal College of Physicians, was
the husband of Margaret Giggs, kinswoman of More, whom
we see in Holbein's sketch of the family. Executors were
Roper and More's nephew, Serjeant Rastell, who was also to
go into exile; supervisors, James Courtenay, Basset's cousin,
and Dean Cole of St Paul's, who preached the disgraceful
sermon before Cranmer's burning at Oxford. Cole was
shortly to be replaced by an abler man, Alexander
Nowell—and indeed Cardinal Pole observed that the Protestants had the abler men, and also the younger generation
with them.

Basset's will was redolent of his Catholic faith: £40 to pray
for his soul and all Christian souls; £40 to monks and nuns
chosen by his executors, £20 to the restored Blackfriars of
Smithfield. Queen Mary had re-founded the monks and nuns
at the joint royal foundations of Sion and Sheen. The late
Earl of Devon had made over some properties jointly to him
and those religious houses at his persuasion. Basset now
bequeathed them his share—hoping to be named as a
founder—'for evermore.' 'Evermore' was to be just a matter
of months before they vanished for ever.

On the secular side the will was long and complicated, for
it is evident that James had bitten off more than he could
chew, and he was dying 'indebted in sundry great sums.'
Hence he expresses regret several times that he could not do
more for his kin and friends: only £5 each to his sisters,
Mary Woolacombe and Philippa Pitts, 'for if my debts were
not so great as they be I would better have remembered
them.' For his niece, Honor Basset, called after her grandmother, he provided maintenance at 20 marks a year until his
nephew Arthur reached his majority at twenty-one. Arthur's

wardship he estimates at 1000 marks and he seems anxious to provide the reversion to his estate for the future head of the family.

A small annuity is provided for 'my cousin Easton', of that family who still keep guard over St Thomas More's relics. Similar small sums were appointed for a number of servants, among them 'my nephew and servant, John Courtenay.' Most of these payments were to come out of the manor of Torrington—and that would make trouble for his heir when he succeeded. Nothing whatever was said about his mother, not even a gift for remembrance. Was she still out of her wits?

Philip was now only eight—so his father would have married in Edward VI's reign—and succeeded to an inheritance that was much encumbered with mortgages and his father's bequests. However, if one held on to one's land its value increased with the increasing prosperity of Elizabeth's time. This Philip was unable to do, as we see from the letters he wrote to Lord Burghley some thirty years later.[26] We get the impression from them of a feeble creature, totally unable to make anything out of what was left to him or of his chances in life.

In May 1588 Philip was writing that he had hoped to be called to the Bar, but his creditors stood in the way. He had been an ancient of Lincoln's Inn twelve years, and wished a way to gain a livelihood. Would Burghley speak to the Solicitor General and the Bench that he might be admitted? Four years later he complains that he has been set upon in Lincoln's Inn by several men who drove him to the waterside, and carried him off, threatening to hand him over to the Counter, if he did not sign an extent upon his lands. So this was on account of debt, the men set on by his creditors. Burghley had listened sympathetically to his brother-in-law Verney's case—Philip had married a Verney: but for Burghley's clemency 'it would have been the end of his house.' He said that he had never received the sums Mr Carew was claiming. In November 1592 he is sending his wife, 'the unfeigned and faultless partner of my unhappy fortunes', to ask Burghley to continue his goodness to him. Through her he receives 'the grievous notice of your lordship's displeasure

towards me'—evidently Burghley thought he had himself
only to blame. He does not '*lurk*', but *lives* in Lincoln's Inn.

During these years a complicated Exchequer case
concerning the manor of Torrington dragged on between the
Fortescues, and Basset and his brother-in-law. Basset was
indebted some £4000 to the Crown; and Fortescue had 'by
private information to her majesty' procured a lease of it
under the great seal: 'so that now sitting in the darkness and
horror of my estate, I have no other refuge but to the merciful
goodness of your lordship.' In a petition of 1595 Basset
recites the tale of the considerable inheritance left him by his
father: Columb John, Poundisford, and Padbroke, formerly
of the Marquis of Exeter's; Coleridge, a manor of the Duke
of Suffolk's, ten miles in compass with a goodly park and
demesnes (that should have served any sensible man to live
contentedly upon); various lands which had been Sir Gawen
Carew's; besides Torrington, 'the cause of so much trouble
to your lordship.'

Now he is nearly 'worn out of all, with mortgages and
forfeitures, and the double dealing of others to whom he
committed his affairs while he was yet too young to look to
it himself; so that now he has not the revenue of a penny in
the world.' With the single sum of £300 he had done his best
to satisfy his creditors. In July he begs that the composition
Burghley has effected may not 'leave him so extremely poor
as not to have one penny for his lingering extremities.'

That is the last we hear of him: this is what James Basset's
success and assiduous striving had come to. The main stock
of the Bassets of Umberleigh continued on there, and then
moved to Heanton Punchardon beside the Taw, until the
male line petered out with an old bachelor in 1802. The more
ancient inheritance of Tehidy in Cornwall was settled upon
the second son of Sir John Basset and Honor Grenville—
George, who lived there, conformed to the Elizabethan
consensus in religion, served several times in Parliament, and
died in 1580.

It was the Cornish branch that thrived and came to great
wealth with the development of the mines on that estate—
they were said to have received £1 million alone from
royalties on Dolcoath, most famous of Cornish mines, of
which all Cornishmen were still proud in my youth. This

branch produced a remarkable man in Francis Basset (1757–1835),[27] promoter of the Industrial Revolution in Cornwall, patron of science and the arts, whose monument stands high on Carn Brea overlooking all West Cornwall, which he dominated while he lived. Created a peer, he went back to the Norman origins of the family and became Lord de Dunstanville. He built a fine mansion at Tehidy and filled it with works of art and science. In our disgraceful time, an unworthy descendant, Arthur Basset—that name going back to Lord Lisle—sold house, furniture, pictures, estate, every stitch of land his ancestors had owned for so many centuries. Thereupon the great house of Tehidy burned down.

Such is the end of the story with its various morals.

Notes

1. Cf. the notice of him in *Dictionary of National Biography*.
2. At last they have been edited by Miss St Clair Byrne in more accessible fashion and in modern spelling: *The Lisle Letters*, 5 vols (Chicago University Press, 1982).
3. See my *The Tower of London*, p. 98.
4. *The Letters of Stephen Gardiner*, ed. J. A. Muller (Cambridge University Press, 1933) pp. 57, 62.
5. *Ibid.*, pp. 76, 79.
6. A mark equalled two-thirds of a pound.
7. For this decisive Parliament v. S. E. Lehmberg's excellent *The Reformation Parliament, 1529–1536* (Cambridge University Press, 1970).
8. i.e. young herons.
9. For the last days of this decrepit institution v. my *Tudor Cornwall: Portrait of a Society* (Cape, 1941; new edn. Macmillan, 1969) pp. 166–8.
10. Muller, *op. cit.*, p. 81.
11. Dr Barnes was burned in 1540.
12. Something like a whistle.
13. A conserve made of codlings or quinces.
14. I.e. poniet, or wristband.
15. A stout plain silk.
16. I.e. young herons. The word sometimes appears as hearnshaw or handsaw, cf. *Oxford English Dictionary*, as in *Hamlet*, II. 397, 'I know a hawk from a handsaw.' The meaning is perfectly simple, though the amount of ludicrous commentary on it is hardly believable. The Shakespearean scholar, G. L. Kittredge, thought it a piece of Hamlet's nonsense, when in fact the professor did not know his Elizabethan English. C. J. Sisson gets it right, *New Readings in Shakespeare* (Cambridge University Press, 1956) Vol. II, p. 217.

17. *Letters and Papers of Henry VIII, (L. and P.), Henry VIII*, Vol. XV. p. 1223 ff.
18. *The Heralds' Visitations of . . . Devon*, ed. J. L. Vivian, (1895) p. 46.
19. For the following two paragraphs cf. refs in *Cal. Pat. Rolls, Mary*.
20. *Acts of the Privy Council, 1550–1552*, 401.
21. *Return of M.P.s, Pt I.*, 383, 387, 389, 393, 396.
22. See my edition of it, *A Man of Singular Virtue*, with a selection of More's Letters. (Folio Society, 1980).
23. See later p. 85.
24. Particulars for Grants, 2122. (P.R.O.)
25. Cf. 'Lord Chamberlain Hunsdon', in my *Eminent Elizabethans* (Macmillan, 1983).
26. Lansdowne Mss, British Library, Vol. **59**, 28; Vol. **72**, 55, 64, 77, 78; Vol. **78**, 25, 41; Vol. **79**, 79, 89.
27. Cf. notice of him in *Dictionary of National Biography*.

2

Edward Courtenay, Last Earl of Devon of the Elder Line

The Courtenays are the most historic and long-continuing of West Country families. They were honoured with a special Digression, as he calls it, in Gibbon's *Decline and Fall*[1]—like having one's name inscribed on the dome of St Paul's. A footnote has a characteristic flout at the Devonshire clergyman to whom Gibbon owed some of his information—the great historian never feared to say what he thought: 'the rector of Honiton has more gratitude than industry, and more industry than criticism.' Gibbon takes them back to the companions of Hugh Capet and the castle of Courtenay, in the Isle de France, from which they took their name; to the First Crusade and the principalities of the Franks in the Middle East, when the Courtenays ruled one astride the Euphrates at Edessa briefly, for 'examples of genius or virtue must be rare in the annals of the oldest families.'

A Courtenay married the daughter of Louis VI, 'le Gros'; one or two more royal marriages grandified and, in the end, endangered the family. In France, 'while the elder brothers dissipated their wealth in romantic adventures, and the castle of Courtenay was profaned by a plebeian owner, the younger branches of that adopted name were propagated and multiplied.' A scion of the family came to England to make his fortune in the train of Eleanor of Aquitaine, received favour and office in Devon from Henry II, and married a daughter of the Redvers Earl. Thence from Edward III in 1335 came their elevation to the earldom; after that, through many operations and services, acquisitions and misfortunes, they remained of the first rank.

Gibbon continues: 'by sea and land they fought under

the standard of the Edwards and Henries; their names are
conspicuous in battles, in tournaments, and in the original
list of the order of the Garter; three brothers shared the
Spanish victory of the Black Prince. . . . In peace, the earls
of Devon resided in their numerous castles and manors of
the West.' They were a prolific family, 'and in a contest
with John of Lancaster, a Courtenay bishop of London, and
afterwards archbishop of Canterbury, might be accused of
profane confidence in the strength and number of his
kindred.' This was William, son of the second earl, the able
suppressor of the Oxford movement of the time, that of
Wyclif and the Lollards.

Then, 'in the quarrel of the two Roses, the earls of Devon
adhered to the house of Lancaster'—as did most of the
country—'and three brothers successively died either in the
field or on the scaffold.' These were Thomas, the 6th Earl,
taken prisoner at the battle of Towton in 1461 and beheaded;
his brother and heir, Henry, beheaded in 1466; and the next
brother and heir killed at Tewkesbury in 1471.

The family was so prolific that one finds descendants of
it, down among the people in Cornwall to this day, spelling
themselves Courtney. In Devon one sees relics of that senior
line in their ruined castles in the valley by the roadside going
down into Okehampton, or above the sounding Exe at
Tiverton, or the remains—in spite of the removal of their
monuments from the chapel at Tiverton in the eighteenth
century (to make room for unmemorable congregations)—as
in that of the second earl and his wife in Exeter cathedral, of
1377, or the brass of his son Sir Peter Courtenay. In the
Close, by the north-east gate, they had their town-house, of
which something remains from medieval times.

After the fratricidal slaughter of the struggle between Lancaster and York for power, to find an heir to the earldom,
resort had to be made to a kinsman of the Cornish branch,
Sir Edward Courtenay of Boconnoc. Upon the usurpation
of Richard III Edward, now head of the family, and his
cousins, the bishop of Exeter and his brother—of the junior
Powderham line—joined in proclaiming the Lancastrian heir,
Henry VII. They were premature, forced to take refuge with
him in Brittany, and came back with him in 1485. After

Bosworth the earldom was properly revived in Edward, and the family estates restored.

His son William married Catherine, sister of Henry VII's wife, both daughters of Edward IV, and this Yorkist marriage brought the family its troubles under the Tudors. Sir William Courtenay was in favour and took a prominent position at Court so long as his sister-in-law the Queen lived. After her death suspicion fell upon him of corresponding with Edmund de la Pole, the 'White Rose', the Yorkist claimant abroad. Sir William was sent to the Tower, and attainted. On the accession of the promising young Henry VIII, Courtenay was allowed to succeed to the earldom, but died in 1511 before he was restored in blood. He was succeeded by his only son, Henry, still a youth, who was treated by his cousin, the King, with favour and gradually—not all at once—restored to all the honours of the family.

This brings us to the threshold of our story.

In 1511 Henry VIII entered upon the first of his French wars. It was always his ambition to shine in the field, like his successful grandfather, Edward IV, after whom he turned. Sir Thomas More, who understood him well, one day said, when complimented on Henry's familiarity with him— walking in the garden at Chelsea with his arm around his neck: 'if my head could purchase him a castle in France, it should not fail to fall.' We may regard this failing as an inheritance from his ancestors, but in fact it was no other than his contemporaries'. In the war the young Earl served at sea.

From 1520 he began to reap the rewards of favour: as gentleman of the Privy Chamber he was in close attendance on the King and was promoted to the Privy Council, a member of the governing circle. Next year he profited from the Duke of Buckingham's fall, succeeding him in the order of the Garter and in his London mansion in St Lawrence Pountney, and of course he was present at the extravagant, exhibitionist show of the Field of the Cloth of Gold.

Rewards and offices in the West Country, where the primacy of the Courtenays was made, followed; he was also made Constable of Windsor Castle, and in 1525 created Marquis of Exeter. In all Henry's proceedings regarding the divorce from Catherine of Aragon, Exeter gave support—the country, however much it sympathised with the blameless Queen, appreciated the necessity of a male heir and certainty in the succession to the throne. Doubt with regard to the validity of the marriage had existed from the first. Both Henry and Catherine were equally, and genuinely, convinced—but on opposite sides of the question. So much for people's 'convictions': they believe what they wish.

As the revolution in the Church unfolded itself under the impetus of Cromwell, Exeter had doubts; after all, he belonged to the aristocratic old order, not the new deal of rising gentry and middle class, which Cromwell and the Commons represented. With the Pilgrimage of Grace his doubts grew; sent to the North with Norfolk to suppress the rebellion, Exeter somewhat hurriedly retired and suspicion of him grew. His wife, as a Catholic *dévote*, was a liability.[2] She was Gertrude Blount (pronounced Blunt), daughter of Lord Mountjoy, and had incriminated herself by dealings with the Holy Nun of Kent. This silly woman gained much publicity by her prophecies of ill that would betide the King, if he did not mend his ways. This, of course, was dangerous; her folly touched other exposed people whose opposition was suspect—More and Fisher, for example—before she reaped her reward, confessing that she had been led on by the desire to draw attention to herself, on the gibbet.

The Marchioness begged the King to pardon her contacts with the Nun, but henceforward the Courtenays lay wide open. When Sir Geoffrey Pole turned traitor against his family the old charges were brought up: how the Marchioness had gone down to Canterbury in disguise to consult the Nun, who had said that the time would come when the King would flee his kingdom. And Lady Exeter had entertained this nuisance of a prophetess in their country mansion at West Horsley near Guildford.

The crisis of the reign was upon them all. The King's cousin, Reginald Pole, denounced Henry's new deal before the public opinion of Europe in his formidable work on the Unity of the Church, and had been made a Cardinal for his pronouncement. The Pope sent him north as Legate, to cooperate with the rebellion—which, however, had been suppressed by the time he arrived in Flanders. There he remained for several months in 1537 awaiting his chance.

Henry retorted savagely against his family; Geoffrey Pole's evidence incriminated not only his brother, Lord Montagu, but the Marquis of Exeter. Both were sent to the Tower in November 1538. Montagu confessed that the Marquis had offered 'in counsel to be bound body for body' with him. Exeter would give no evidence against his cousin, when prompted by Cromwell. All that year incriminating circumstances had accumulated against him. In February his bearward was attainted of treason—he must have uttered dangerous sentiments; idiotic servants said that they hoped that their master would wear the garland at the last. During the recent rebellion bright prospects circulated among the opponents of the new deal, of marrying the Lady Mary, no longer Princess, to the Marquis' son, Edward, 'and so they to enjoy the realm.' Early that year he had been deprived of his offices of Constable of Windsor and gentleman of the Privy Chamber, in dangerous proximity to the King. The Marquis grieved most at this, his wife said—naturally, for it was an overt sign of distrust: one could not have one who might kill the King in a position to do so. Someone commented on the indignity of his being dismissed and 'made to take abbey land': where others profited enormously from the suppression, Exeter garnered only the little priory of Breamore in Hampshire.

He was now framed—along with the inaccessible Cardinal (whom Henry, Stalin-like, would have had assassinated if he could)—as head of the Opposition. It cannot be said that he made an effective one; a French envoy wrote, 'il semble qu'il cherche toutes les occasions qu'on peut penser pour se ruiner et détruire.' A servant of Geoffrey Pole gave evidence that the Marquis had visited him for secret collogue, speaking French or Latin: 'he had a long beard, and a great cut upon his cheek as with a sword, and another upon his nose.' Geoffrey Pole returned the visit and lay all night with the Marquis, so no one knew what was said; but the latter had kept his distance from Montagu 'because there is noted a certain suspicion between us.'

Exeter would give no evidence, but the women talked. Lady Salisbury said that if she had her rights she would

be Countess of Warwick—she was Clarence's daughter, her
brother Warwick executed by Henry VII at the demand of
the Spaniards before they would give Catherine of Aragon
in marriage—and that Exeter should be Earl of March. Both
these were Yorkist royal titles (Henry VIII, however, was
both Lancastrian and Yorkist rightful heir and would brook
no challenge from any quarter.) The Marchioness confessed
that she had heard Sir Edward Neville sing in the garden at
Horsley that Peter Mewtas had been sent overseas to slay
Cardinal Pole; at other times he would sing merrily that he
trusted this world would amend. They all knew what was
meant. The Marquis' chief agent in Cornwall, Walter
Kendall, was sent to the Tower with him, charged with
raising men there for him.

Swiftly in December Exeter and Montagu were executed;
Lady Salisbury, mother of the Poles, remained in the Tower
for the next two years, Lady Exeter for a matter of months,
when she was pardoned; the Exeters' son, Edward Courtenay, for the next fifteen years, until the accession of Queen
Mary freed him. Among the mass of papers regarding the
so-called 'Exeter Conspiracy' (compare the contemporary
'conspiracies' and 'confessions' of Soviet Russia), we have a
scrap of evidence about the boy of eight. His schoolmaster
was an Oxford man, one Robert Taylor, who had fled overseas that August to Antwerp; he had been threatened by
some young gentlemen of the household for ministering
correction to the boy.

From the detailed evidences we can reconstruct something
of the grand household: 'the articles in my young Lord's
chamber, the chamber next it, the school-house', all the
chambers of the mansion; the Marchioness' jewels and
apparel there (she and Lady Salisbury had not sufficient in the
Tower); eighty-four items of plate; the musical instruments,
virginals, regals (small organs), no less than nine viols. We
see what a part music played in a Tudor household. Among
the grooms, one 'can sing properly in three-man songs',
another 'can play somewhat on divers instruments, and his
knowledge is to teach men to do things in music which he
himself cannot express nor utter; and yet he can perfectly
teach it, wherefore he was master of the musicians.' A third
'can play well with a harp, sing, juggle and other proper

conceits and make pastimes'; a fourth 'luteth and singeth well, and playeth cunningly upon the viols and divers other instruments.' It is not surprising that Sir Edward Neville *sang* politics in the garden at West Horsley: the Henrician world rang with music.

The Marquis had a Cornish jester, William Tremayle, and several of the servants were good wrestlers—as such the Cornish were adepts. Thomas Godolphin was 'meet and diligent in serving about a nobleman, with honest and decent qualities'—he was keeper of Restormel park; Jasper Horsey was keeper of Dartington park; George Daubeney one of the foresters of Dartmoor, 'a tall man of stature.' The household contained eighteen gentlemen and five gentlewomen, of whom one was a Spaniard. Among the servants were four gentlemen; twenty-two yeomen and grooms. The estates needed twenty-six keepers of parks, receiving fees, not wages.

One sees what a catastrophe it was when a noble house fell—like a great ship going down at sea. People manoeuvred round hoping to pick up flotsam and jetsam. Lord Lisle put in for the parks at Okehampton and Chittlehampton (with their supply of venison). He did not get them. Okehampton went to Sir Peter Carew. Indeed the Carews did best, for they were on the spot in Devon, and they were supporters of the new deal—in spite of Sir Nicholas Carew, Master of the Horse, losing his head on account of the Marquis. Sir George Carew got several of the Courtenay manors in Devon; Sir Gawen Carew bought a couple more. Anthony Harvey got the receivership of the estates in the western counties, with the mansion at Cullompton to reside in. Many smaller people put in for properties. The greatest beneficiary was wise Lord Russell, who succeeded to the Marquis' prime position in the West.

His son was held behind the walls of the Tower—we have Cromwell's memoranda and, after he vanished behind them, the Council's instructions for Courtenay's diets and apparel. Early in 1546, when he was rising sixteen, he made an attempt at escape. 'I rejoice with you the taking of Courtenay,' wrote the poet Earl of Surrey to Paget, 'and in the grace that God hath given our master that never yet attempt of treason against his royal person took effect.' (Surrey's own turn was to come next year.) In June, in view of the youth's sickness, the King granted him 'the liberty of the garden and gallery, with one sober man always in his company to see that no-one conferred with him secretly.' In September Courtenay had an interview with the Lord Chancellor and the Lord Great Master on the 'matter touching his allegiance. The young man showed himself very humble and desirous to make amends for his late folly.'

Courtenay confirmed in writing what he had told them 'concerning the Spaniard here prisoner who has often tried to persuade me to break prison.' If he could have got abroad, he would have made a valuable tool in the hands of the country's enemies. Considering the King's 'abundant mercies and manifold goodness to me', he begged their intercession with the King 'to have pity and compassion on this my miserable imprisonment.' Not much pity or compassion was to be found in that quarter; but next year a considerable sum, £20, was allowed his doctor 'for his continual attendance and painstaking about Courtenay, being sick in the Tower, as also to his apothecary for medicines to him ministered.'

The Act of Attainder had stripped him of his titles, and in the various pardons for other people, he is always excepted— as too dangerously near the throne. Edward VI and he were alike legitimate great-grandsons of Edward IV. Some part of his time he employed in translating an Italian work of Reforming sympathies, dedicating the manuscript to the wife of Protector Somerset. If the idea was to propitiate the powers that were, it had no effect; Courtenay remained incarcerated. It was reported to Charles V that the young man applied himself to his studies and to music, so that his imprisonment was not grievous. But in the crisis that arose from Edward VI's dying, rumour ran that he would be put out of the way to checkmate those who wished to marry him to the Princess Mary.

Mary's accession to the throne had not been expected, with the reversal of the new deal that had been gathering impetus in the past twenty years. The new Queen was no fool, but a convinced reactionary; unfortunately she was twenty years out of date and out of touch. Unlike her father and her sister, she was no politician and had no thought of moving with the times. Indeed she thought that her accession was providential, and that Providence had raised her up to put back the clock twenty years. This kind of thinking is always a mistake.

Edward VI himself had tried to wrest the succession from both her and Elizabeth, as being 'but of the half-blood'—though Northumberland bore the responsibility for trying to carry out his wishes, in the pathetic episode of Queen Jane, and suffered for it. The country wanted the continuance of Henry VIII's obvious line. On 3 August Mary entered London in state, attended by those figures of the past and the future, Elizabeth, the duchess of Norfolk and the marchioness of Exeter. Two days later Bishop Bonner was released from the Marshalsea, where the Protestant dean of Westminster took his place, and Courtenay from the Tower. The new Queen was graciousness itself to those who had been victims along with her, expressed her sorrow for it and that they should have suffered so long. Several days later Bishop Gardiner was released: there could never be complete confidence between him and Mary, for he had been implicated in every move in the divorce of her mother and the breach with Rome. But his political ability and experience were indispensable; he was ready to back-track and express regret at the divorce from Rome.

We see something of the difficulties the régime would face in the uproar that took place when the Queen's chaplain enjoined Catholic doctrine at Paul's Cross. The London merchant, Machyn, reports 'a great uproar and shouting at his sermon, as it were like mad people, what young people and women as ever was heard, as hurly-burly and casting up of caps. If my lord mayor and lord Courtenay had not been there, there had been great mischief done.'³ The young man was at once taking his place among the leading figures of the realm. The Earl of Pembroke made him handsome presents to get back on the Council, and the Marchioness won him favour with the Queen.

On Sunday, 3 September, Courtenay was created Earl of Devon at Richmond, the earldom having been extinguished by attainder. We have a manuscript account of the stately occasion, Courtenay being led between the earls of Arundel and Oxford.⁴ He knelt before the Queen, Secretary Petre reading the patent, 'and at the words of *gladii centuariam* the Queen put the sword about his neck hanging down before him baldric-wise, and at *cape circuli possessionem* she put the coronal on his head.' After the ceremony the procession re-formed, trumpets blowing, until they came to the chamber where they dined, he alone remaining 'in his kirtle and hood . . . and after dinner he shifted him, and went and gave the Queen thanks or otherwise at his pleasure.'

Immediately she took steps to provide handsomely for him and his mother, and restore them to their rank. The Marchioness had been living on the moderate pension of some £160 a year allotted out of her late husband's lands, plus presumably her jointure. She became a lady of the Bedchamber, Mary's companion until her marriage, and received an annuity as well as a large grant, of the value of £666.13.4 a year, 'for the better support of her estate and rank', of properties that Northumberland had swallowed from Somerset, and he from whom?[5] For her apartment at Court she was given eight pieces of tapestry, of hawking and hunting, and five with the story of Brute, four Turkey carpets, and window pieces of verdure; a bedstead of Windsor making, apparelled with cloth of gold and crimson velvet embroidered with fagots and falcons, and the necessary equipment of a bedroom, presumably at Richmond.[6]

Her son was given similar equipment: six pieces of tapestry, of hawking and hunting, a Windsor bedstead with its equipment of cloth of gold and crimson velvet, curtains of sarcenet, cushions of cloth of silver, etc. However, in December a vastly larger grant was made of his late father's, evidently to set the Earl up in housekeeping for his house at Kew—bedsteads and equipment for several rooms. We can select only a number of items to illustrate the taste and furnishings of the time. Tapestries: no less than fourteen pieces of hawking and hunting, nine of the Passion, four of the story of Jupiter, two of the history of St Paul, besides several more. 'Pieces of imagery' would refer to painted cloth or arras hangings, of which there were many; of verdure, no less than thirty-three pieces for a gallery, besides many 'window pieces', and a number of carpets—these were not placed on the floor but on tables or boards. Chairs, stools, cushions were covered with a variety of materials, velvet, silk, tissue, cloth: of gold or tinsel; one black velvet cushion embroidered with H. and G. (Henry and Gertrude). It had all been moved evidently from West Horsley or their London house to the Wardrobe at Richmond.

The nine viols, the regals and virginals from Horsley make their appearance again, along with the chapel equipment: altar frontals of cloth of gold, of green cloth of silver embroidered with 'Jesus', of tinsel with crimson velvet embroidered with 'Jesus, Maria'; others of black velvet, and of purple, yellow and Bruges white satin. Pictures: one of Jesus, Mary and Saint Elizabeth, a table of our Lady giving our Lord suck, another of 'a woman having St John's head in a dish.' A secular picture in needlework depicted the popular theme of Pyramus and Thisbe.

We are taken behind the scenes in another schedule, which intimately illustrates how these Tudor magnates ate each other up; for we have lists of the goods the Earl bought or was given from the belongings of Northumberland, and his son Warwick who died shortly after his release from the Tower, and of the Marquis of Northampton, Queen Catherine Parr's brother, who narrowly escaped execution. Devon bought Northumberland's cloak of white felt lined with white satin, his very shirts, some of them wrought with gold and silver, and his shaving cloths garnished with gold. He bought the Duke's walnut writing desk with its equipment mostly of silver; 'a card of England and Scotland wrought in silver and gold', and two maps of 'the destruction of the Scottish Field', i.e. Northumberland's victory at Pinkie. A marginal note says 'the abbot of Westminster hath them: given to the Earl of Devon.' (This was Dr Feckenham, of the restored Abbey.) The Duke's personal weapons: a little dag, i.e. pistol; a skene (dagger) with gilt hilts, a bodkin and a knife; a fistulate (pipe or whistle), with bodkin and knife; a flask and touchbox garnished with silver; a rapier with engraved russet hilts, with a dag. Devon bought altogether 144 ells of tapestry of various kinds, 60 ells of arras, along with more beds, chairs, stools, cushions; a fireshovel and a pair of andirons point up the housekeeping upon which he was embarking.

We have a longer list of Northampton's goods: more tapestry and arras and a great deal of bed equipment; three

English carpets of Turkey making—if actually of English manufacture, the earliest I know of; chairs, cushions, stools—one of these last 'for a chapel, covered with crimson velvet and gold embroidery'; a new close-stool without bottom. Given to Devon and to Lord Rich—More's betrayer, who ended up Catholically: two pairs of gloves, one pair with 'thirty-one pair of aglets of gold, white enamelled, and fifteen buttons of like work'—they must have been gauntlets. We see the luxury of the time in the clothing more than anything, except for the jewels and plate.

Of the dead Warwick's goods Devon received 'a black cape of velvet, with twenty-three aglets of gold and sixty-five buttons of gold.' The clothes of the time were very valuable, and of materials to last. Another cloak was also of white felt lined with white velvet, buttons of silver; along with Warwick's Parliament robes of scarlet, in time for its opening.

Along with the earldom Devon received a very large grant of all the historic Courtenay estates in the West—at the service of a Red Rose, be it noticed.[7] He did not get back his father's home at West Horsley, nor the house in London; nor the offices that had added to his wealth. But he now succeeded to the old holdings in Devon, Tiverton, Okehampton, Colcombe castles, with Plympton; nearly thirty manors big and small, hundreds and boroughs, stannary rights, advowsons and detached holdings. In Cornwall were some seventeen manors, besides advowsons and stannary works; in Somerset another dozen, and a few more in Wiltshire, Berkshire, Surrey and Hampshire, including Breamore priory and its lands, which his father had acquired. It was all done in accordance with law and custom, and re-created a handsome appanage of some £1250 a year—a full-time job for anyone to supervise. Most grandees left that to their agents and servants—and lost in consequence.

Having spent most of his life in the Tower, the Earl was not trained to such close attention, and so sudden a reversal of fortune went to his head. The Emperor's ambassador reported that he threatened he would kill Sir Geoffrey Pole, on his return to England, for his part in the deaths of the Marquis and Lady Salisbury. The young man was giving himself airs of importance; some people knelt to him as if it was a settled matter that he would marry the Queen. This was far from the Emperor's intention. Cardinal Pole wrote his cousin a friendly letter with good expectations of the future. This was enough for Charles V to hold up Pole's mission as Legate to reconcile England to the faith, until the marriage of Mary to his son was safely concluded. The difficulty was to get the English people to accept it. There was the young Earl in the public eye, the only male of the blood royal.

Thus equipped and upheld he was ready to take a foremost place among the Queen's faithful following. The fact that he and his mother had suffered as had Mary herself, for their opposition to the new course upon which her father had set the country, made a bond between them. For the coronation on 1 October he was made a Knight of the Bath, the ceremonies taking place in the Tower, too familiar to him. He took a leading part in procession and in the Abbey, bearing the sword of state before the Queen and again at the opening of Parliament, at which he was formally restored in blood. In November we find him lending his presence to a sermon by Abbot Feckenham at St Mary Overy's (now Southwark cathedral)—not that the Earl was a religious devotee like his mother.[8] Rumours ran that his life was ill-regulated, while in the streets signs of jealous rivalry in love were displayed. The Chancellor, Waldegrave, and his kinsman Lord Hastings were lobbying Parliament for a motion to urge Mary not to marry a foreigner.

In January 1554 the Spanish ambassadors landed at Tower Wharf, and the Earl officially received them into the city. The Queen's marriage was a question of national importance, and a matter of urgency for her, if she was to produce an heir; for she was rising thirty-six, and she had never been strong. From her point of view there was everything to be said for her following the advice of her cousin, the Emperor, and marrying his son. All through her troubles Charles V had been her support and strength. A queen had never ruled in England; Mary needed a man beside her, and she desperately needed a son. Moreover, England's natural and commercial ally was the Netherlands, where Charles V ruled and Philip was shortly to succeed him. Philip was eleven years younger than Mary, but a serious young man, already

a king and always a good Catholic; while Mary on her
mother's side was even more of a Spaniard than he was, and
a religious fanatic, unlike her father.

On the other hand, the insular English were the most
xenophobic of nations, and the idea of Philip coming to rule
in England was met with resistance from the start and from
the top to the bottom. It divided her Council, the majority
being opposed to it at first, and Devon had a party in his
favour. Along the Channel coast there was apprehension,
especially in Kent and the West Country. The West had an
English candidate for Mary's hand in the Earl of Devon,
and so had many other people, including himself. Ten years
younger than the Queen, he was no younger than Philip.
Mary, however, never thought of him as a serious candidate:
she evidently regarded him as a delayed adolescent—which
he was.

All the same the modern historian of this period cannot
but reflect on how many people were ready to throw their
lives away on desperate gambles. Canny Henry VII had
waited until the cup was filled by Richard III's crime and he
had turned the country's stomach—so that the march to
Bosworth was well considered, well prepared, and well worth
it. But most Tudor conspirators simply threw their lives
away taking bad chances. Resenting Mary's refusal to
consider him—in spite of her goodness to him and her
continuing affection for the sake of his mother's and his own
sufferings—he went into opposition to the marriage and lent
himself to conspiracy. The Protestant left-wing was in favour
of replacing Mary by Elizabeth, their candidate, now at
twenty of an age to marry, and whom but Courtenay? And
so, suffering from a sense of rejection by the Queen, he
fancied himself.

The official announcement of the Spanish marriage was
made on 15 January 1554; at once the good feeling which had
been shown on Mary's accession vanished, and opposition
declared itself. In the West the activists were the Carews,
Killigrews, Tremaynes—all to be treated with favour when
Elizabeth came to the throne: they were her men. The simple
primitive feeling was openly expressed, in familiar terms,
by a Devonshire gentleman in Exeter cathedral that, if the
Spaniards entered the realm, 'they would ravish their wives

and daughters, and rob and spoil the commons.'⁹ At Plymouth there was strong feeling against the Spaniards being allowed to land there.

It was suspected that the Carews intended an attempt on Exeter, and Sir Peter Carew laid posts to bring the Earl to Devon. But divided counsels forced the would-be rebels to give up, and Carew fled across Channel in a boat belonging to Walter Ralegh's father. (One sees the Elizabethan future foreshadowed.) At the other end of the Channel Wyatt's rebellion gravely threatened London: a personal appeal of the Queen to the City stiffened resistance. It was a narrow shave for the new régime. Mary did not know whom to trust, and the French—alarmed at the prospect of a Habsburg entrenched in London—were in touch with the Opposition. Bonvisi put it about that the Pope favoured the French and would not grant a dispensation for Mary's marriage to her cousin. The Earl feared that if Carew were captured he would reveal the secrets that are imprecisely known to us. Mary charged that he was keeping company with ruffians and heretics, while his mother withdrew from intimacy with the Queen and spoke of her son no more. Gardiner proposed an honourable mission for him to the Emperor, who the Queen hoped would find a match for him abroad. (At one point Charles V's niece, the Duchess of Lorraine, was suggested.)

At the outbreak of Wyatt's rebellion Devon talked in a vain, irresponsible way—he was no leader, unlike Wyatt; all was lost, he repaired to Court, where the Queen reproached him with failure to do his duty. Under suspicion, he was arrested at the Earl of Sussex's house, and on 12 February was returned to his old quarters in the Tower—after only six months of freedom!

Protected from further punishment by the Queen and Gardiner, in March he was conducted under the care of Sir Thomas Tresham to more salubrious, at least more distant, confinement at Fotheringay, sufficiently removed from the popular demonstrations against the entry of Philip and his Spaniards into London that summer. By Easter 1555 the régime had achieved some stability, and in the euphoria of Mary's expectation of an heir, the Earl was released. In April he went to Court to kiss hands on obtaining leave to go abroad—really into exile.

The Earl's early death meant that his correspondence came back to England, and in such fulness as to be rare. This constitutes its historical value: it is very infrequent to find the letters to and from a great noble of the time, from day to day, sometimes several letters, or drafts, a day.[10] Meanwhile, he was so close to the succession, an obvious candidate for the hand of Elizabeth, that his movements were closely observed at home and abroad, and rumours circulated freely—for the opposition to Mary's régime continued.

An agent of his reported that he had delivered his farewell messages to the rulers at Court, and expedited his commission for carts and post-horses, 'with one or two more than you speak of for the better furnishing of the Spanish friar—whereat my Lord Chancellor [Gardiner] and certain others of the Council did laugh most heartily.' A useful commendation to a merchant friend was enclosed, 'who was imbrued with the new-found faith, but since, he is reclaimed'; also to other English merchants in Flanders 'who will do you such service and pleasure as men of their calling may do unto a man of honour.'

On 3 May James Basset wrote to the Earl at Calais, on his way to Flanders, thanking him for 'the great horse which your lordship would needs give me.' From Court Philip's attendant, the Count of Horn, sent an introduction to his brother, while the King's Secretary, Ruy Gomez, said that Philip had instructed the Duke of Alba to present the Earl to the Emperor. Basset advised him not to tarry at Antwerp to equip himself, but to repair at once to Brussels. 'I know with the more expedition you arrive there the better it will be accepted, and if you should long delay it would be suspicious; wishing earnestly your lordship should by all possible means avoid all kind of occasions that might be suspected.' Basset had explained to Bonvisi 'how freely you are delivered without any condition', and that, since he had the King's recommendation, none at Brussels need fear to be friendly and do him pleasure. Bonvisi would advance him a credit of 1000 ducats; Basset and Sir Francis Englefield, to whom the Earl entrusted his affairs, were considering how the funds he needed might best be raised.

Anthony Bonvisi was a rich Italian merchant, a friend of Sir Thomas More, who lived in the City at Crosby Place—

the house from which Richard III planned his usurpation of his nephew's throne. More himself had owned the house at one time, and would know its story—though indeed he had several sources of intimate information about Richard.

Basset assured Devon of the good will of Sir William Cordell, the Queen's Solicitor, to whom the Earl was 'more bounden and that did stand you in more stead than you would ween.' From Calais he reported to his aunt, Lady Berkeley, his arrival 'safe but scant sound, for I was a little touched with the seas.' He thanked her for the pains she had taken for him, 'which oftentimes since I have been very sorry for when I thought of your broken brow.' He asks Basset to procure a licence to travel for John Blount, his mother's young brother. His mother had been at work for him checking the inventories of his stuff from Richmond, at Kew and 'also of the stuff of London', and concentrating his goods at Kew, 'leaving your house wholly furnished, every chamber as you left them.' She spelt phonetically—'Your loving mothar, Gartrude Exetar': it was regular then to pronounce 'er', 'ar', as we still do in serjeant or clerk. She also inserted emphatic h's, 'hit' for it, 'has' for as, 'hown' for own.

The Earl remained at Brussels, sometimes referred to as 'the White Rose', for several months during Charles V's last residence there before his abdication and retirement to Spain. The Emperor had come down from the Habsburg family consultation at Augsburg which divided the inheritance: the Austrian territories and the Empire to his brother Ferdinand, the Spanish empire to his son Philip, along with the Netherlands—the source of so much later trouble. Devon reported to Gardiner that Alba presented him to the Emperor, who 'sat up in his chair [as we see him in the Titian portrait] and had, as it appeared, his health very well.' In fact Charles was racked by gout and rheumatism, worn out by the incessant burden of rule over so many lands. He, 'according to his own honourable and good nature, used me in such wise as I could not have desired better.'

We have an account of Devon's reception from Mason, the English ambassador, who promised to advise the young man according to the Council's instructions. He had demeaned himself well, acknowledging Philip's help in delivering him from custody and procuring him leave to see

the world, which 'displeasant fortune' had caused him hitherto to lack. The Emperor promised his favour, on account
of the Earl's father, 'of whose ill fortune a great piece, he
thought, was for the good will he [Charles V] bare to his
well-doings.' Devon wrote conveying his thanks to Philip in
Italian, which he knew—though he had a secretary with him.
He had delivered Ruy Gomez' letter to Don Luis, 'from
whom I find much courtesy', but had not yet used the Count
of Horn's introduction. A dozen years later Horn was
executed by Alba, along with Egmont—a theme to provide
inspiration in European drama and music in later centuries.

Basset reports that the Earl's letters had been well received
by King and Queen and that it was right to send them
through Secretary Petre, 'for it is the ordinary way and will
be best taken.' Moreover he was beholden to the Secretary
for his good will and helping to retain that of their Majesties.
This is the tone of both Basset and Englefield towards the
errant Earl—they, too, clearly regarded him as still
adolescent: perhaps no wonder after his life spent in the
Tower. As his trustees they desired further instruction as to
what he wished about his business affairs. Solicitor Cordell
advised that he could not sell outright land that was entailed
upon his heirs male, and that to raise the money he needed
it would be necessary to have a perfect Survey made of his
estates.

He admitted to Basset that he had left the state of his living
'in a raw case by means of my hasty departure', and agreed
to the Survey being made. King Philip had promised him
licence to go to Italy: would Basset make suit for a written
licence in form? The disease he has in his hip, 'which now
in my last trouble I took by a great cold, groweth so fast on
that I am constrained to seek some speedy remedy . . .
which, as physicians do say, is there in the baths presently
to be had.' He is at such extraordinary charges, 'which of
force I am compelled here to be at', that with the further
expense of his journey in view he is forced to make 'an
extreme shift' for money. This theme recurs again and
again—understandably, for besides a posse of servants, he
had gentlemen attendants in his retinue. The journey to Italy
was reasonable in itself: nearly all Tudor magnates made
what came to be known as 'the Continental tour', to qualify

themselves for service to the state on their return. This theme also recurs. 'I pray you consider my going into Italy as a matter that—as this messenger shall tell you—standeth me wonderfully upon.' Messengers and messages went frequently to and fro across the Channel.

Thomas Martin had moved Gardiner for licence to go to King Philip's territories, Milan or Naples, 'whereby your lordship should have less occasion to look homeward, and better means to advance yourself in further knowledge, and therewithal do yet more notable service at your return.' Gardiner's opinion was that 'your being at Brussels was but very dull, and I think no less.' Martin was at Calais in attendance upon the Chancellor, who was, with Cardinal Pole, commissioner engaged in negotiation with the French— 'tomorrow we shall have a great aim whether we shall have peace or war.' At Rome was a Papal conclave: 'there are four rumoured in the likelihood to be popes—Pole, Theatini, Morini, and De Fano. We have sundry letters from Rome that the first is most like to speed. If it be so, it will be a good occasion for your lordship to have the conduct of your own kinsman to his see at Rome, and I doubt not but it will come to pass.' It did not.

The Earl paid a visit to Calais, 'having been here [at Brussels] ever since my coming utterly idle, whereof I am somewhat weary; I intend tomorrow to go to Louvain, to pass the time for a while and so to visit Mr Bonvisi', about the money he was advancing on Basset's credit. His attitude to his mother appears distinctly cool and formal. The poor lady reproaches him, 'sorry to parseef [perceive] that you have so much business you have no lessar [leisure] to write in your hoan [own] hand to your hoan [own] mother, and yet seldom to hear from you.' She adds that 'if my waiting [i.e. on the Queen] can do you good, if I may get a chamber I will wait, and although my years require ease.'

From Mantua Pole's confidential attendant, Michael Throckmorton,[11] wrote a welcoming letter, in God's name 'who not once, but divers times, hath so graciously redeemed you out of captivity and bondage.' Though unknown to him, Throckmorton was deeply bound to his mother, and was all the more glad of his 'prosperous deliverance' by the Queen's favour. 'No man living would be more gladder to see you and enjoy you than I, your poor servant, in my poor house.'

John Haydon, the Earl's man of business in Lincoln's Inn, sent over by John Walker, his bailiff in the West, half-year's rents of £438.17.8. In addition to this there would be fines and dues enabling Devon to spend at the rate of £1200 a year, not more. One would have thought that this was enough for a young Tudor peer to jog along with, but a Continental tour would involve much extra expense. During Devon's 'last detainment' the deer in his parks were 'most shamefully spoiled and destroyed, and your woods in the same not best favoured . . . I had rather serve you the days of my life for no penny than any of your inheritance should be departed withal.'

John Haydon was an Ottery St Mary man who did well as a lawyer in London; purchasing lands of the collegiate church, he built the pretty Tudor house of Cadhay in the meadows nearby, which happily survives intact. John Strode came from the family at Newnham, which produced the poet, William Strode in the next generation—one still sees their ancient house with Tudor chimneys crouching down in its hollow, from the railway line near Plympton. We observe how large the West Country element was in the Earl's following: the old loyalty remained through the disaster to the family and the long imprisonment.

In June John Strode was writing, from the Camp at Namur, news of the war between the Emperor and the French—which was to drag England in and lead to the loss of Calais. Some four hundred 'swert rutters', i.e. German heavy horsemen, and five bands of ordinary (light) horse had arrived. The French had sent into Marienbourg five hundred pioners (i.e. sappers) 'clothed all in red. The place where the Emperor doth fortify is likely to be strong. Desiring your honour to accept this my rude letter, for I am a very simple inditer . . . Yours to command to the hour of death.'

Writing to Lord Abergavenny—as a Neville, a kinsman—Devon appears as companionable. 'I would have seen you at my coming over, saving that I was not sure to find you at home'—it would seem that he had paid a brief surreptitious visit. 'I would spend an hundred pounds to have your company here one month, for I lack such a companion.' He asked his help to obtain bucks and does, to replace those spoiled from his parks. He trusted one day to see him in England again 'with your broad dagger on your back.'

On his way the Earl had called on Thomas Gresham at Antwerp—to be so celebrated as the leading financial expert of the day—for he thanks him for his good cheer and sends a friendly message to the English merchants he met there. Would Gresham get him a cittern (a kind of guitar), and enough good black velvet to make a long night-gown (i.e. dressing gown), and 'cause your man Clough to make a bill how much money the whole cometh to.' Richard Clough was to become celebrated and rich too, builder of Plâs Clough in his native Denbigh, husband of Catherine of Berain, daughter of a by-blow of Henry VII.[12]

On 1 July the Earl was excusing himself to his mother for not writing or sending very often, there was so little to tell her. 'I like my being here very well, saving that my purse waxeth too light.' At Brussels 'the Emperor, the French Queen, the Regent and the Duchess of Lorraine have their continual abode. But I, for my part, sometimes go abroad unto the notable towns and places in this country, where I pass the time much to my contentation.' He ended with a rather facetious postscript about their household companion, William Daubeney, 'who now handleth me even as he did when I was at Fotheringay. Since I saw him last he never would ask for me, nor send to me, nor write me commendations. But I see the old proverb is true in him: seldom seen soon forgotten.'

To Thomas Smith, to whom he was under a debt of obligation for standing by him in his trouble, he wrote more warmly, concerned also that Sir Thomas Tresham had been very ill. If it had been his chance to remain in England, 'we might have been there this summer together practising with our crossbows among his deer—supposing I should have shot better this year at my mark than I did last time we were at Lyveden.' He had a goshawk for Smith, when he had means of having her well conveyed to him. To Gardiner's official, Dr Thomas Martin, he sent 'a plan of the fortifications in these parts.'

On 12 July Secretary Petre wrote that 'the Queen's good

hour of delivery is now looked for daily and as we trust is
very near at hand.' The Earl forwards the news to Bonvisi,
and the King, having done his marital duty, 'is here looked
for shortly.' The sum of 1000 crowns which Bonvisi was
forwarding through Gresham would be repaid at Christmas.
Lord Cobham proposed to make a gift of a great horse; the
Earl is rather delicate about accepting it as a gift, though
much in need of one. He would prefer a loan, since 'the
noblemen here do commonly ride daily upon some jennet [a
light horse], bastard jennet or great horse fair to the eye.'

   Those whom he trusted with his affairs at Court besides
Englefield and Basset, were Sir Robert Rochester,
Comptroller of the Household, Sir Edward Waldegrave,
Privy Councillor, and Solicitor Cordell. Since the Survey of
his lands was being made he was anxious that it should be
made clear everywhere that he was in favour with the King
and Queen; for it is elsewhere 'bruited that I am here either
as one in captivity and prison, or at leastwise banished.' Such
a rumour would redound unfavourably upon his credit in
bargaining for his land. Meanwhile, 'I do cut off all superfluous, yea and many necessary, charges here'; yet he needs
an extra supply of money besides his revenues, 'such is the
dearth of all things in these parts [chiefly about the Court],
and the charges importable, especially to one that both am a
stranger and also lack all manner of provisions.' He gave
instructions for John Walker and Thomas Browne, attending
his business at Kew, to receive board wages.

   He had arranged with Gresham for some plate; now he
wishes to supplement that with a similar basin and ewer,
another salt like the other without cover, and 'two quart pots
with covers for wine, of the prettiest and best fashion you
can devise, all plain and white. I do see my lord ambassador
[Sir John Mason] hath two very large and fair, which, as he
saith, come to but £17 a piece.' He did not wish to exceed
that sum. 'You must give great charge to the goldsmiths that
they make the parcels no weightier than my proportion . . .
for else you know they will make all heavy, for the more
ounces the more their advantage.' The spoons he wished to
be the best fashion of the sort he had specified; 'also devise
the forks some pretty thing on the top of each, and to have
fair proportion and not too great. Also I pray you provide

me of a pan to set in pots with wine to make the wine cold, of brass of Nuremberg making, neither too great nor too little.'

Here we have him at his most intimate: a young nobleman of taste, who does not want objects that are ornate—as much Renaissance plate was—and in fact does consider the expense. He had got as far as Malines on his way to see Gresham, when urgent business called him back to Brussels, 'where I mind not long to make my abode'; so would Gresham 'make some haste with my plate, for I have need thereof.' To Sir Thomas Tresham: 'your son is merry, who doth yet, I thank him, remain here with me.'

In August he writes a rather formal letter to his mother, who had been called again to the Queen's Privy Chamber, commenting sententiously that 'as you have always borne a true and faithful heart towards her Majesty, so your continuance therein, with your honourable wise and virtuous behaviour besides, shall both nourish and increase the same.' Really—from him! He regrets that, at this time when his mother was having some trouble over her business affairs, 'it was not my chance to have been in place where I might have done your ladyship some service.' Chance!—it was his own meddling with high politics that had burned his fingers.

His mother had sent over her man with a token, but on his return the ship he was in was forced back to Calais by a fight between the French and Spaniards. She was taking her journey to Canford-ward—her house in the country— though staying as usual on her way with Sir William Warham at Malsanger. He was the heir of Archbishop Warham who had built the house, of which an octagonal turret remains. Her law affairs would determine her movements; a daughter of Warham's accompanies her, 'the which is a wife—with others. If wiving take place you should be that [there] . . . Praying hour [our] Lord to pressarf [preserve] you both in honour and virtue, and to give his grace to avoid all ill and sinful company.' This monition was in place, to judge from rumours as to his conduct in London after his release. She signs herself as usual, 'your loving mothar'; he never returns with 'your loving son.'

He is 'your loving friend' to Lord Paget, the Lord Privy Seal, but then he wants him to advance his licence for his

journey to Italy—'I hope thereby in time to come to do the
King's and Queen's Majesties the better service. I am neither
good secretary nor orator, but I pray you be persuaded by
these few words.' For the rest he referred him to Mason, the
ambassador's letters. He made the same excuse to Basset,
who reproached him with slackness in writing to his friends:
'ye know of old how ill a secretary I am.' In fact, he
employed a good secretary, and the letters that flew to and
fro are numerous. Thomas Harvey—one of the Queen's
Pensioners (her bodyguard), and another Devonshire
name—wrote from Greenwich assuring the Earl of his devotion, 'without the Italian's dissimulation.' Certainly he
seems, with his name and descent, to have had the loyalty
of a great many people, as well as the friendship and favour
of others.

Harvey had forwarded Devon's letter to Lord Worcester,
another friend in the Catholic circle around the Queen. 'The
many fair promises sugared with numbers of feigned words,
and the effect with deed following so small', he wrote again,
to say that licence would be necessary from both King and
Queen: 'your lordship's wholly without dissimulation.' He
seems a sententious fellow, very conscious of the Italian
atmosphere around Philip, who spoke neither English nor
French, but Spanish and Italian. Lord Chancellor Gardiner
was inditing a curious Italianate tract on the succession as
his testament. Disregarding Elizabeth, of whom he was a
determined enemy, he considered the possibility of Philip's
continued rule. Certainly Bishop Gardiner was quite as much
of a Machiavellian as Thomas Cromwell.

In Flanders so conspicuous a figure was having some
trouble; the ambassador reported to the Council that the Earl
had been 'molested and troubled with varlets.' Several attacks
were made on his attendants by Spaniards—perhaps in return
for the manhandling of Spaniards in the streets of
London—culminating in an affray in September in which
several were hurt. This was a feature of the time (like mugging
today); but everywhere he went the Earl, as a royal
personage, was a conspicuous target. He went in fear of his
life, and it was said that he thought of nothing but preserving
it.

The Queen was 'much offended that you should be so

misused there' and complained to Philip, who 'would write immediately over for the reformation thereof and would himself see it at his coming.' Basset advised the Earl by no means to ask for leave 'while the King is there, for it might be construed evil, that you have no fancy to be where he is. His Majesty's abode there cannot be long, for the writs of summons of a new Parliament' have gone out, and it is most requisite he should be present. Then the Earl could 'wait upon his Majesty hither, which I think will not be denied', or ask for leave for Italy. We see the difficulties the Earl's precarious exaltation placed him in.

Basset would take his opportunity to go over and explain the situation fully. When Philip came over he advised the Earl 'to leave your accustomed solitariness and keeping of your house alone.' He should be more of 'a good fellow and more companionable among the noblemen, which is the only means to great good will amongst them—and now there is such plenty of noblemen that your lordship hath no cause, as you had before, to do as you did.' It would appear that on account of the molestation of his attendants he had withdrawn from the public gaze. This was uncongenial in the Court society of Brussels; one sees how much he was a target for suspicion.

He took Basset's advice, and accompanied the English ambassador, Sir John Mason, to meet Philip at the Louvain gate on his arrival at Brussels. He was able to assure Basset that 'I find such courtesy that I am become so far in love with waiting that meseemeth I find not myself well satisfied if I be not there once or twice a day.' This was in October; the news was that the Emperor's departure was postponed for a month and that then Philip would return to England. Devon was troubled by the news of Gardiner's renewed illness—as well he might be, he owed him so much. He had a chance of speaking with Philip, who asked him when he intended his journey. Now he was awaiting formal leave from the Queen, and dispatched letters to her and her principal ministers, Gardiner, Pole and Secretary Petre.

He was kept kicking his heels in Brussels and grew discouraged. The Emperor would take no hand in expediting him on his way to Italy, while Philip was preventing him from a farewell visit to England to look to his affairs. An Imperial agent wrote that he had no heart now for the undertaking of marrying Elizabeth, *'nor would she accept him, for she has big ideas.'* This is much closer the mark in this matter than historians have hitherto realised.

Philip had a heavy burden on his mind, for he was just about to take over one half of his father's intolerable responsibilities. On 25 October took place the historic scene, in the hall of the Castle at Brussels, of the Emperor's abdication. He leaned on the arm of the Prince of Orange, attended by all the Flemish grandees, among them Counts Egmont and Horn, Philip kneeling before his father to receive his charge— what vistas of the tragic future it presents! Nothing of this transpires in Devon's correspondence, nor is it likely that he, a foreigner, was present at this intimate scene, the whole assembly dissolved in tears.

Meanwhile his mother had a good deal of business to transact at Canford—where the large medieval kitchen of her house remains, beneath Barry's towering masterpiece. She had bought various offices and bargains, on her counsel's advice, 'the which I bear the great charge of and you are like to have the profit, if you be to me as ['has'] God and nature command you.' She followed this up with her usual warning 'to fly sin and evil counsel and company.' Is one wrong to detect a note of distrust, a certain disaccord, between mother and son?

He was anxious to pay a farewell visit to England before leaving for Italy, for the Survey of his lands was being made by the most experienced surveyor of the time, Humberston. Basset made suit to the Queen, putting it diplomatically that he wished to take his leave of her and his mother. Mary replied that, if the King approved, she was well content. When the Earl applied to Philip, he replied diplomatically that he himself would make his excuse to the Queen—a polite way of saying that he did not want him in England.

All sorts of rumours flew round—we cannot tell how far true or not, probably not. One was that the Earl would have to accompany Philip to Spain—if so, no wonder he was keen on getting to Italy. Another was that the Emperor would marry him to Elizabeth. This had something to recommend it from the Habsburg point of view—to keep him loyal and Elizabeth Catholic. For the Habsburgs England was a strategic keystone in the arch—all that was missing was the English determination on independence, and Elizabeth's with it. But Mary was now, after Wyatt's rebellion, irrevocably opposed to such a marriage.

His mother was grateful for a letter—'one way comfortable to perceive you do not forget your mother who esteemed you above her own life'—and longed to see him before he left.

> I trust, according to your bounden duty, you will first come into England to see the Queen's highness, and your poor mother, who has as little worldly comfort as [has] ever woman had, saving only the goodness and comfort of the Queen's highness . . . I am at this present so pained with the colic and the stone that I have much ado to write. . . . If you come into England I trust I shall see you, or else I will shortly write to you, if I be alive.

When suit was made for his return, it was 'not well taken.'

Much of the remaining correspondence is taken up with the Survey and the necessity to sell land. Secretary Petre, himself a Devonshireman, was very keen to buy the manor of Whitford. 'I would be right glad to satisfy his desire, although mine own affection be specially bent to reserve my land in Devon.' Petre pressed again for Whitford; Devon was reluctant, especially 'having consideration of the goodness of the lands in those parts'—a note one is glad to hear. However, a mortgage would take as much time as an outright sale, and both time and the need for money were pressing. 'He buyeth for pleasure, I sell for need. He is a continual [i.e. permanent] gainer, I having occasion to spend. He is well able to pay, and I not in state to give, specially where there is no alms' deed.' But the Secretary of State was a man to consider—so, Whitford it had to be.

On 6 November he took formal leave of the Emperor, King Philip, the Queens, Duchess and all the States, Philip entertaining him courteously and giving him no less than thirteen letters of commendation to various states and ambassadors, as well as his general passport. Personal troubles incommoded his departure. He needed to disembarrass himself of some of his following; young Tresham flung away in a rage saying that he was dismissed out of disfavour, refusing both money and persuasions. He threatened some

of the Earl's servants going about on his necessary business—
Devon reported this to his father in case of mishap.

A more congenial letter went off to the Earl's kinsman,
John Trelawny, a remote cousin who was to inherit some of
his property, including his papers. 'I have amongst the rest
sent home your son, whose honest diligence I have so well
tried in my service, with his courage right well witnessing
the heart of a gentleman.' He thanked the father that 'without
any acquaintance you have committed him unto me, being
your eldest and most dearest son.' He can hardly have
expected that the Trelawnys would be succeeding to some of
his possessions.

The Earl moved to Louvain for his last weeks in Flanders,
prevented by Philip of his intention of visiting England. He
had Petre to thank for the transport of forty tuns of beer for
his household, the rest for his friends. Money had been raised
for him by his commissioners: 'the more money I have in
bank the better I shall live by my living [i.e. rents] and be
subject to the fewer extremities in so far distance from my
country.' With the winter approaching, he expected to have
to make some stay in Germany. From his mother he extracted
her cook, 'as he is a most necessary man for my
purpose. . . . Because your ladyship should not be utterly
destitute I have sent you Herman, who hath served my turn
well since my cook died . . . he hath a good will to learn
and take pains to serve you.' It sounds rather casual of him,
though no doubt his need was greater than hers. She asked
for a prebend lately fallen to his appointment for a dependent
of hers. This he refused: 'Dabney being an old man unlearned
and without possibility to be priest, I see the order both of
my lord Cardinal and of all bishops such as he can by no
means be admitted . . . a prebend being a spiritual
promotion.' He had bestowed the prebend on the bearer, for
his long service; 'I trust it shall not displease you.' He asks
her blessing in thus taking leave 'for a long time and many
years, as I suppose.' It was to be for ever.

From ambassador Mason he heard of Lord Chancellor
Gardiner's death, 'glad to understand he hath made so good
and charitable an end, as he hath well declared by his
reconciliation with my lord Paget.' They had been at daggers
drawn within the Council for power, and over rival policies.

Basset now wrote apologising for delay, for the Chancellor 'my especial good lord and your very friend (whose soul Jesu pardon, as I doubt not he hath) lay then *in extremis*. What with watching with him, what with grief and sorrow (and as I had most cause), so that I could think upon nothing else but spent day and night altogether with him until he died.' He now advised against Gresham's terms for credit as exorbitant, at 10 or 12 per cent: the commissioners for the sale of Devon's land—some £100 a year in value—would not agree to it. Bonvisi's terms were more agreeable and he would supply him with 6000 ducats' credit in Italy.

Meanwhile Cardinal Pole was warning those who would have care of him there against the companion he was taking with him, urging them to endeavour to rid him of this bad company. We do not know who this companion was, or what made him undesirable. Secretary Petre also wrote a farewell word of warning:

> this ill world is full of rumours and reports, and the same for the more part to the worst. And therefore your lordship will in your journeys, companies, choice of places use that foresight that no occasion may be given to the ill men to speak ill, whereof might follow any impairment of the good opinion the Queen's Majesty hath conceived of you.

The Earl sought to justify this good opinion by reporting his meeting at Antwerp with Sir Peter Carew, who was anxious to make submission and return home to serve King and Queen. He had been misled by conscience touching religion; though Devon had talked it over with him 'there resteth in that point a piece of work for you to bring him to a more perfection.' To Sir Gawen Carew the Earl sent his bailiff of the manor of Crewkerne to explain a conflict of interest which he imputed to the ill dealing of lawyer Haydon, 'whose hollow heart to me and false in mine affairs by more means than one I have intelligence of.' He bursts out in an angry long letter: 'he cannot be content to be my steward, mine auditor and receiver . . . but he will handle the matter so as he will be my governor, which I would be loth any subject should be, much less such a varlet', etc. To Englefield and Basset he complained that it was Haydon's 'duty to do as he is bidden', whereas he has done his best 'to overthrow my determinations . . . that of mine own ought to

have that I command. . . . So that, where my debts hath
grown by mine imprisonment and service to the Queen's
Majesty, he seemeth to impute it to my misguiding, by the
abusion of my men—which imputeth a very light opinion of
me to give such sentence over me.'

This takes us into the heart of Courtenay's character and
situation; no doubt these various elements entered in. We
see also how dependent the owner of great estates was upon
servants, agents, lawyers, intermediaries. Those people did
best who could manage their own affairs. Devon was angered
to the point of incoherence by Haydon's suggestion that he
should be guided by the Earl of Bedford, 'for whom he is
an officer.' Tactless, to say the least, for Bedford now
enjoyed the primacy in the West that the Courtenays
formerly had. Apparently Bedford's present insufficiency of
funds, on embassy abroad, was given as a lesson to Devon
'to take a more sufficient bank.' Bedford may 'measure it as
he thinks good for himself, being Earl of Bedford, a married
man and a chief at home. . . . It passeth not solicitor's office
or any other to control me of that I should think good for
myself, being all otherwise unburdened [i.e. unmarried]—
albeit I meant indeed to spend more and make my proportion
larger than he.' Actually Henry VIII's largesse had made
Bedford the richer man, even apart from his offices. 'The
stay [holding up] of my business moveth me to passions as
I cannot contain them.'

However, his commissioners finally dispatched it to his
satisfaction, and the Earl expressed himself particularly
grateful to Basset. 'What pangs and passions I have been in
by the circumstance of my case you may consider; but now
you have brought my business so friendly and wisely to pass
as the same hath well confirmed the hope and confidence I
have always had in you.' He was equally satisfied with
Bonvisi, 'whose conscience is so upright and just as that a
man may safely without fear have to do with him.' A good
quality in a banker, we may say; but then Bonvisi was a
religious banker.

His bills of credit serve me but for Venice only . . . wherefore, albeit I
have in my purse 7 or 8 hundred crowns already, and think to spend
but a small portion thereof in my journey, yet, because I have no credit

between this and Italy, I have taken up here of Mr Bonvisi 400 crowns, to the intent that if—by sickness, hurt, or mischance—I shall be enforced to stay by the way, I should not be put to any extreme shift.

He instructed Basset to pay the 100 marks owing to Gresham and to see the bonds discharged. And 'where you have given me counsel to play the good husband . . . I pray you play the husband for me at home.' This was his last letter from his abode at Louvain, for next day, 30 November 1555, he was setting out.

He had hoped to see his kinsman, Lord Hastings, in Italy next year; now he promises to write to him often from thence, hoping he would keep in touch. He made a similar promise to his aunt, Lady Berkeley, with whom his relations were warmer than with his mother. 'Every month letters may be sent on both parts'; but, after he has acquainted himself with the states and princes of Christendom, and the manners of their Courts, he may go further 'to see the Great Turk's Court at Constantinople or peradventure beyond.' In that case, look for no letters; 'but as I shall pray for you, so, I pray you, pray for me, for the voyage will be somewhat dangerous.'

Thus he goes over the horizon southward to Italy.

We can, however, trace his progress from the State Papers, for his every step was watched as a person of state—or, in Shakespeare's phrase for Southampton, 'a child of state.' On 10 December he was at Cologne, thanking the English merchant, Aldersay, for the bill for 400 crowns. By 21 December he had arrived at Speyer, where there was plague; so he crossed the Rhine to the village of Rheinhausen. He could 'write much of the barbarous character of the people, but dare not for fear of his life.' Arrived at Augsburg by 29 December he chose a new guide; he had received his stuff and equipment at Mainz. The news was that plague was raging at Venice. Next day he was writing to Sir Philip Hoby of Bisham—the Montagus' burying place—the scholarly diplomat who knew Italy and was acquainted with Titian and Aretino.[13] The Earl had a wider circle of acquaintance than one would expect from a life-long prisoner—but, then, the Tower was by no means solitary.

From the end of December we have a suspicious bit of information that may or may not be true—to the effect that Ruy Gomez was in touch with a Dalmatian to assassinate the Earl in Venice. So at least this individual, Marco da Risano, deposed to the Council of Ten: the assassins would carry three arquebuses, he would know the place and be able to find boats for their escape. One would not put this past Ruy Gomez—after all, Philip's later Secretary, Antonio Perez, arranged the assassination of Don John's Secretary, Escobedo. That there was something in it we may infer from the Council of Ten giving the Earl licence for twenty-five men to attend him. The Council had entertained him, but apologised for not receiving him with 'royal honours.'

His kinsman Lord Hastings writes that Philip's return to England has been long looked for. By 15 January 1556 Devon had arrived at Padua, for Peter Vannes, England's ambassador, invited him to Venice next day for a grand ceremony. John Blount sent forward a bearer with news of his mother and aunt. In mid-February ambassador Mason was writing that a truce had been concluded between the Empire and France, that the Estates were to assemble at Brussels and Philip shortly go to England. Most interesting historically is his information that the great part of the English clergy wished the Cardinal back again in Rome. This is important information coming from a government source. By his thorough-going reform of displacing and replacing all married clergy and making them put away their wives—clerical marriage had been permitted under Edward VI—Pole upset far more secular clergy than any of the changes had so far done, or were to do again with Elizabeth. It must have been a considerable factor in increasing the unpopularity of Mary's reaction, and reconciling even conservatives to the Elizabethan settlement when it came.

The egregious Dr Story—who wished Elizabeth put away—prays for the Earl's prosperous estate, so useful in the future to the Christian religion and his native land. (His prayers were unanswered.) The Queen and Cardinal have both spiritual and civil matters much on their minds. In the absence of Philip, Mary was now leaning chiefly on Pole; together they were embarking on the full Catholic programme and hotting up the burnings. Justice, wrote

Story, himself a civil lawyer, was being reduced to order by Archbishop Heath, the new Lord Chancellor. The spirit of Mary's rule was religious indeed.

News from the Court at Greenwich was that the King's prolonged absence makes the Queen melancholy. (But, after all, he had done his best to impregnate her: no more hope in that quarter.) Mason has forwarded the Earl's letter to Ruy Gomez, who would communicate it to the King. The Earl of Pembroke is sending him a fine gelding. Meanwhile Devon has been entertained at Venice by Doge and Senate, and would visit Throckmorton at Mantua about Easter. This last introduces an Italian merchant who will be useful financially, and he sends on the news that Pole, now made Archbishop, would at last proceed to priest's orders—hitherto he had been but a deacon. Religious affairs progress coldly enough in England, though seven heretics have been recently burnt. Mason sends on the news that, among these, was Archbishop Cranmer, 'standing steadfast to his opinions.' At the last, harassed by Spanish friars, he came clean and, emerging from doubts, at last spoke out what he really thought.

These developments were accompanied by renewed resistance to the régime and yet another conspiracy. Headed by Henry Dudley, it inculpated a considerable number of people, including the prominent Sir Nicholas Throckmorton. This numerous family included some Catholics, but the majority were Protestants; Sir Nicholas' previous acquittal had made the Queen ill: he now fled overseas. So did others of the West Country gentry previously involved: Tremaynes, Killigrews, Horseys and others. The aim this time was to raid the Exchequer, and stop English money going over to Philip for his purposes—one would have thought a proper aim. Many arrests were made, including Walker, Devon's agent in the West, and others whom he knew. So suspicion came to rest on the Earl once more.

All kinds of rumours flew round abroad, obviously exaggerated or untrue. People said that, if a Spanish marriage were forced on Elizabeth, the French would back marrying the Earl to Mary Queen of Scots. Such were the chessboard politics of Habsburg versus Valois that continued to be played well into Elizabeth's reign. That Mary's government was alerted to these contingencies is evident from the questions put to those arrested about placing Elizabeth on the throne and contacts with Devon. Many were examined, his servant Walker sent to the Tower. The Venetian ambassador, reporting this, added that there were contemptuous demonstrations in the churches and that Catholic preachers were shouted down. For Philip's part, he instructed his ambassador in Venice to keep careful watch on the Earl and find out everything he was up to; if he left Venice for Milan or Piedmont—i.e. into the sphere of French influence—to let him know.

At the end of March Mason wrote that Philip's departure for England was further deferred by a visit from the King of Bohemia. At Padua the Earl was present at a grand reception for the Queen of Poland, and at Ferrara he was entertained by the Duke at his palace. In April he wrote to protest against Walker's imprisonment and made the point that the numerous arrests created an unfavourable opinion of England in Venice. In lighter vein he wrote that a hundred courtesans had been converted at Rome during Lent, but that at Easter they went back to their old trade. On the other hand, a hundred of the fairest Venetian gentlewomen were to attend upon the Queen of Poland.

In May Lord Paget over in Flanders pounced on Sir Peter Carew and the famous scholar, Sir John Cheke, who had been Edward VI's Secretary of State. Travelling between Brussels and Antwerp, 'they were unhorsed, blindfolded, bound, thrown into a wagon, conveyed to the nearest harbour, put on board a ship under hatches and brought to the Tower of London.' Philip was not responsible for this ruse, which was much resented by the English, but it added to his unpopularity. In the Tower they were joined by Sir William Courtenay of Powderham, who was indicted at the Guildhall in the autumn with Sir John Pollard as participants in the Dudley conspiracy, at least to the extent of concealing the knowledge they were made party to.

From Venice Devon admits that Walker's arrest was excusable. Mason said that he would be shortly released—though he was not; meanwhile, would the Earl report himself more often to his friends at home, as it is not well known in England where he is, or what has become of him. In June a servant, Humphrey Mitchell, evidently a West Countryman, offended the Earl by arriving on him unexpected at Padua, for suspicions continued. An English envoy in Paris reported that the Dudley conspirators had sent Henry Killigrew (the later Elizabethan diplomat) to the Earl, but that they had had no reply. 'They say that he is persuaded that, if he should return into England, it would cost him his life.' Mary's rebels continued to have hopes of him, but he pleaded that suspicions of him were unfounded as events would prove. However, a packet of his letters had been opened in Flanders. In July Mason wrote that the Queen retained her good opinion of him—but Walker was still held in prison; he enclosed an extract exonerating both Elizabeth and the Earl, as having too much wisdom and honour to be parties to the late conspiracy. Indeed, the best course was to wait for Mary's death—though meanwhile people burned.

In September the Earl was dead himself; we have details of his last days from a dispatch of Peter Vannes, Mary's ambassador, within hours of the event on 18th of the month. The Earl had gone out to the Lido to see his hawk fly over the waste, when he was overtaken by a storm, so that he could not return by his gondola. He managed to get back to Venice in a searcher's boat wet through, but refused to change his clothing. Five days later he had a fall within doors. To avoid the tediousness of journeying by water, and the cost of horses, he returned to Padua shaken up in a waggon. When Vannes visited him he found him in high fever and very weak. Two of the best physicians in Padua attended him.

He had died a good Christian, receiving ghostly comfort at the last, lifting up his eyes and knocking his breast, 'in repentance of his sin.' Vannes brought in a priest with the sacrament; but 'his tongue had so stopped his mouth, and his teeth so cloven together, that in no wise could he receive that same. And after this sort this gentleman is gone, as I do not doubt, to God's mercy.' Vannes was now about to see to his burial 'with as much sparing and as much honour as can be done.' He besought the Queen to pay the funeral expenses and to extend charity to his servants, 'about ten in number, masterless, moneyless, not able to live here nor come home without her help.' He had given instructions for

his papers to be inventoried to await royal commands—
evidently as a record of his innocence, the terminus of so
many hopes.

It seems a pitiable end—in keeping with his life.

It remains to gather together the scraps that remain from the
foundering of a great house, in the senior line, in the person
of this unfortunate young Earl, wrecked by his royal blood.

We must not linger over the portion of the Survey of his
lands that we have, though it does give an insight into the
historic holdings, some of them, of the Courtenays in
Cornwall.[14] Humberston has interesting general reflections
as to the nature of land-holding at the time. The customs in
each manor are distinct, 'for every lord within his own manor
devised such customs for his own tenants as to his own
contentation seemed best.' The Cornish manors yielded not
only rents and fines, waifs and strays, and heriots, but the
toll-tin on the stream works in such a manor as Treverbyn
Courtenay, in the uplands above St Austell, now solid china
clay. Heriots meant that, on the death of a tenant, the heir
had 'to gratify the lord with the best beast or some other
best parcel of their movable goods in token of a remembrance.' Tenants still had to work 'due days' for the lord 'in
time of tillage, hay time and harvest', according to the
particular custom.

'These things knit such a knot of collateral amity . . . that
the lord tendered his tenant as his child. And the tenants
again loved and obeyed the lord as naturally as the child the
father.' This offers a somewhat idealised picture, unrecognis-
able by any Marxist historian. But what follows is illuminating: if the lord commanded 'the tenants would leave wife,
children and substance, and follow their lord and adventure
their lives with him and had no care of their lives.' If he were
'left in the field, the wife so long as she kept herself sole
and unmarried should enjoy the whole living towards the
education and bringing up of their children without any fine.'
Thus we see how it was that 'feudal' lords could bring their
following to the field, and this retained its importance right
up to the Civil War, especially in the West.

'Now and then friendship causeth concealment of things'—
that was true enough: tenants everywhere took what advan-

tage they could, especially on large estates—like the Duchy of Cornwall—where the lord was a perpetual absentee. Humberston notes that on most manors the ancient manor house was either in decay, or occupied by a farmer. He specifies that on several of the Cornish manors there were no common fields, 'but every man his land to himself to use and employ as he shall think most meet for his profit and advantage' (no doubt a predisposing factor, over the ages, towards the individualism of the Cornish). In East Cornwall the people were 'more civil than in the West part of Cornwall, and better disposed to plant and set, and furnish their habitations with orchards, and do use the making of cider as they do in Devonshire.'

Everywhere along the coast fishing was an important part of the economy. The manor of West Looe had a number of prosperous merchants trading into France, Brittany, Spain and elsewhere,

and the town is well furnished with small ships and crayers; but the great number of the inhabitants are fishermen and mariners. The most part of all the East country as far as Exeter are served with fish from the haven every week, and a continual resort of rippers [fish-carriers] is thither for the same. The inhabitants hereof are stout men, hardy and adventurous upon the seas; and in the last wars against France did more harm to the Frenchmen and took more prizes, as the report is, than any one haven or port within all the West parts.

So much will serve us for an insight into the sources of the Courtenays' wealth and what had so long upheld their grandeur in the West. Among the manuscript *Nachlass* that came to the Trelawnys we have accounts of the rents arising in the West, signed and sealed by the Earl, something under £1000 in his first year. A token sum of £20 was 'to be bestowed in charitable use among the poor and scholars of the universities'—it does not seem that he made a will. Hence some dispute arose between his mother and his executors as to some of his possessions.

'We would be very loth', they wrote, 'to detain and withhold anything that of right that belongs to your ladyship, so we doubt not you will restore such stuff as belonged to the said Earl to be employed to such uses as we stand charged to perform . . . i.e. the satisfaction of his debts, the relief of his poor servants, and in such good and charitable uses as your ladyship shall have no cause to judge that we mind to take any benefit thereby.' This was pretty sharp talk to the Marchioness from Rochester, Englefield, Waldegrave and Basset: 'the part your ladyship doth challenge is comprised within the warrant given to his lordship, and much more which we be informed remain in your possession. As for the tale of cloth of gold and tinsel, we mind not if the gift of them may be duly proved from your son to your ladyship to detain them any longer.' This was in January 1557.

It was natural enough that some of his stuff should adhere to her, for we learn that she had her own chamber at Kew: there were the furniture we recognise, the tapestries, the 'falcon and fagot' work, a new 'tapestry counterpane of the Salutation of our Lady.' We remember too the furnishings of 'my lord's chamber', the chamber next to it, the pallet chamber with tapestries of wild beasts, birds and flowers. Then William Daubeney had his room: evidently a gentleman companion, who was probably steward of the household. A number of coats are specified as coming to the Lady Marquis. We have an immensely long schedule of her son's garments and personal equipment. It would be anachronistic to describe him as a dandy, but evidently in the short period during which he enjoyed liberty, he went splendidly clad.

We note a few things only, to bring him back: the night-gown, i.e. dressing-gown, of violet cloth guarded with velvet, the fine black cloak made after the Dutch fashion; the capes and coats, doublets and jerkins, the velvet breeches edged with satin, the buskins and the velvet shoes after the Spanish fashion; the shirts wrought with red silk, or striped with black silk. We note the rapiers of damascene work, the daggers, girdles and spurs. Printed books in Latin and English number sixty score—these would be the family library more than his personal books, for we have seen that he was not much of a reading or writing man. He had his 'writings', i.e. leases and patents, in a chest; another chest of viols and a couple of lutes. We recall perhaps the pair of virginals.

We will not detail here all the household equipment of hall, kitchen, buttery, pantry, pastry, bakehouse, boiling house, etc.—merely note 'two great staffs to run at the ring

withal', likely to have been his sportive father's. The equipment of the chapel is mostly recognisable, the three pictures
set in tables upon the altar, evidently a little reredos, the
super-altar, and corporas case.

On 25 September of that year the Marchioness made her
will, 'in good and perfect memory', reciting all the magnificent titles of Philip and Mary.[15] She left money for a dirge
and a trental of masses, fifty marks to the poor at the time
of her burial; another fifty marks to them at her month's
mind, with a dirge and a trental of masses, and the same at
her year's mind. £10 for the poor 'to pray for me, my
husband, my father and mother'—nothing whatever said
about her son. To Lady Berkeley a black velvet gown and a
diamond ring; to sister Blewett a velvet gown and a silver
gilt cup; to cousin Sir Richard Blount a gilt standing bowl;
brother John Blount £20 and a silver gilt cup; to cousin Anne
Kevill, £20.

Her sole executor was 'my trusty and well beloved friend,
Anthony Harvey, esquire', whose daughter was to have a
black velvet gown furred with sables and two flagons of silver
gilt. Harvey was to have the entire disposition of the rest of
her estate. The will was witnessed on 26 December and
proved on 8 January 1558: she would have died between
those dates. Harvey provided her with a fine tomb, on the
right hand of the altar, in Wimborne Minister—a medieval
tomb chest in the conservative Marian manner, in keeping
with her life. It must be concluded that it was a sad one, for
all the bright promise of her grand marriage in its early days.

Since the Earl died unmarried, and the males of the family
had suffered so severely from both Yorkists and then Tudors,
to find the heirs to his personal estate one had to go right back
to the daughters of his great-great-grandfather, Sir Hugh
Courtenay of Boconnoc, killed at Tewkesbury. These had
been married in Cornwall: Isabel Mohun, Elizabeth Trethurf,
Maud Arundell of Tolvern in the Roseland, Florence
Trelawny. The descendants of these were coheirs, the inheritance divided among them: Reynold Mohun—hence the
Mohuns moved up-river from Hall by Polruan to beautiful
Boconnoc; John Vyvyan, Margaret Buller, John
Trelawny—and so the Trelawnys came by the personal
manuscripts.

The male line at Powderham, though a cadet line, always held that the earldom had not been extinguished by Edward Courtenay's death in 1556; for it had been re-created by Queen Mary with remainder to his heirs male. They were the male heirs. In 1831 they achieved the recognition of their title, in a famous peerage case which occupies a whole volume.[16] The case, however, was simple: the descent of a peerage did not go by the same law as the descent of land, and the claim was allowed. In any case, the Earls of Devon at Powderham Castle—no longer in possession of Tiverton, Okehampton, Colcombe, Plympton castles, and the rest—go back in unbroken male line, so rare as to be almost unique, to the ancient Courtenays of Gibbon's *Decline and Fall*.

Notes

1. Edward Gibbon, *The Decline and Fall of the Roman Empire*, ed. J. B. Bury, (1896) Vol. VI. pp. 446–54.
2. Courtenay had been first married to Elizabeth Grey, liable to be confused with her aunt, the Elizabeth Grey who was Lord Lisle's first wife. But in a letter to Cromwell, Lisle makes clear that the niece 'died ere she came to the age of fourteen.' This clears up a confusion. *L. and P.*, Vol. XIII, p. 346.
3. *The Diary of Henry Machyn*, ed. J. G. Nichols (Camden Soc., 1848) p. 41.
4. Additional Mss, 6113, British Library.
5. S.P. 12/1.64.
6. Courtenay Mss., originally at Trelawne, Cornwall.
7. *Cal. Pat. Rolls, Philip and Mary*, I. 250–7.
8. *Machyn, op. cit.*, pp. 48, 50.
9. *The Life and Times of Sir Peter Carew*, ed. J. Maclean, (1857) pp. 180–1.
10. The Lisle Letters are of course the great exception.
11. For him see my *Ralegh and the Throckmortons*, (Macmillan and St. Martin's, 1962) pp. 2, 6, 11.
12. Clough, sometimes known as Sir Richard, though not an English knight, was a Knight of the Holy Sepulchre. For Catherine of Berain, v. my *The Expansion of Elizabethan England* (Cardinal, 1973) pp. 68–70.
13. For him v. 'Bisham and the Hobys', in my *Times, Persons, Places: Essays in Literature* (Macmillan, 1965).
14. Harleian Mss., British Library, 71.
15. Prerogative Court of Canterbury, (P.C.C.) 1 Noodes. This corrects the *Dictionary of National Biography*, which gives the date of the will as that of her death.

16. Sir Harris Nicolas, *Report of the Proceedings on the Claim to the Earldom of Devon*, (1832).

3

Sir Peter Carew, Soldier of Fortune

Sir Peter Carew has the rarity of having had a contemporary biography devoted to him. This is a distinction indeed, for one can think of very few such, to rank along with Cavendish's life of Wolsey, Roper's of More, or Fulke Greville's Philip Sidney. Like those books Carew's biography was written by one who knew him well and much admired him; the historian of Tudor Ireland calls it 'a delightful book', as it is; but little known.

It was written by John Hooker of Exeter—uncle of the Richard Hooker, philosopher of the Anglican Church—and himself one of the most eminent antiquarian scholars of his time. He is best known as the editor of the second edition of Holinshed's *Chronicles*, to which Shakespeare owed so much for his English history plays. Chamberlain of Exeter, a kind of town clerk, he wrote an account of the city, a number of tracts on its customs, and a catalogue of the bishops; various works on the keeping and constitution of Parliament in both England and Ireland; kept diaries and left a mass of manuscripts on antiquarian matters. He was a good scholar, though, when he came to write his biography of Carew, he wrote it in no rebarbative academic fashion, but simply and humanly.[1]

His antiquarian researches encouraged his hero in the last of his many adventures—the revival of the claims of the medieval Carews to large domains in Ireland, which had lain dormant for nearly a couple of centuries. It led to a lot of trouble there, engulfed in a mass of troubles already—though we must see it in the perspective of the heart-breaking attempts of the Elizabethans to impose order on an incoherent, pre-medieval society, and to plant 'civility', as they saw it. Never can antiquarian research have led to such disturbing effects—except for the Parliamentarian anti-quarianism which helped on the Civil War.

A more congenial aspect of the biography is that it tells us much about the youth, personality and circumstances of its subject—just what we miss so much with eminent Elizab-ethans. If only we had such a biography of Marlowe or Shakespeare, or of Drake or Walter Ralegh—the last two of whom Hooker knew! Sir Peter Carew was his hero, and we have reason to be grateful for that: a striking, exceptional career, a marked personality, but also one characteristic of the age.

By Tudor times the Carews were an enormous clan, with several branches. The name was pronounced Cary—and so in Cornwall right up to our time. It is convenient to distinguish between this bunch as Carew, keeping Cary for their kinsmen and neighbours of Cockington near Torquay, and Carey for Queen Elizabeth's cousins, the Hunsdon family. The Carews were a Norman family, originally Montgomery; they seem to have taken the name Carew from the castle in Pembrokeshire which they came by through marrying a Welsh heiress. It was from these parts that the Normans progressed from their conquest of England to the conquest of Ireland, under Strongbow, and the Carews were in the following. Later in the middle ages the Norman impulse receded and the Celtic tide flowed back, obliterating Carew landmarks.

They were, however, powerfully planted in the West Country, particularly in Devon. In those days, when sea-travel in their little craft was easier than travel by land, they were in their element crossing the Bristol and English Channels, and again—when the expansion of the Tudor state got going—the Irish Channel. Nothing is more striking in Peter Carew than his restless journeying about—just like his Norman ancestors—all over Europe.

By the fourteenth century the family had come by Mohun's Ottery—through a marriage to a Mohun heiress—on rising ground above the river, a defensible spot, in the parish of Luppitt, church higher up towards the beetling tree-crowned eminence above and the exposed ridgeway along Luppitt Common. It would seem that Peter Carew mostly built the

big mansion, of which little survives, for his initials appear
above the Tudor door; something of the gatehouse remains.
In the church is the big barbaric font in which they were all
baptised: centaur fighting dragons, men fighting each other
with clubs, animals in the forest—all very appropriate for
such fighting folk—and the fine roofs that looked down on
their devotions.

Peter was born here in 1514, a younger son of Sir William,
whose father, Sir Edmund, baron of Carew, mortgaged that
castle and the South Wales properties to Sir Rhys ap Thomas
to go and fight in Henry VIII's first war in France. There
Sir Edmund was killed by a gunshot, in modern fashion, at
the siege of Térouanne in 1513. Of his grandchildren the
eldest was George who was drowned in the capsizing of the
Mary Rose; Peter was a second son; Philip disappears over
the horizon as a knight of Malta.

As a boy, very spirited and forward, Peter was put to
school in Exeter; but there proved unruly, 'a daily truant
and always ranging.' Once, escaping to a top turret of the
city wall, he threatened to throw himself down when
pursued. The alderman, of the house where he lodged,
reported his doings to Sir William, who had him leashed like
a hound to one of his servants and taken home. There he
coupled him to a hound for a time, until he thought of giving
him another chance at schooling, in London at St Paul's.
There too the schoolmaster 'in no wise could frame this
young Peter to smell to a book, or to like of any schooling.'
What do with him?

Walking in St Paul's one day Sir William met with an
acquaintance who served in the French Court and rather fell
for the boy, 'perceiving him to be very forward and of a
pregnant wit.' He took him to France as a page, where for
a time he 'made much of him.' But his 'master's hot love
soon waxed cold and faint'; the boy was made a lackey of,
and then reduced to serving in the stables. One of the Carews
of Haccombe, 'a cousin german of Sir William in the fifth
degree' was at the French Court one day when he heard the
lackeys and horseboys calling out to 'Carew Anglais! Carew
Anglais!' Inquiring who the youth was and to what this
gentleman's son had been reduced, he reproved his patron
and took him under his own wing. He recommended him to

the service of the Marquis of Saluzzo who, going with the French to Pavia, was slain there.

The battle, 1526, was a disaster for the French, with Francis I taken prisoner by the Emperor and held captive in Spain. Hereupon the young soldier of fortune recruited himself to Charles V's camp and took service with Philibert, Prince of Orange. Upon the Prince's death at the siege of Florence in 1530, Peter found favour with the Princess, his mother, who wished to retain him in her service. Peter, however, wanted to see home and friends again, having grown to man's estate. She dismissed him with a gold chain, money in his purse, and good commendations to Henry VIII and Sir William.

He made a favourable impression on the King at Greenwich, who took him into service as one of his henchmen, and gave him leave to visit his parents who had lost all touch with him—so like the time and lack of communication. Returned to Court, 'the King had great delight and pleasure in him, for he had not only the French tongue—which was as ripe in him as his own natural English tongue—but was also very witty [i.e. intelligent] and altogether given to all such honest exercises as do appertain to a gentleman, and especially in riding, for therein he had a special love and desire.'

Henry was inspired by jealousy of, and rivalry with, Francis I, and was descended from the Valois himself. So he took pleasure in conversing about the French Court with Peter, and made him a gentleman of the Privy Chamber, who 'could name every nobleman in France, in what credit and countenance he was in the Court, that the King the more he talked with him the more he delighted in him.' Part of Anne Boleyn's attraction for Henry was that she had the sophistication of the French Court—his love letters to her were in French. When the Lord Admiral of France came over, Carew was placed in attendance on him; as also on the grand occasion in October 1532, when Henry took Anne Boleyn over as Marchioness of Pembroke to present her officially to Francis as his wife to be.

The Scottish Court was hardly less French than Scotch, so Carew was chosen to accompany Lord William Howard to present the Garter to James V; where his French manners and fluency made people think him a French lord. Again, for the reception of Anne of Cleves as Queen at Calais, Carew was appointed 'among sundry other lusty gentlemen meet for this service.'

Restlessness and the desire for foreign travel thereupon set in. Carew was anxious to see the war raging in the plains of Hungary, where Charles V's brother, Ferdinand, had lost Buda to the Turks and was now besieging it in force. Carew was joined in his request for leave by John Champernowne, a cousin, and at last Henry granted it, with a generous grant towards the journey. Next spring they travelled through France to Venice, where they procured a safe-conduct from the Turkish ambassador, took shipping to Ragusa, thence by land—a perilous journey— to Constantinople. They passed themselves off as merchants seeking alum, and so managed to penetrate the Court and see the Grand Turk 'twice or thrice in his greatest royalty and glory.' When suspicions were aroused they were befriended by the French ambassador on account of Carew's fluency in the language and 'behaviour tasting after the French manner.' Thus they got away in a merchant ship to Venice, with a Spanish gentleman whom they redeemed after six years' captivity.

In Venice and Milan they were aided by Italian magnates in the pay of Henry VIII, and thus went straight to Buda, where mighty hosts were gathered within and without the city. At length the Turks brought up reinforcements and raised the siege. With no further service to be done, they betook themselves to Vienna, where Champernowne and Wingfield died of dysentery, and Carew moved back to Venice to recover from it.

Returning to Court, the King was fascinated to hear of his travels, especially of the Turkish Court and manner of wars; while 'in singing, vaulting and especially for riding, he was not inferior to any.' Henry was passionately fond of music, a composer himself, and sang with a light tenor voice. Carew, 'having a pleasant voice, the King would very often use him to sing with him certain songs then called "three-men songs", as namely "By the bank as I lay", and "As I walked in the wood so wild." ' It sounds a pleasant interlude from the lurid politics of those years—we recall Sir Edward Neville *singing* politics in the garden at West Horsley. We should retain both things in mind, singing and weeping, music and the scaffold, the lute and the fall of the axe.

In Henry's last French war—into which Charles V manoeuvred him and then renegued on him, leaving England alone to face a France three times bigger and stronger—Sir George Carew, the elder brother, was a lieutenant of horse, the younger brother a captain of foot, whom he equipped at his own charge: the 'Black Band.' In a pursuit near Cambrai Sir George, 'being more forward than circumspect', was taken prisoner. Peter took a French gentleman, whom he hoped to exchange for his brother, and brought him to Calais; the Frenchman departing, newly apparalled by his captor, went back on his word and did nothing.

Next year, 1544, Carew served under Suffolk as captain of horse and was one of the first to enter Boulogne, the walls of which had been undermined by Cornish miners under the lead of Sir William Godolphin. Carew was given command of a castle five miles from the town, when Suffolk sent for him, Peter leaving his charge to his lieutenant, a fellow Devonshireman. The Duke sent Carew with a message to the King, and this won him a reproof from irate Majesty. Henry asked him by what warrant he had left his charge. When Carew answered by the Duke's, his general, the ageing monarch said: 'Learn this for a rule: so long as we ourselves are present there is no other general but ourselves. Neither can any man depart from his charge without our special warrant. And therefore you, being thus come hither without our commandment, are not able to answer for the same, if we should minister that which by law we may do.' Thus Henry kept discipline in that undisciplined age: it is very revealing of him—as also the fact that no one could take the slightest liberty with him. Straight talk 'the King would give and not take', says Fuller. Peter's cousin, Sir Nicholas Carew, Master of the Horse, had been a great favourite; but he was secretly a supporter of the Marquis of Exeter and used opprobrious language of Henry—and so had ended on the scaffold four years before.

The year 1545 saw the height of the naval war, with the French concentrating a powerful fleet of galleys in the Channel. Peter Carew kept the seas, on guard, all winter and in the summer was given command of a great Venetian, of

700 tons. In calm weather the French Galleys had the advantage; when the wind blew the ships under sail prevailed in the actions that swung to and fro in the Channel. When the reinforced French fleet took station off Portsmouth, Henry—ageing and bulky, but indomitable—had himself carried in a chair to the coast: 'he fretted, and his teeth stood on edge to see the bravery of his enemies to come so near his nose, and he not able to encounter with them.'

Sir George Carew, released from captivity, was Vice-Admiral in the *Mary Rose*, in which Roger Grenville was captain: one of the fairest and strongest ships in the fleet. The King dined aboard the *Great Harry* with the Lord Admiral, attended by both Carews and their young uncle, Sir Gawen (Celtic for John). Henry asked if anything could be spied at sea: 'the word was no sooner spoken but that Peter Carew was as forward', climbed to the masthead and reported a fleet approaching. Henry ordered everyone to action stations, himself taken in the long boat on land. Regally generous, he took the chain from his neck with a great gold whistle and put it around Sir George's.

After an exchange of gunfire the gunports of the *Mary Rose* were left open, when a sudden wind arose and she began to heel over. Sir Gawen, passing in his ship, called out to his nephew to know what was happening: Sir George said he had a sort of knaves he could not rule. The ship heeled more and more over until she capsized, some seven hundred men drowned. The disaster seemed inexplicable; in later centuries many relics have been recovered, most of all quite recently. Hooker gives us a clue, which must come direct from Peter Carew:

> It chanced unto this gentleman [Sir George] as the common proverb is: the more cooks the worse pottage. He had in his ship a hundred mariners, the worst of them being able to be a Master in the best ship within the realm. These so maligned and disdained one the other that, refusing to do that which they should do, were careless to do that which was most needful and necessary; and so, contending in envy, perished in frowardness.'

It shows how necessary Henry's sharp discipline was. From the shore he watched the tragedy, along with Sir George's wife, whom it was his royal duty to comfort though 'oppressed with sorrow on every side.' This he did, encouraging morale, 'hoping that of a hard beginning there would follow a better ending.' The service went forward; a fleet of a hundred and five sails took the seas. This was largely Henry's creation. The French went back to port.

Next year, the Channel clear—the galleys gone back to the Mediterranean—an assault on Tréport near Dieppe was made. William Courtenay, son of Sir William of Powderham and captain of the *Mary James*, climbed the cliff with Carew. The inhabitants fled, the town spoiled, ships in harbour burned—the usual amenities of war. The Lord Admiral witnessed the exploit and dubbed both Devon men knights. Carew was sent to the King with dispatches, who made to knight him, but reading the letters 'perceived that he was already advanced to that degree.'

By the death of his elder brother he was to succeed to the inheritance: 'many a man would have gone home to enter into possession of those great livelihoods as which were then left to him.' Not so Peter: he remained in service at Court. Next year he attended the ambassador to make peace in France. The young Earl of Worcester was at Court there, being trained up and to learn fashions; when somewhat manhandled by a Frenchman, he was too young to revenge himself. Peter did it for him, boxing the offender's ears in public, before King and Dauphin. At first put out by this, the King appreciated the spirit of it, took to Peter and carried him with him hunting. Once, when in a sweat, the King could not find his handkerchief; Carew humbly offered his, which was accepted. I think that handkerchiefs were a French fashion. It was noticed that, at Anne Boleyn's coronation feast in Westminster Hall, the Queen delicately held a handkerchief before her face when she spat.

Hooker, a good middle-class citizen, did not approve of Carew's aristocratic extravagance; he once mentions his spending 'wastefully.' Now in France 'he gave not only away that which he received there, but whatsoever he brought of his own with him; insomuch that he left scarce either jewel, horse, or apparel but he gave it.' It was high time that Sir Peter, now head of the family, should marry. Again, it was exceptional for a soldier of fortune that one hears not a

murmur of impropriety throughout his life: he was on his
way to being a respectable Protestant.

He made suit to a Lincolnshire lady, daughter of a Skip-
with and a Dymoke, who was the widow of Lord Talboys.
Sir Peter's suit did not advance until he addressed himself to
the King; reluctant at first, Henry promised to incline the
lady, with a handsome £100 a year grant in land to them and
their heirs. Before the marriage could be solemnized Henry
died, and it fell upon Edward VI's coronation day. At the
jousts to celebrate the coronation 'this Ulysses in honour of
his Penelope wore her glove upon his headpiece, and
acquitted himself very honourably.'

The marriage turned out happily, though sadly without
children—and this ultimately brought down Mohun's
Ottery. It was financially so advantageous to marry a widow,
with her widow's thirds and her jointure, that in Elizabeth's
time we find some celebrated widows married three or four
times, and Parliamentary legislation was suggested against it.
For the disadvantage was that these later marriages were apt
to be childless, as it turned out with Carew. However, he
departed briskly enough to Lincolnshire for a time, 'where
her living lay'; the lady kept her former title, as was usual
when her rank by her previous husband was superior.

What would happen when Henry VIII's mighty hand was
removed was shortly revealed—and it showed that in fact he
had been too patient over the divorce from Catherine and
delayed too long in begetting a son to succeed him. Though
religiously a conservative, Henry as a politician was releasing
the forward impulse again when he died: he placed the
progressives around his son, and kept out Gardiner, ablest
of the conservatives. With a boy-king, the circle around him
took advantage of the weakness of the Crown—guardian of
the nation's interests—to help themselves largely to the spoils
of the Church. No matter about the titles—a dukedom for
Somerset, earldoms, baronies and such things—enormous
grants of land were ladled out. Russell, for example, whom
Henry had made richer than the Courtenays, with some
£1500 a year, now acquired another £300 a year in lands
alone, apart from offices, to support his earldom of
Bedford—the foundation of the historic dukedom and gran-

deur of all the Russells, up to the late Bertrand, Earl Russell. ('I am drunk as a lord; but then I am a lord—so what of it?', said this notorious Leftist.)

Protector Somerset displayed an unsuccessful combination of arrogance towards his equals and liberal-minded lenity towards the people—who repaid him as might be expected: with disorder and rebellion. Within a year of Henry's death there were riots in Cornwall, where the successor to Wolsey's illegitimate son as Archdeacon (what was wrong with clerical marriage?) was murdered. Next year, 1549, the reasonable introduction of the Mass in English instead of Latin provoked two risings in Devon and Cornwall, which coalesced into one, instigated by priests and led by a handful of light-headed gentry. Somerset proposed to deal with this leniently, and indited a long proclamation arguing the matter and putting the government's case. (Fancy reasoning with the people!— naturally the rebellion grew worse.)

The Council decided to send Sir Gawen and Sir Peter down to the West to see what local influence could do. Uncle and nephew were much of an age and we find them henceforth cooperating closely in Devon, though Peter took precedence as head of the family at Mohun's Ottery, Gawen from Tiverton. Both these men of a younger generation were Protestants, and had to protect the preachers, Dean Haynes and William Alley, from the Catholic-minded congregation in the cathedral at Exeter.

In June they arrived there, recruiting such men as they could. Moving on to Crediton, Sir Peter found the entrance to the town barred against him by a rampire. Someone— apparently not on Carew's orders—set fire to the barns on either side of this. The people fled, but the rumour spread all round that 'the gentlemen were altogether bent to overrun, spoil and destroy them; and in this rage, as it were a swarm of wasps . . .'—the image is a good one—the Rising spread. Walter Ralegh's father, another known Protestant (like Drake's father, a clergyman who was forced to leave Devon), had a narrow escape but was rescued by some mariners who knew him. Carew marched out of Exeter east to Clyst St Mary, where he found himself held up by another defended rampire at the bridge (I often think of it when travelling over it today). Here he might have been shot, for, going

confidently ahead, he was recognised and a gun levelled at
him, when another stayed the gunman's hand.

The whole country around Exeter was now up, the
Cornish joining with the Devon rebels to besiege the city.
Nothing for it but for Carew to ride to London for reinforcements. The government was distracted—disorder and riots
in a number of counties, shortly a major rebellion in Norfolk,
no money in the Treasury to pay troops, though German
mercenaries had to be hired and brought in. Carew put the
case in the West Country to the Council but, the 'moderation' of Somerset prevailing, found himself charged with
excesses in the burning of the barns at Crediton.

Bedford was sent to the West as his primary responsibility
and took up his post at Mohun's Ottery. He seems to have
been in a defeatist mood and thought of retreating, when
Carew overtook him on Blackdown and forcefully put the
case that, if he withdrew, there would spread thereby 'a
greater fire than all the waters of five shires about would
be able to quench.' Reinforcements arrived, including the
German mercenaries (war and soldiering their national
vocation throughout the ages), and Bedford turned west to
the relief of Exeter. After a month's siege, it had been a
narrow thing—there were many Catholic sympathisers in the
city, though they did not wish to be plundered by a multitude
of peasants. At a skirmish at Fenny Bridges Sir Gawen was
wounded in the arm by an arrow; government troops had
few casualties.

Bedford sent the Carews on to Launceston, whither the
Cornish had retreated across the Tamar, their leaders—
Humphry Arundell and Winslade—captured. These men had
little importance in themselves, belonging to the lesser
gentry. But Arundell was a grandson of the house at
Lanherne, grandest of Cornish families, who were henceforth
incriminated by their Catholicism and left out of the running.
The Carews got their reward for their services, and the
considerable expenses they had been at in raising and arming
men against the 'wasps'. Sir Peter got John Winslade's lands
in Devon, to the clear annual value of £73.14.10, a nice
addition to his well-being; Sir Gawen, Arundell's lands in
Devon worth some £53.9.10 a year with a lesser amount in
Cornwall—another nice nest-egg.[2]

We have indications of the Carews' increasing importance in their county as the result of these events in the licence to both Sir Peter and Sir Gawen to retain a retinue of forty, over and above their daily servants. Sir Peter had sat for Tavistock in the last Parliament of Henry VIII's reign, from 30 January to 23 November 1545; this was dissolved 31 January 1547. In Edward VI's reign he moved up to represent his county in the Parliament of 1 to 31 March 1553, and the first of Mary's reign, 5 October to 5 December 1553 when the course her reign would be set upon was not yet decided.

For the rest he divided his time between his wife's estates in Lincolnshire and his own in Devon, with attendance at Court. In 1551 he was one of the knights accompanying the Marquis of Northampton to France to present the Garter to the King. In Devon the two Carews joined Bedford in a project to exploit coal and iron in the forests of Dartmoor and Exmoor—with not much prospect, one would think. We find his name on the commissions of the peace, and some of those for special purposes, such as those to keep down engrossers from increasing prices of corn and victuals; or to apprehend ships engaged in questionable dealings in the Channel. He himself had ships based in Dartmouth. In the summer of 1552 he was authorised by Northumberland's government to inquire into disturbances regarding preaching in Exeter. He and his brother had to escort Protestant preachers like Dean Haynes and William Alley to the pulpit, to protect them against the conservatism of the congregation. This led to a jar between the brothers and their supporters among the gentry on one side, and the citizens on the other. It foreshadowed events to come.

There was no sign of resistance to Mary's accession in the West—Carew himself proclaimed her. It was the Spanish marriage that crystallised opposition and, from what we have seen, the Carews would have led open rebellion in Devon, if they had had enough support—as Wyatt had in Kent. But the 'Commotion' of 1549 was hardly five years away, and the West Country wanted no more disturbance. Though anti-Spanish feeling was widespread, especially in the Channel ports, the moderates, like Sir Arthur Champernowne, would not join in open action. The activists and convinced

Protestants were apt to be those with sea-interests: Carews,
Killigrews, Tremaynes.

It is difficult to find out what precisely was intended by
projected action that did not come off—perhaps the movers
were not clear themselves; but it looks as if the capture of
the city of Exeter by them was feared. Much was made of
Sir Gawen's descent over the city walls in his riding boots
to join his nephew at Mohun's Ottery to raise a following,
while Sir Peter was said to have laid posts to enable the Earl
of Devon to come West to take the lead. There is no doubt
of the conspiracy, but it was abortive. We have the letters of
the brothers, with the usual implausibility of would-be rebels
in their circumstances. In January 1554 the Privy Council
summoned Sir Peter to appear before it. The brothers excused
themselves thus to the sheriff:

> Being informed that you prepare yourself with power to apprehend and
> take us, for what matter we know not, we have thought good to advertise
> you that we are as true and as faithful subjects unto the Queen's High-
> ness as any whatsoever they be within the realm, and intend to follow
> and observe her religion as faithfully as they that most are affected unto
> it.

This is an interesting pointer to the attitude of the
governing class. Responsible people, like Elizabeth or Sir
William Cecil, were prepared to conform to the law when
the law was changed. We have the certificate of Cecil and
his wife going to confession and receiving the sacrament
at their parish church at Wimbledon at Easter. They were
Protestants, as the Carews were. It was first the Spanish
marriage, then the full programme of return to Rome,
enforcement of clerical celibacy and the burnings, that alien-
ated the country from Mary's régime and wrecked Catholic
hopes for good.

The Queen replied instructing the authorities in the West
to answer

> the many false rumours of the coming of the high and mighty prince,
> our dearest cousin the Prince of Spain, and others of that nation into
> this our realm . . . and to set forth their devilish seditious purposes,
> some to the hindrance of the true Catholic religion and divine service
> now restored within this our realm, others of a traitorous conspiracy
> against our state royal.

To Protestants, of course, theirs was the 'true' religion. We are reminded of Gibbon's summing up of the various modes of worship in ancient Rome: 'considered by the people as equally true; by the philosopher, as equally false; and by the magistrate [i.e. politician] as equally useful.'

Sir Gawen wrote further to the sheriff defending himself.

> It should seem by slanderous bruits you have shut and chained the gates [of Exeter], laid ordnance upon the walls, keep watch and ward as it should be besieged by the Queen's highness's enemies . . . and blown abroad to the utter undoing and clear defaming of the most part of gentlemen of the county, and to our own discrediting among our neighbours, that the gentlemen practise to take the Queen's highness's city.

For his part he had no more with him than he accustomably rode with, eight persons, and Sir Peter Carew his household servants. The occasion of his repair to Mohun's Ottery was the rumour that they were to be apprehended.

The city authorities, though divided in religion, had no doubt of Sir Peter's intention in bringing in half-a-dozen horses laden with harness from Dartmouth. When he thought it the better part of valour to fly across Channel, it was given in evidence at Sir Gawen's indictment that his brother, in league with the Duke of Suffolk, had said, 'If the Queen would forbear this marriage with the Spaniards and use a moderation in matters of religion, I would die at her feet. But otherwise I will do the best to place the Lady Elizabeth in her stead.' He durst be one of the hundred gentlemen that should take the Queen and put her in the Tower. Such is the irony of history that it turned out that Carew's blueprint offered the best prospect of success for Mary's reign: no Spanish marriage, and a 'moderation in religion.' By Mary's circle, however, Carew was regarded as 'long of impious and erroneous religion.'

In the game of battledore and shuttlecock of 'ins' and 'outs' in the party conflict—we may reasonably call it that of progressives against regressives—Sir Peter Carew lost Mohun's Ottery to James Basset. The park of Okehampton was leased to George Jerningham, sewer of the Chamber, of that faithful Catholic family. By Carew's attainder the estates of his wife, Lady Talboys, worth a little over £200 a year, came to the Crown; she was allowed two-thirds of it for her subsistence. We have an inventory of the mansion at Mohun's Ottery, to tell us what it was like.

It was not a large house—just such a Tudor place as one still can see at Collacombe near Tavistock; most of that survives, the home of his cousins, the Tremaynes. There in their parish church of Lamerton one sees those brothers, with whom Carew had his adventures under Queen Mary, sculpted on their monument. The most successful of them, Edmund, became Clerk of the Privy Council under Elizabeth, when he celebrated in his hall with decorative coat-of-arms and initials, 1574.

Mohun's Ottery too had its hall and little gallery at end; the gatehouse was a feature, with its chamber above. Within were the King's chamber, the steward's, the maidens', the yellow bedchamber, the corner chamber next to the garden, the corner chamber next to the barn, that next over the gatehouse, lodge, kitchen, buttery, etc. Not large; nor was it furnished with any luxury; evidently Sir Peter lived in more style in London—he was not continuously in residence in Devon. Thus the steward's chamber was best furnished, joined bedstead with tapestry coverlets, damask tester with silk curtains, hangings of black and yellow say. These were the dominant colours in the bedchambers, a few pieces of tapestry, linen sheets of Dowlas, i.e. from Brittany; some chairs covered with crimson satin or red cloth, hangings of arras, window cloths of green say. Not much in the way of plate—probably the Carews kept that in London, and carried it about with them for use, for ever moving about, restless and active as Sir Peter was into age.

Carew was on familiar ground in exile in France, and was said to have been received by the King and Constable, though they denied it when representations were made by Mary's ambassador. He, the Killigrews and Tremaynes had ships at their disposal, and Carew moved easily from Normandy to Brittany and back again to join the French forces near Abbéville, leaving John Courtenay to look after his ships. By May he was in want of money and was promised a pardon if he would confess everything. The government was out for evidence against Elizabeth and the Earl of Devon, but no one would inculpate them—Wyatt on the scaffold specifically exculpated them. In July Carew wrote a letter of submission: he had rashly decided not to bear servitude under a foreign prince, but was now ready to accept and serve. At home the wives were making the best of their misfortunes and lobbying in their husbands' behalf. Both Carews had made good matches; Lady Talboys was buying back her husband's goods, Lady Guildford—Sir Gawen's wife—managed to get him liberated from the Tower. She was the sister of Dr Wotton, the English ambassador in France. All in the family.

Hooker is able to tell us of Carew's adventures while abroad—he would have got them from his own lips: how, on getting aboard at Weymouth, his foot slipped and he might have been drowned if someone had not taken hold of him. Storm drove their bark back into Weymouth, where some were willing to give up. Not so Carew, who kept the company close aboard until a better wind served, and they arrived at Rouen. Thence he rode to Court, and had offers to serve with the French forces. These he refused and left for Venice.

There the English ambassador, Peter Vannes, sought to have him extradited, and made suit to the state for the purpose. Carew had a friend in Foscarini, the advocate general, with whom he had been acquainted at Edward VI's Court. Frustrated of his purpose, Vannes hired some ruffians to capture him at a dark corner in a street, *ruga causa*. Carew, alerted, made his attendants pass the corner two by two, himself in the midst, so that the ruffians could not identify him, and thus he escaped.

Foscarini helped him to take up money so that he could move to Strasbourg, where a body of Marian exiles were gathered, notably Ponet, late bishop of Winchester. Ponet's house caught fire—not so bad anyway as being burned himself in England; Carew managed to enter the house and save Ponet's money in a cupboard, just in time before the building fell in. Meanwhile, Carew's wife, who had been trying to obtain his pardon in England, travelled over to Brussels to make suit to Philip.

Sir John Mason, the ambassador there, made interest for him at home, with conviction: 'he is not a man to be lost, if he may be won unfeignedly. This fall may be to him *felix culpa* [a happy fault], and the Queen hath thereby occasion

to win such a servant as for sundry qualities there be not
many in the realm of England.' This is strong testimony as
to his character, and in fact there is general agreement that
little could be said against him. In spite of his adventurous
career and the usual solicitations to a soldier of fortune, he
was singularly moral and upright; we know his aptitudes in
horsemanship and languages, his spiritedness and courage
from a boy; and, except for this bad break under Mary, he
was generally regarded as a responsible servant of the state.

It made the worse impression therefore when he and Cheke
were humiliatingly captured and brought back to the Tower,
by a ruse of Paget's—nor did it add to the latter's popularity,
who was markedly ignored when Elizabeth succeeded, in
spite of his expressed wish to serve. It was made easy for
Carew to obtain pardon, by a large payment in cash. His
grandfather, Sir Edmund, had owed the Crown some £1200;
various payments had been made, but there remained £800
to pay. On arranging to pay this Sir Peter was freed; it was,
however, a large sum to raise, and must have made a hole in
his pocket. By 1557 his properties were restored, and he
was back in administration as a responsible member of the
governing class, commissioned by the Privy Council, with
the Lord Admiral and Paulet, to settle the suitors for the
government of the Isles of Scilly.

At the next turn of the wheel of fortune—no wonder it
was such a favourite image with Tudor writers—Carew was
in favour and regarded with confidence. Mary's war with
France, on behalf of Philip, had gone badly: Calais was lost
and the French were entrenched in Scotland, with a strong
force in Leith. The most urgent task, after the return of
religion to its Edwardian basis, was to get them out. But the
English assault on Leith failed. Why? Carew was sent on a
confidential mission to find out.

It was a highly responsible job from every point of view.
Not only were the reasons for failure to be inquired into and
reported on, but the Scots needed assurance that the English
would not give up. The Duke of Norfolk was in command,
but he was quarrelling with Lord Grey de Wilton, Warden
of the East Marches and Governor of Berwick. We have
Carew's instructions in full: the reasons for the failure of the
assault, to report the number of the French forces in the

town, to consult with experienced officers how best to take it; to confer with Sir William Winter, the commander of the fleet blockading the town, regarding the sea-force necessary in these combined operations; to assure the men that reinforcements and money were on their way, and the Scottish lords that the Queen would not give up the enterprise. Norfolk was referred to Carew for his instructions.

It was the first external test of the new régime, and it was crucial for William Cecil; for Elizabeth, new to her job and having learnt caution from adversity, doubted the enterprise. Cecil had to force her hand by threatening to resign: the French hold on Scotland *had* to be ended. Carew performed his task with efficiency and tact, and reported in full. The failure had been due to insufficient breaches in the fortifications and ladders to mount the walls; 2300 trained French soldiers held the town, with 200 people besides; no provisions had got through to them for three weeks; he had comforted all with assurances of aid. Cecil's opposite number in Scotland, the politic Maitland of Lethington, reported to him that Carew had been well received, 'yet doth his own honesty, with your good report, and also being your dear friend', increase his credit in Scotland.

Cecil himself now went north to supervise the ending of French power in Scotland with the Treaty of Edinburgh. It was his first triumph and confirmed Elizabeth's confidence in him, which was never to be withdrawn. In July Carew was travelling back, post haste from Edinburgh, with a private letter to the Queen which Cecil had confided to him, when he was detained at Darlington by an attack of ague—presumably malaria, which was widespread in those days. The reward he received six months later was a licence to him as the 'Queen's servant' to import at Dartmouth as much wheat, barley etc., as would be necessary to brew beer for export to friendly countries, up to 1000 tons, not more. This would have brought him a good profit, and Dartmouth was his port.

Earlier, in March 1559, he had been commissioned with Sir William St Loe, captain of the Queen's guard—and husband of the redoubtable Bess of Hardwick—to survey the Tower, familiar territory. It was the country's chief arsenal, and this meant a survey of ordnance, munitions, etc. These commissions seem to have been his last for some time at the centre of affairs. It was said that he lost favour for outspokenly urging the Queen's marriage in Parliament. This was the Protestant line, and he was candid and outspoken; it was, however, always resented by Elizabeth, who regarded it as an impertinent intrusion into her own sphere of prerogative, and anyway had seen the unfortunate consequences of her sister's marriage.

For the next few years we find Carew in the West, employed on his own affairs and those of his county, where he was the leading figure after Bedford, the Lord Lieutenant. Bedford was not a resident; Carew was and, from 1562, Custos Rotulorum. The usual activities as such fell to his lot: reporting to Bedford regarding the stamping of coins at Exeter, in the re-coinage which established the currency on a sound basis at last—after the inflation of the past two decades: the real foundation for the financial stability and economic prosperity of the reign.

Maritime matters come increasingly to the fore. With the religious wars developing in France and the Netherlands, the Huguenots fought their battles at sea. The Channel was filled with privateering and questionable doings: it was hard to draw the line between privateering and piracy. In 1562, in the confused conditions of war with France—in the hope of regaining Calais—Carew was instructed to apprehend the victuallers of pirates in the West Country. In September 1564 he was commissioned to fit out two vessels to clear the coasts of Devon and Cornwall of pirates. He proceeded on rather a large scale and expensively: 246 personnel to pay for in *three* ships. And not altogether successfully, for some pirates took refuge in Bere Haven under the protection of O'Sullivan Bere's castle. He had arrested Stucley's hulk at Cork, but it had not produced half the wages due; much of the charges had fallen on his own purse. Events were drawing his attention to Irish waters.

Meanwhile, since the impost on wines, Dartmouth shipping had been hit. In 1565 he was to deliver a hulk from Zealand detained at Dartmouth; and, with Sir John Chichester with whom he had been serving at sea, to investigate the broil between Killigrews and Godolphins on one side, and Reynold Mohun on the other. In August 1568 we find the two Carews again, Peter and Gawen, complaining of captures made in English waters, under colour of commissions, or letters of marque, from the King of Sweden. It was indeed difficult to keep order in the Western approaches.

The last phase of Carew's career is not the least venturesome, and that by which he is best known: the revival of the medieval claims of his family to a large appanage in Ireland. Family memory would tell him how important the Carews had been there in the fourteenth century, when his ancestor, Sir John Carew (d. 1362), had been Escheator of Ireland, and for a time Justiciar, equivalent to an Elizabethan Lord Deputy. He had possessed the barony of Idrone, to which Sir Peter had the title deeds, but himself could not read their medieval script. So he called to his aid the redoubtable John Hooker, who undertook his researches with enthusiasm and became Sir Peter's right-hand man in his new venture. Much of his biography is devoted to it and he naturally sees it in individual personal terms. We, however, must see it in proper perspective, as part of the movement of the time.

All the new national states were expansionist, most of all Spain; and by a kind of law of human movement, of which all history gives evidence, more powerful and efficient societies move over their borders into weaker ones, especially if they are backward and present a power-vacuum. The Celtic fringe around Northern Europe presented such areas, all the way round from the Scottish Highlands and Hebrides to Brittany.[3] Ireland was inevitably such a challenge to the Tudor state; in any case it could not be ignored for strategic reasons, though a territory almost as large as England was beyond her resources to lick satisfactorily into shape, as the Elizabethans wished. They were almost all shocked by what they saw there, had no sympathy for a Celtic culture which seemed to them barbarous and savage—and did not have our advantage of courses in anthropology to appreciate it.

In the fifteenth century there had been a marked recession of Anglo-Norman power in Ireland, what with the long wars with France and the Wars of the Roses in England. The result was that the Celtic tide now lapped up to the English Pale, and over it. The Pale roughly meant where English was the dominant language, i.e. not only in the arable country around

Dublin (not in the neighbouring mountains), but in the towns planted around the island—for Celtic civilisation, if that is the word for it, was averse to city life, which is after all what civilisation means.

In these areas the Old English—it is more convenient to call them the Anglo-Irish—held out, somewhat beleaguered. Beyond them were the territories of the great Norman lords, chieftains of their tribal following, who had intermarried with the Celts, spoke Irish and had gone native in differing degrees. These were the Fitzgeralds, earls of Desmond in the south-west, the Burkes, earls of Clanricarde in Connaught, the Butlers, earls of Ormonde. Henry VIII had broken the power of the Fitzgeralds of Kildare, after a rebellion; gunpowder reduced their stronghold of Maynooth. Beyond these were the indigenous Celtic septs under their chieftains, MacCarthys and such in the far west; above all, in untouched Ulster the O'Neills, whose power was contested by the O'Donnells. Into this maelstrom there were constant incursions from their Scottish kin, the Macdonalds, some of them coming to settle across the narrow waste of waters. They all lived to fight each other. Altogether it was an appalling mess.

With the Reformation the English state, gathering power, intervened more and more in the hope of enforcing order, establishing English power and developing the neglected resources of the other island. This brought in an increasing number of new English, officials and soldiers, adding a further conflict of interest with the Anglo-Irish, apt to remain Catholic, when the new men were Protestants. The Reformation itself was accepted quietly enough by the Dublin Parliament, along with the dissolution of the monasteries to reward the obedient with their lands. For the next thirty years there was a submissive quiet. Actual plantation, outwards from the Pale into inefficiently cultivated or waste areas, began under the Catholic Philip and Mary, with the turning of Leix and Offaly into proper shire-ground as King's and Queen's counties (today regressed to the old names).

Elizabeth I always favoured the Butlers—who themselves were half Celts and spoke the language—for they were her cousins, through her Boleyn grandfather, who for a time held the title of Earl of Ormonde (her cousins, the Hunsdons, were always hoping for it). Black Tom, the tenth earl, was always loyal to her and could be relied on to keep order in his area; but he was away at her Court in the years 1565–9. This left a power-vacuum, and gave opportunity for new ventures and disorders. Moreover, these years witnessed the gathering crisis of the reign: the rising of the Northern Earls, the Papal excommunication and 'deposition' of the Queen, in Ireland the direct confrontation with the Counter-Reformation in the rebellion of James Fitzmaurice of Desmond, who proposed to enact the Papal Bull.

Plantation in Munster was already under way, and it was very much the enterprise of Devon men from across the water. The St Legers and Grenvilles from North Devon were active in Cork, with their base in the walled city. The Earl of Desmond had mortgaged tracts of land for large sums outside the walls, and Grenville hoped to cultivate and plant the monastic domains of Traghton abbey, as his grandfather had bought and planted Buckland abbey in Devon. Historically it was a further wave of the same secular impulse.

Devon to the fore. St Leger was sheriff in Cork; Sir John Pollard was to be Lord President of Munster, with the Exeter lawyer, Periam, as his Chief Justice. Henry Davells, married to a Kilkenny woman, was a Devon man serving a life sentence as sheriff and provost-marshal in Munster, until he was murdered by Desmond's brother, young Sir John, whom he had taken to his bosom. Thomas Stucley, the adventurer who afterwards went over to the enemy, tried his fortune in Ireland. Humphrey Gilbert and Walter Ralegh won their spurs fighting there—Ralegh taking up land on the grand scale forfeited in the great Desmond rebellion. Sir Peter Carew's young cousin and heir was to make his career there, until butchered after the rout at Glenmalure in 1580; his brother, Sir George, afterwards killed his murderer. Such was Ireland.

This is the perspective in which we must see Sir Peter's Irish enterprise—characteristic, and yet idiosyncratic, for it was based upon reviving medieval claims which had lain dormant for a hundred and fifty years. No doubt he was looking for a new field of enterprise, though a man in years; but the antiquarian enthusiasm of John Hooker pushed him on. Hardly ever can antiquarianism have had such disturbing consequences.

Hooker says that Carew being at last 'at some leisure' bethought him of his Irish inheritance. In the fourteenth century the Carews had possessed not only the barony of Idrone, on the borders of Wexford, but large estates in Munster. It was decided to follow up these claims, with the good will of the government, and a regular legal campaign ensued.

Hooker was sent on ahead to Dublin to research into the records in Dublin Castle. We have a long letter of May 1568 recounting his activities. He had got a house for Carew and his company, conveniently down on the quay—Carew, like Grenville, had his own ships, which gave them free movement to and fro. Leighlin castle had been the house of Carew's ancestors, head of the barony, and during their long absence their seneschals had taken over their lands. He could keep as good a house in Dublin as in Exeter, only he would need money and to import spices, sugar, etc. 'Bring over your two physicians and George Carew's cook.' Hooker's wife was to send over his stuff in Sir Peter's bark; evidently he was contemplating a long stay, and we have his notes collected from the records at the Castle.[4]

Hooker won much unpopularity at the Dublin Parliament of 1569. This marked a new phase in the amenities of Irish history, which he wrote up in a section of Holinshed's *Chronicles* he later edited. Shane O'Neill had been virtually an independent prince in Ulster, but he had been defeated by a combination of the O'Donnells of Donegal with Scots MacDonnells, who had infiltrated Antrim—to Elizabeth's dislike as much as Shane's—and these had killed the old brute, who was a murderer of his kinsmen in his own right. The Dublin Parliament passed an Act opening up most of Ulster for settlement—and this paved the way for the first Earl of Essex's optimistic enterprise, in which he lost life and fortune. We must remember that the Irish semi-princes claimed authority every bit as 'autocratic as any in Europe':[5] their rule was a tyranny which lesser lords and septs much resented. English rule would have been a rational liberation for them, but for language, religion and sentiment—all that was irrational.

Hooker sat as M.P. for Athenry, and he was a recognised authority on Parliamentary procedure. The Anglo-Irish objected to the new English returned for places they knew not, and Sir Edmund Butler, Ormonde's brother, was a principal malcontent, fearing that their captainries would be taken away, the burdens of coign and livery on their tenants abolished, 'and such other like disorders redressed.' These are Hooker's words, and the point was only too well taken. Hooker described the Opposition as 'kerne', a very derogatory term.[6] For good measure he asserted the absolute authority of the Queen to impose customs without any of their consents. Indignation was such that he had to be escorted home for safety to Carew's house.

The progress of Carew's claim to the barony of Idrone drove Butler into open rebellion, for the claim disputed some land in Butler's occupation. Both the Lord Deputy, Sir Henry Sidney, and the Earl of Ormonde were absent in England, so the mice could play. Carew and Davells were on the commission to keep order during Sidney's absence, when Butler broke out, joined forces with his enemy, James Fitzmaurice of Desmond, and went native with him, who was spoiling and massacring planters where he could catch them.

Carew decided to make a test-case of his claims upon the property of Maston, not far from Dublin, then in the possession of Sir Christopher Chivers. We need not go into the legal proceedings to and fro; suffice it to say that Carew's claim was held good. He treated Sir Christopher generously, 'the whole land re-leased unto him almost for nothing, saving a drinking nut of silver worth about £20, and three or four horses worth about £30.' This decision made way for deciding his claim to the whole barony of Idrone, largely occupied by Cavanaghs, in his favour. After some doubt the country folk were brought 'to such a quiet state as that it was rid from all oppressors, kernes and other loose people, which lived upon the spoil and rapine of others.' These words express the Elizabethan bias: no doubt some native Irish regretted the loss of their little fun.

Hooker continues that Sir Peter 'erected certain courts baron in sundry places within his barony, for maintenance of peace and quietness among them, according to the laws and usages of England, which to them before that time was not known.' The barony extended north and south along the

River Barrow, which divided it from the Butlers' Kilkenny on the west; on the east, Wexford. Thus 'his name and fame so increased that the most part of the people thought themselves most happy that so good a man was come amongst them. Nevertheless, some there were who being accustomed to reap what other men do sow and to spend what other men do get, could not abide the dwelling so near such a worthy man.' There were decent folk in Ireland as elsewhere, who preferred peace and quiet, only there the lunatic fringe was (and is) larger.

At one time an ambush was laid for him at Bolton Hill, along the highway from Dublin to his stronghold at Leighlin Castle, guarding the bridge across the Barrow. The keepership of the castle belonged to the Crown; Stucley was replaced by Carew in it, a more trustworthy keeper, with command of its garrison. Carew was alert to such traps from his years abroad and familiarity with war conditions; he had his 'espials' and travelled with an escort, so that he avoided the danger—unlike poor Davells, who trusted to friendship and was murdered by one whom he regarded as a 'son'. Carew's imposition of order in his barony, which he wished to see blossoming and fruitful as an English county, aroused the ire of all who had a vested interest in disorder. He suppressed the customary but burdensome usages—discouraging to settled cultivation of the soil—of 'coign and livery, cessries and cesses, and such other Irish customs: being but the spoiling of the honest subject and the labourer, and the maintenance of thieves, murderers, and all loose and disordered people.' Here speaks the honest Elizabethan, the Elizabethan point of view.

What rendered the situation critical in 1569 was the conjunction of the Butlers, Ormonde's three younger brothers, with the fire-eating James Fitzmaurice, who represented the irreducible Gaelic spirit (though himself of Norman descent, of course). Sir Edmund Butler put out self-justifying declarations that he was not fighting against the Queen, but Carew. Actually his castle of Cloghgrennan and its dependency had been taken by his father from the Cavanaghs, and lay in the barony of Idrone now declared to be Carew's. James Fitzmaurice on the other hand put out a long declaration citing the authority of the Papal 'deposition' of the Queen. He followed it up by putting Grenville's planters outside Cork to the sword and calling on the city to surrender.[7] It did not.

The crisis demanded the return of the Lord Deputy, Sir Henry Sidney, who had a high opinion of Carew, and sent him south with young Humphry Gilbert as Colonel of the forces. Carew had no difficulty in taking Cloghgrennan, whence they marched to Kilkenny. Neither had this town surrendered, in spite of its sympathy with the Butlers, for it was Ormonde's capital. Outside the town lay Sir Edmund's forces, who were administered a sharp defeat. Carew, however, had a narrow escape in the grounds of the Castle, whence an Irishman aimed a caliver shot at him three days running without effect, and was prevented by a friendly hand at the last. The Earl now returned from England, and soon procured the submission of his brothers.

James Fitzmaurice was left high and dry with his rabble. Gilbert ran through Munster with fire and sword, sparing no rebels. Fitzmaurice surrendered on his knee at Kilmallock, promising faithful obedience, but ready to rise at the next opportunity—as ten years later he faithfully did, instigated the great Desmond rebellion and was responsible for the ruin of the Fitzgerald earldom.

Hooker agreed with Gilbert that only fear would keep such people in order; as he wrote in Holinshed's *Chronicles*, 'no longer fear, no longer obedience . . . false, truce-breakers, and traitorous.' After the appalling experience of the later Desmond rebellion and the subjugation of Munster he wrote of 'this wicked and perverse generation, constant always in that they be inconstant, treacherous and untrustworthy. They do nothing but imagine mischief and have no delight in any good thing . . . their feet swift to shed blood and their hands imbrued in the blood of innocents.'—As in Ulster today, we may add.

There were of course exceptions, and Hooker has to make one for Brian MacCahir, a faithful follower of Carew, 'with whom he never brake his promise, but stood him in good stead as well in matters of counsel as of any service to be done in those parts. A man (which is rare among these people) very constant of his word, and so faithfully he served and so much honoured Sir Peter Carew that after his death, being as one maimed, he consumed and pined away and died in peace.'[8]

After these Irish amenities Carew returned in 1570 to Court, where he found himself not best received by the Queen. Ambivalent as ever—or seeing both sides—she held him responsible for the Butlers' rebellion, as in part he was by establishing his claim to Idrone. But his claim had been backed by the government in both England and Ireland, and ratified by law. If they wanted the extension of English law and order in Ireland, what better instrument could there be? Carew was much respected as a person, and he was investing his own money in the enterprise. Like most other planters in Irish soil—St Leger, Grenville, Ralegh, Edmund Spenser— little of his investment did he see back.

While at home Carew engaged in his usual avocations, carrying out various tasks wished upon him by government. In May he writes from Edmund Tremayne's Collacombe that he had delivered over an impounded hulk to its Flemish owner, £200 due in all. Next year he makes suit to have the lands of his barony freed from cess, i.e. the customary imposition of a levy upon all the tenantry and peasantry to support soldiers or, with the Irish chiefs, kerne and gallowglass to maintain their power. His uncle, Sir Gawen, would attend at Court to pursue his suit.

Tremayne reports that both Sidney and Carew were in disfavour. The truth is that the Queen did not like Sidney's expensive forward policy, at any rate in Munster; she preferred to rely there on Ormonde keeping order. The government in Dublin was instructed to keep Carew from putting forward his larger claims in Munster, now that it was pacified; with this Sir John Perrot, successfully and sympathetically ruling there, agreed. Hooker was left to look after Carew's interests, and he pursued his researches—to find that his claims in Munster were as good, according to the records, as that to Idrone. Tremayne himself was an authority on Irish affairs; dispatched by the government to report on them, he presented a thorough and knowledgable account of their complexities.

By 1572 the worst crisis of the reign was surmounted and the turning point reached, both internal and external: the Northern Rising, Norfolk's plots with Mary Queen of Scots and contacts with Alba in the Netherlands; the arrest of Spanish treasure ships, consequent upon the overthrow of Hawkins' third Caribbean enterprise, the suspension of trade. In August Carew was placed, with Christopher Hatton and two others, to go into the whole business of the Spanish ships taken up since 1568, to inquire into the people who had got their goods and merchandise into their hands, to view all books and accounts, and to report. It must have taken many months, for next year the commission was renewed.

When down in Devon we find him performing the duties of a J.P., inquiring into the lunacy of Richard Drake of Otterton, and such matters. Again in the autumn he was at the Tower, inquiring into deficiencies and needs, a military assignment as before. In the winter of 1572–3 he was engaged in surveying the defences of the ports in Devon and Cornwall: we have his bond for payment of the large sum of £663.6.8 for ordnance and ammunition delivered to them. In June another matter at the Tower was consigned to him: the dispute between the tiresome second Earl of Southampton, imprisoned for his part in the Mary Stuart-Norfolk plots, and the Lieutenant of the Tower regarding the charges for his diets.[9]

Meanwhile Hooker was weaseling away at the records in Dublin Castle and drawing up Carew's titles to the old Carew lands in Cork. After James Fitzmaurice's submission Munster was quiet, and various lords had expressed their willingness to come in with Carew's claims. Of the Cavanaghs Hooker reported, 'every one of them is enemy to other', and that they were supporting the thieves depredating in Wexford and Carlow. In January 1573 a commission of inquiry into Carew's claims were to go to the Lord President of Munster, whether he liked them or not. A long account of debts to be paid was submitted. Hooker would procure a hawk for Sir Peter—hawks and hounds were Irish products the Elizabethans much valued. In London, from his house in Great St Bartholomew's, Carew was following his suit for the relief of cess upon his barony.

Next month, March 1573, he received a sharp letter from Hooker. 'Your cess cannot be released without your presence. If your evidence be not brought hither in due time and

against the next term, you must impute it to your own folly.
I have so often written to you herein that I am both weary
and ashamed thereof.' Upon this Carew asked permission of
the Privy Council to return to Ireland. He reckoned that the
rebellion had cost him some £3000 one way and another—
no doubt an over-estimate. In return he asked for the fee-
simple of Leighlin Castle, that his barony should be freed
from cess, and for permission to perambulate and 'mere'
(measure out) its bounds. We learn that the Queen now
favoured his suit. There was an important new development
in Ireland, and Carew's help would be valuable.

Ulster was the most recessive of the provinces, the least
touched by English power, though open to the coming and
going of Celts with their common Gaelic culture, their feuds
and marriages and murders, across Scottish waters. Essex—
father of Elizabeth's later favourite—proposed to penetrate
these recesses and to plant there. The Earl optimistically put
all he had into it, raised forces and support for it, and had
the Queen's backing. She wanted to see order and authority
extended there as in Munster.

Carew returned to Ireland, whence he reported to
Burghley that he thought that Essex had sufficient force to
reduce Ulster, but he lacked full authority to punish traitors.
Carew promised not to create trouble by pushing his Munster
titles at this juncture; Hooker returned to England. Hardly
anything is known of his impecunious brother, father of the
famous Richard Hooker, of the *Laws of Ecclesiastical Polity*:
a mention of him as Dean of Leighlin shows that he too
found sustenance with Carew. Tremayne wrote from Collacombe to Burghley that Secretary of State Smith's misliking
of Carew's persuading Essex to plant the Ards was
unfounded. Naturally Sir Peter favoured a forward policy,
and wrote to 'cousin Tremayne' that ministering the sword
on one hand and justice, i.e. English law, on the other were
the only means of redress. The Earl of Desmond had widespread contacts with the resistance chiefs; while the Ulster
septs were spoiling down to the gates of Dublin. He
recommended Henry Davells for promotion, who had done
very good service for a long time. (Like Mountbatten, he
was to meet his fate in Ireland.)

In Ulster Essex came up against the usual difficulties: sickness, probably malaria and dysentery, decimated his troops and he himself sickened. The enterprise halted; the Queen, thinking it strange it should be abandoned without her knowledge, when it had been so costly to her, directed its resumption and ordered Carew to second Essex as his Lieutenant, with twenty horse in pay and a band of horse or foot. It was nothing like enough, as usual. Carew, his health affected, withdrew from the border to Leighlin; Essex died; the reduction of Ulster had to wait till the end of the century.

From Leighlin Sir Peter summoned over his wife and friends, with Hooker to take up the business of his Munster titles. Hooker took ship from Exmouth to Cork, 'but through foul and stormy weather the ship was driven into the town of Wexford, which is about fifteen miles from Leighlin. He landed, leaving the ship which not long after, with foul weather, was cast away, both men and goods.' Such losses too were the frequent risks of Irish enterprise. Determining now to go forward in Munster, Carew made over Leighlin Castle and the charge of the country to the younger Peter Carew, and settled in the town of Ross until he heard news of Hooker's mission in Munster.

Hooker went forward with his usual promptitude, and at Waterford got the agreement, for what it was worth, of the Munster lords and chieftains to Carew's claim. 'And for that which was past they would, in recompense thereof, give him three thousand kine or cows [the Irish currency], which they accounted to be about one year's rent of so much land as they did hold'—though there were further signories and territories far exceeding that. At Cork the Earl of Desmond, Lord Barrymore, Lord Roche and others 'had great conference with this agent [Hooker], and pretended great joy and much gladness that Sir Peter Carew would come to dwell among them and that they should have the neighbourhood of so good and noble a gentleman.' The grand Earl of Desmond, the fifteenth and last—a sad and vacillating man, who was pushed into his fatal revolt by the uncompromising James Fitzmaurice—even wrote welcoming Sir Peter into Munster. With the advice of Henry Davells, Hooker took a house for Carew in Cork and another in Kinsale, provisioning them from Bristol and Exeter. Meanwhile Sir Peter freighted a ship to transport his household stuff and was ready for his journey, when 'it was God's pleasure to appoint him to another journey.'

At Ross he unexpectedly fell ill with 'an imposthume [abscess] in the bladder' and stoppage of urine, which, though exceedingly painful, he bore with exemplary patience. He died there on 27 November 1575, his body transported by water to Waterford, where he was given a grand funeral attended by the Lord Deputy and all the Council. Philip Sidney's father pronounced the valediction at the graveside: 'Here lieth now, in his last rest, a most worthy and noble gentle knight, whose faith to his prince was never yet stained, his truth to his country never spotted, and his valiantness in service never doubted: a better subject the prince never had.' Sir Henry Sidney, with whom Carew was a favourite, seems to have forgotten the episode under Queen Mary; but let that pass. In general, in every sphere, even among opponents, Carew seems to have had universal respect—exceptional for a soldier of fortune.

Exceptionally too, for such a career, he seems to have had himself under discipline; no rumour of scandal, particularly with regard to sex, ever touched him—again singular in a *condottiere*, a young man at Henry VIII's Court. No doubt he owed his unspotted character in part to his religion, for—like Burghley and the Tremaynes—he was a religious-minded Protestant. Hooker puts it down also to the standards of his parentage, 'the ancient line of the barons of Carew, and the other of the noble house of the Courtenays, which is a great ornament and the first degree of nobility. Yet, when virtue, the subsistence and ground of nobility faileth, the nobility also itself decayeth.' Buried at Waterford, Sir Peter has his monument in the cathedral at Exeter so familiar to him: solitary at a prayer-desk, surrounded by all those quarterings.

Hooker gives us his appearance: of middle stature, 'but very well compact and somewhat broad, big-boned and strongly sinewed, his face of a very good countenance, his complexion swart or choleric [i.e. ruddy, sanguine], his hair black and his beard thick and great'—as we see from his portrait at Hampton Court, fine eyes and arched eyebrows, prominent nose, an alert, inquiring expression. Both Sir Peter and Sir Gawen, as we see from his portrait at Antony in

Cornwall, were very swarthy. Sir Peter was muscular and strong, full of energy from a boy, skilful at all martial exercises. Considering this, his way of life abroad and the atmosphere of the time, it is odd that Hooker should be able to say of him, in his quaint language: 'albeit he had his imperfections, yet was he not known to be wrapped in the dissolute net of Venus, nor imbrued with the cup of Bacchus, he was not carried with the covetousness of Plutus, nor yet subject to malice, envy or any notorious crime.' His chief imperfections were a quick temper, though soon over, and a measure of extravagance: he was too liberal in giving.

His range of competence was considerable, and Hooker enumerates his skills:

> whether it were for the building of a house, moulding of a ship, devising of a fort, making of a platform [i.e. for ordnance], his advice was ready and his skill good. Wherein he took such pleasure that he did not only bestow great masses of money therein of his own, as in making of houses, building of ships, for erecting of mills and many other like, but would also edge, procure and cause others to do the like.

Evidently he spread himself, so that we have no one monument of his, like Sir Richard Grenville's in Buckland Abbey, still less Bess of Hardwick's, that grand builder. He must have had an enjoyable life.

If he had lived out his full span of three score and ten years he would have had the opportunity, when all Munster lay open after the Desmond rebellion, of building a ducal appanage there. As it was, his heir, the younger Sir Peter, lost his life in it and all the efforts of John Hooker and his patron proved in vain—as did Ralegh's later. Others reaped where they had sown; the vast patrimony came to Richard Boyle, the Great Earl of Cork, and thus to Bess of Hardwick's descendants, the Cavendishes.

What makes Carew so representative of his age is not only his adventurous, aspiring career but his combination of Protestant religion with a Ciceronian temperance of mind. Cicero was his favourite reading, as he was the great Burghley's, whom he resembled in this:

> he did so moderate the lusts of the body and the affections of the mind by the rule of reason that he was not known, at any times, to be

outrageous in malice, envy, anger, lusts, sensualities and such like; neither would he in words utter any speeches which favoured any ribaldry, filthiness, or uncomeliness; neither in act would do the thing which was dishonest and foul. . . . He neither would gladly be in company with any woman of a suspected name, whereby he himself might be had or grow into any suspicion.

It adds a corrective to our usual picture of a Renaissance soldier of fortune.

Hooker compared him to Paulus Aemilius and Publius Scipio. Even the antiquarianism that inspired Hooker and Carew was characteristic of the age. It is by a singular propriety that his faithful aide should have been the editor of, and a chief contributor to, Holinshed's *Chronicles*.

It must have been a disappointment to him that he had no progeny to carry on his name and house at Mohun's Ottery. Thus it is that, by a singular oversight, he does not appear in John Prince's roll-call of *Worthies of Devon*, among others less worthy of remembrance. It was an occupational risk to marry a well-endowed widow that one was apt to have no children, and it would seem that his wife played little rôle in his life. But that the marriage was one of affection and that he had entire confidence in the Lady Talboys appears from his will, of which he made her sole executrix.[10]

We have a glimpse of them in his last request: 'I do heartily desire and beseech my loving wife, Lady Margaret Talboys, of all loves and as she hath ever hitherto used herself most kind and loving to me that she will forbear to levy any part of the profits of the said Barony [of Idrone] until all my said debts and legacies shall be well and truly paid.' From the scale of these there would not be much left over, he had spent so much on his Irish *ignis fatuus*. He made his wife's brother a trustee of the Barony, along with his friends, Edmund Tremayne, Jacques Wingfield of Dublin, John Harrington of Stepney, Jasper Horsey (another West Countryman in Dublin), and faithful Hooker. These were made trustees of one half of the barony, the other half to his wife for life, thence to his heirs male. Carews did go on in Ireland, into the peerage, so that his efforts were not entirely in vain. The younger Peter's brother, George, succeeded as keeper of Leighlin Castle in 1580 and made a military career in Ireland. He ended up as an earl; marrying the heiress of

Clopton house at Stratford, he is to be seen on his grand monument in the church there, surrounded by all the accoutrements of war.

Henry Davells appears as the first of Sir Peter's creditors to be paid. To half-a-dozen of his following he left £40 each; among them appears Roger Hooker, the elusive father of the great scholar; George Harvey, esquire, was another trustee, husband of the Hookers' sister. Two more substantial bequests to followers, then 20s each to Denis of the buttery, Watt of the kitchen, £3 to 'Bess my laundress' and 20 nobles to 'my man Parks', evidently a personal valet.

Mohun's Ottery he had settled upon Thomas Southcote, who had married a niece, Thomasine Kirkham. The Southcotes remained there for a century or so, until after the Civil War when the estate came to co-heiresses and the manor was dismembered. Thus it descended to a farmhouse, and there is little memory of its most famous occupant thereabouts.

Notes

1. Hooker is at last coming into his own, with W. J. Harte's edition of his book on Exeter, and V. F. Snow's of that on Parliament. His biography of Carew was edited by John Maclean in 1857.
2. Particulars for Grants, Edward VI, 1467 and 1468. (P.R.O.)
3. Cf. the original book of David Mathew, *The Celtic Peoples and Renaissance Europe: A Study of the Celtic and Spanish Influences on Elizabethan History* (Sheed & Ward, 1933).
4. I have consulted some of these in Narcissus Marsh's Library in Dublin.
5. R. Dudley Edwards, 'Ireland, Elizabeth I and the Counter Reformation', in *Essays in Elizabethan Government and Society*, Presented to Sir John Neale.
6. The wild kerne continued the old Celtic habit from prehistoric times of cutting off the heads of their victims, cf. C. Lennon, 'Richard Stanihurst (1547–1618) and Old English Identity', *Irish Historical Studies*, Sept. 1978, 121 ff.
7. Cf. my *Sir Richard Grenville of the Revenge*, Ch. 3.
8. *Holinshed's Chronicles of England, Scotland and Ireland*, (1808 edn.), Vol. VI. p. 372.
9. Cf. my *Shakespeare's Southampton: patron of Virginia* (Macmillan, 1965) Ch. 2.
10. P.C.C. Prob/11/58.

4

The Diary of William Carnsew, Country Gentleman

Elizabethan diaries are very few and far between, and are apt to be terse and extrovert—except for tiresome Puritan diaries, favouring us with their religious experiences. Even the Lady Margaret Hoby is a religious bore—poor lady, she had little else to console her, with such a husband as spindle-shanked Sir Thomas Posthumus, and no children. Simon Forman is certainly not a bore, but he is exceptional in every way— very revealing of Elizabethan sex-life. For a normal picture of what Elizabethan country life was like—the daily routine of a small country gentleman in the 1570s—I know no better introduction than that of William Carnsew of Bokelly in St Kew in North Cornwall. And for a Cornishman who knows that endearing countryside, it has a charm upon it. It is such fun going round those parishes knowing who precisely lived in what house—alive and kicking when one knows something about them—in the reign of Elizabeth I, when one hasn't the least idea of the occupants in the reign of Elizabeth II. The inflexion of the true historian: nostalgia for the past.

Our finest contemporary historian, G. M. Trevelyan, assures us:

> at bottom, I think, the appeal of history is imaginative. Our imagination craves to behold our ancestors as they really were, going about their daily business and their daily pleasure. . . . It is the detailed study of history that makes us feel that the past was as real as the present. The world supposes that we historians are absorbed in the dusty records of the dead . . . but to us, as we read, they take form, colour, gesture, passion, thought. It is only by study that we can see our forerunners, remote and recent, in their habits as they lived, intent each on the business of a long-vanished day, riding out to do homage or to poll a

vote; to seize a neighbour's manor house and carry off his ward, or to leave cards on ladies in crinolines. And there is the "fair field full of folk".'[1]

It is precisely the detail—each entry as sharply defined as a spar of Cornish quartz—that is so revealing of life.

I first brought the Diary to life many years ago, from a little-explored corner of the Public Record Office,[2] and used some of its material to light up the social life of the time in *Tudor Cornwall*. I had it completely transcribed for me, with the idea of perhaps publishing it in full one day. But the handwriting is so crabbed, minute and difficult, so full of contractions, initials and signs that spoke only to Carnsew, as to make it hard to read. The Diary has now been published by Professor N. J. G. Pounds, who has been able to illuminate some points from his geographical and economic knowledge, and to identify a number of the people.[3] It still remains to identify others, clothe them with some flesh, solve remaining difficulties, paint in the background to give the picture depth and make it intelligible to the reader. This necessitates, in short, presenting in modern English—no point in 'ye olde Tudor tea-shoppe' spelling.

One needs besides a knowledge of that particular bit of North Cornwall, between Padstow Bay, that tremendous coastline along Portquin and Port Isaac to Tintagel, and the heights of Bodmin Moor dominated by Brown Willy and Rowtor. To the east Camelford, then down along the wooded valley of the River Allen to Wadebridge: the country to the west is 'west the bridge' in the Carnsews' parlance. That vanished medieval bridge over the Camel was the pride of the place and their gateway to West Cornwall.

St Kew parish gives its own impression of ancientry; for it is dominated to the north by the prehistoric encampment of Tregear Rounds and to the south by that of Killibury, while it possesses a megalith with an Ogham inscription, common enough in Ireland, rare elsewhere. Since the parish is mostly good arable soil, it has a fine fifteenth-century church which has kept some of its medieval glass. Before the Reformation, rectory and manor belonged to Plympton priory, which would have helped in the building. Some of the historic houses remain—in particular, beautiful Trewarne with its many mullioned windows, and seventeenth-century Pengenna.

Bokelly itself—the name means the dwelling by the grove—still stands, attractively Georgianised, sheltered by its trees, infrequent in that upland country, and protected by the heave of hill to north and east, fine views over the valleys of the Allen and the Camel. From Carnsew's time there remain a small decorated window, perhaps of a former chapel, and a big buttressed barn which bespeaks the size of the manorial demesne.

When Leland passed by, in Henry VIII's reign, he notes that 'Master Carnsey [evidently the pronunciation of the name] hath a pretty house, fair ground, and pretty wood about it. Thence three miles by good corn ground, but no wood, to Wadebridge.' The old road avoids the valley, where the wood is:

> Whereat now Wadebridge is there was a ferry eighty years since, and men sometimes passing over by horse stood often in great jeopardy. Then one Lovibone, vicar of Wadebridge [i.e. of Egloshayle] moved with pity, began the bridge, and with great pain and study—good people putting their help thereto—finished it with seventeen fair and great uniform arches of stone. One told me that the foundation of certain of the arches was first set on so quick sandy ground that Lovibone almost despaired to perform the bridge until such time as he laid packs of wool for foundation.'[4]

Such was the folklore that remained living up to my time, and such was the finest medieval bridge in the West, until destroyed by a careless County Council, when a new bridge beside it could have been built, preserving the old. However, in an ignorant demotic society, one must expect no pride in the past or anything beautiful.

The Carnsews derived their name from Carnsew in the parish of Mabe, rocky moorland, and it means Blackrock. It seems that they originally came from remote St Keverne near the Lizard, moving east to Carnsew. The place has a characteristic approach for an ancient house, a winding lane between sparse hedgerow trees; then all the way back—the house looks south-west—a magnificent view over the Fal country, hills and silvery creeks of the river. The farmhouse nestles snug into the raw hillside within a Tudor granite wall,

forecourt with porch into the original hall. One window has
the hood mouldings of the sixteenth century still, an arched
doorway into the house. Above, the dark quarried rock from
which they got their name. They moved hence east to the
better land in and around St Kew, for in 1478—when the
church was being rebuilt more grandly—a William Carnsew
of Bokelly was sheriff of the county. By then small gentry,
armigerous—their coat of arms a bearded goat passant.

The sheriff's son married Isabel Cavell of neighbouring
Treharrock, the family that produced the heroic Nurse
Cavell, shot by the bestial Germans in 1915 for helping
soldiers across the frontier from Belgium into Holland.[5] A
son, another William, took his turn as sheriff in 1511, and
married Elizabeth Tregose of Penpoll. Their son, William,
went further afield to marry Jane, a daughter and co-heiress
of Edward Stradling of St Donat's in South Wales. But Stradling had a Cornish mother; coming and going across the
Bristol Channel was frequent from earliest times and we find
their son in correspondence with his Stradling uncle.

Our William Carnsew, fourth of the name at Bokelly,
married Honor, daughter of John Fitz of Tavistock, called
after her aunt, Honor Grenville. This made Carnsew brother-
in-law of John Fitz, whose grandiose monument we see in
the church there—he died in 1589, the year after our William.
This marriage increased his kinship along the Tamar border
into Devon, people whom we meet, as he did in the Diary:
his brothers-in-law John Eliot of St Germans, who had
bought the priory and made it Port Eliot, and William Bond
of Earth near Saltash, where house and medieval chapel still
remain. William and Honor had three sons—Richard,
Matthew and William—with whom we become acquainted
in the Diary, and two daughters, of whom we hear little.

At the beginning Carnsew notes down the events of the
year 1576 which he thought worthy of remembrance. George
Kekewich was sheriff of Cornwall—the walls of his seemly
house, Catchfrench, remain roofless behind the gawky
modern residence; Sir John Fulford, sheriff of Devon—his
fine house in the parish of Dunsford happily remains to us,
Renaissance panelling of Henry VIII's time, courtyard, hall,
chapel. The events of war were, as usual, much to the fore.
The advance of the Turks in central Europe was a menace

present to people's minds, and recurs in the Diary. Carnsew
was conscientious in reporting the rumours that reached him,
and, when subsequently contradicted, wrote in the margin,
A lie. For example,

> The Turk hath summoned Vienna, in Austria. *A lie*. . . . The Saracens
> took Cadiz in Spain in January, as I heard. *A lie*. . . . The King of Spain
> loseth in Barbary daily. . . . It was told me in March that the Great
> Turk was dead, and that Lord John d'Austria is said to be in Flanders
> about 18 November, and he was in Paris also, but secretly with the
> Spanish ambassador. His power and force is thought to be but little.

Don John's name was one to conjure with after his great
victory against the Turks at Lepanto; in our time Chester-
ton's Catholic enthusiasm led him to write a famous ballad,
with its refrain:

> Don John of Austria is marching to the war!

But as Philip II's Viceroy in the Netherlands in these years,
1576–8, he more than met his match in William of Orange,
leader of Dutch resistance and creator of the nation.

'In October report made that the Prince of Orange was
possessed of Flanders, and that the garrisons of Spaniards
there were become prisoners to them. *A lie*. . . . The States
of Belgium do unite themselves in leagues, and do join with
the Prince of Orange to besiege the castle of Antwerp and
to avoid the Spaniards out of those countries.' This refers to
the Pacification of Ghent, which adumbrated the union of
all the rich provinces, North and South, and offered a gleam
of hope of a United Netherlands free of Spanish dominion. It
foundered, of course, on the fatal religious division between
Catholic and Protestant. 'In November report made that the
Spaniard had burned Antwerp partly. *True, and too true*.'

The Spanish Fury, when the soldiery ran amok and
destroyed large parts of the commercial capital of Northern
Europe, made a fearful impression in England. It ended
Antwerp's commercial supremacy; thousands fled north to
build the future of Amsterdam, more thousands emigrated
to England—desirable immigrants, for they brought their
capital and skills with them, and London took the place of

Antwerp as the leading nexus of trade and financial enterprise.

France was torn in two by a series of religious wars, in which politics largely joined—a contest for power, as always in human history. Rumours flowed to and fro, which Carnsew contradicts. Then: 'Pacification proclaimed in France, 14 May, solemnly: which I read, printed in English 24 June. And then informed that it was not established because the eight towns were not delivered, the Protestants keeping their forces about them.' This was correct; the Peace of Monsieur made reasonable concessions to the Huguenots, including the security of eight fortified strongholds. This aroused the opposition of the Catholic extremists, under the Guise family, and next year the two factions returned to their vomit.

The Protestants took to the sea and privateering, from their strongholds at either end of the Channel, Flushing and La Rochelle. West Country sea-going families—Champernownes, Budockshides,[6] Gilberts, Raleghs, Killigrews, Tremaynes—linked up with the Huguenots in France, Plymouth and La Rochelle closely allied. Privateering shaded off into plain piracy, and depredations in the Channel brought the wars close home to Carnsew in his eyrie. 'The Flushingers rob our men in January and February; and yet permitted . . . Flushingers robbed our Londoners, and they of Rochelle spare none, as it is reported by the Papists.' Carnsew had acquaintance among the Papists, the rich Arundells of Lanherne, for instance—their Tudor house today a Carmelite convent—and some among his kinsmen, the Roscarrocks.

The Flushingers took nine ships of Londoners' goods, and denied redelivery unless they might have some £ lent them a year, and liberty of the havens and seas. . . . In August report made that the Flushingers would deliver all that they took, save certain they kept for countervail of that they lost or was taken from them here in this West Country. For restitution whereof the Queen's commission came to Sir John Arundell and others that they should certify jointly and severally the taking and using of them.

This was the last charge of any importance that came to the Lanherne Arundells; for next year the new sheriff, Richard

Grenville, was to lead a showdown with the Cornish Catholics, rounding them up and driving on the execution of the
first seminary priest, Cuthbert Mayne, thereafter venerated as
their proto-martyr. Carnsew knew Grenville well: 'Richard
Grenville sheriff of Cornwall, to whom I with Mr Edge-
cumbe gave his office at Penheale, 14 December.'

Meanwhile the Puritans were stepping up their propaganda
against the Anglican establishment, under the leadership of
Thomas Cartwright, whose boring tracts Carnsew read. They
had a voice in Parliament in the egregious Peter Wentworth,
who sat in all Elizabeth I's Parliaments—no matter for what
seat, provided he had a seat from which to lift up his voice
in long tirades demanding free speech in matters of policy
that were properly the sphere of the executive. In this Parliament he sat for Tregony: no likelihood that he ever visited
the place—he was a carpet-bagger—for Carnsew did not
know him. 'One Wentworth committed to prison for his
speech and his carriage in the Parliament house. A subsidy
demanded.'

Local news:

> This year was John Killigrew made knight in March. In July ambassa-
> dors waited for out of Spain at Plymouth. Our vicar, Sir Robert Gold-
> smith, died 28 April of a putrefaction of his lungs.[7] I saw him opened.
> His son, John Goldsmith, rode for the benefice, obtained it of my Lord
> Keeper, returned by Oxford and Bristol, and came home 20 May with
> the broad seal for it. In July the young vicar rode to London to enter
> his first fruits [i.e. the first year's tithes from the living due to the
> Crown]. . . . The bishop of Canterbury visiteth by Dr Tremayne, which
> is talked opprobriously of, as though they did nothing but take money
> which passed not 2s 6d of a parish. . . . Wines waxed plentifuller than
> before and more cheap. . . . Assizes at Launceston the Ember week in
> September. Bamfield sheriff of Devonshire.

The year ends with, 'great resort of stately gentlemen keeping
their Christmas there at Exeter: Sir William Courtenay, Sir
Arthur Basset, Sir John Gilbert, Sir Gawen Carew, and
divers others, also the bishop and canons of the Close.'

It would seem best to select entries from the Diary each
month to give a lifelike idea of what he did day by day, what
he read, whom he saw and what they said, and where he
went. That should give the proper flow of his life and show

its variety, his interests, avocations and moods. He gives numerous indications as to the weather, of interest no doubt to the climatologists, of whom I am not one—external events in the human sphere are the proper study of the historian. On New Year's day 1576 he notes that he went to church on Christmas eve, perhaps meaning New Year's day, which was a Sunday, for Christmas then referred to the whole period from Christmas eve to Twelfth night. 'One lamb and another falled this day.' Next day he won at cent, or saint, at home—a card game in which a hundred points was the winning number. 4 January: 'heard first of my brother Thomas' death.' Next day: 'sowed some pulse', i.e. peas and beans.

It is remarkable how many letters he wrote and received in those days without posts. Letters to and from John Cosgarne, with whom he was involved in mining ventures in West Cornwall; Blanche, the wife of John St Aubyn of Clowance, son of Thomas, whom we have met with Honor Grenville, Lady Lisle; Adrian Gilbert, the remarkable scientific brother of Sir Humphry and Sir John, with whom Carnsew shared interest in mineral matters. He wrote to the bishop, at this time poor William Bradbridge, distracted between Papists and Puritans with whom he could do nothing, who took to farming and bankrupted himself. Jane Penkivell with her daughters came to visit one day from neighbouring St Minver; next day his nephew John Langford who looked after his western property for him. 19–20 January, '*Extreme storm*: rode to Port Isaac'—he spells it Portysyke: the modern form would seem a piece of folk-etymology, the original meaning the beach by the cornfield. A couple of days later 'my house torn with winds.' This did not prevent him or his wife from riding round to make agreement with tenants as to leases. 22 January, 'dined at Tremeer', across the river and up the hill into the next parish of St Tudy, where Richard Treffry lived. Next day he dined at St Mabyn, at the wedding of John Glyn with Mary Treweek.

On the farm at home on a couple of days he walked about his grounds seeing to things; 'about my lambs, many died.' Or, 'Humphry Nicoll's sheep trespassed me much'; next day 'met Humphry Nicoll, whose wife had a young daughter.'

Nicoll owned the next farm of Trelill, but he lived at Penvose
in St Tudy, a house which long remained much as it was
then, a hall with fine Elizabethan oak screen, panelling, plas-
terwork, till it was demolished in my time. We can still see
Nicoll on his slate monument in St Tudy church, in armour
kneeling with his Roscarrock wife.[8] He died in 1597:

> Whoso with searching eye surveyest this stone
> and thinkst it marble, 'tis not so alone:
> It is a myrrour wherein thou mayst see
> Both what yu shalt and what thou shouldest bee:
> Say that thy line is ancient, so was his
> Whose part of earth to earth departed is . . .

The Nicolls were an ancient line, and in the next century
were to produce a leading Parliamentarian, Anthony Nicoll.

14 January, Carnsew rode to Bodmin, 'met N. Glyn and
Thomas Killiow for Tregarth.' Nicholas Glyn was the head
of the family that lived at Glyn in Cardinham, above the
sounding valley of the upper Fowey river. He and Killiow
from Lansallos were evidently making an offer for the lease
of Tregarth, Carnsew's farm near Camelford. On days when
he remained at home he was sometimes not well, 'diseased
of rheums', i.e. a cold; or he 'read to Matthew and Richard',
or 'read on the French stories.' He was a reading, reflective
man, evidently better educated than most, which gave interest
to his conversation and extended his acquaintance. We shall
find him entertaining and being entertained a great deal.

January was a quiet month; with February the year woke
up for Carnsew and he became more active. '1 February, at
home about my business. 2 February, *Purification* [of the
Virgin Mary, otherwise Candlemas day]: rode to Roscarrock,
lay there; a great storm; won at play, lost health. 3 February,
came home. A ship lost at Padstow.' Roscarrock is in the
next parish of St Endellion, up on the cliffs between Portquin
and Port Isaac: Georgian front, but at the back is the Tudor
house Carnsew knew so well, with its view over the Camel
estuary. Next day, 'my wife and Jane Penkivell went a-
gossiping to Penvose', i.e. as 'gossips', god-parents at the
christening of the new baby.

6 February he set off on a ten-day excursion westward
transacting business, chiefly concerning his mining interests,

in which he was something of a pioneer, second only to Sir Francis Godolphin. 'Lay at Trerice'—this was the home of the Protestant branch of the Arundells: most beautiful of West Country Elizabethan houses, with its decorative gables and finials, kept in prime condition by the National Trust. The new part of the house had just been built, the plaster-work of the fine hall dated 1572, that of the great chamber upstairs 1573. Carnsew stopped a second night, and 'heard that the bishop of Exeter should be removed to Salisbury.' The see of Salisbury was indeed vacant, but Bradbridge did not get it, though he wanted to give up the distractions of his diocese to get back to the quietude of the deanery at Salisbury. In this he had succeeded, oddly enough, the Italian Peter Vannes—Mary's ambassador at Venice—who held on to his English preferments under Elizabeth.

Next day Carnsew moved on to Roskrow, where he stayed, not at his own Carnsew next door, which was occupied by his tenant and bailiff, Henry Thomas. (This family also took the name Carnsew later, to the confusion of geneal-ogists.) 'At home Jane Penkivell's boy ran away with her money.' His next stage took him to Clowance of the St Aubyns; 10 February, 'John St Aubyn rode with me to see the work at Binnerton', in his metalliferous parish of Crowan. That night he slept at Lelant near St Ives, and back to Clowance next day.

Bargained with Roger Tregantallon for to work the work; viz. he to work the hole and to take that only which he can make tin of, and blow it. Then, being blown and not coigned [i.e. smelted into pieces, the corners or coigns not being chipped for the Duchy's toll], to deliver one-third to Mr St Aubyn for his portion; and to deliver me clear of eight parts three; and to keep to his own use the other five. John St Aubyn must find wood and coal for the work in Binnerton.

This was a major problem in treeless West Cornwall.

The terms of the joint enterprise are clear enough; Carnsew and St Aubyn were partners, Tregantallon their manager. 13 February, 'lay at John Nance's.' This was at Nance in the (later mining) parish of Illogan. The Nances were more generally known by their name of Trengove; we see the tendency, when surnames were not yet settled in Cornwall, to take the name of the place where one lived. John Nance's wife was the daughter of Sir John Arundell of Trerice; these Arundells narrowly escaped becoming known as Trerices, but pride in their Norman name prevailed.

Here 'Richardson delivered unto me a Book of Discipline, I think put forth by Cartwright, *incerto authore sine nomine.*' It was indeed Cartwright's famous book putting forward his Presbyterian scheme to take the place of that of the Anglican Church. Next day, 'took money at Truro for Creegbrawse tin', near Chacewater, a property where Carnsew held the right of toll tin. 'Lay at Trencreek, with whom I communed for Henry Thomas of Carnsew, that he should order the same.' It would seem that Carnsew stopped at Robert Trencreek's Treworgan in the parish of St Erme, a charming sequestered place where much of the house is recognisable. So too Robert Trencreek, with wife and four daughters on his brass in the rebuilt church: 'counsellor at law, 30 years Justice of the Peace and Quorum, a lover of his country, friendly to his neighbours, liberal to the poor; his painful travail in the one, his ready advice for the other and bountiful hospitality to all did manifest a man of a constant resolution in the carriage of his life.' Such were the values the Elizabethans esteemed and promulgated—of more worth than those that prevail in our shiftless society.

Thus back to Wadebridge, where he learned of 'the taking of Jane Penkivell's boy at Barnstaple.' The next two days at home: 'talked with Richard [the eldest son] for his going to London. Frances Carnsew very sick'—this was his daughter, who lived on to be an old maid. Then, 'rode to Roscarrock, met there Doctor Francis, found Mary Roscarrock very sick. William Glyn came hither.' 19 February, 'my brother John Carnsew and his wife with me all day.' They came over from their farm at Trecarne in the upper Camel valley, the moorland spaces of Advent above it. Then, 'gave my brother a chair. Two ploughs at work. Richard and Matthew went to St Germans'—to their uncle Eliot's. The next three days, he sent wheat to Bodmin, dealt with business, and 'conceived matter in writing to convey Matthew forth', i.e. the important letters he was to carry to the Court.

24 February, 'went to meet Mr Mohun at Penvose, of whom I won.' This was Sir William Mohun of Boconnoc, the fine estate the family inherited at the death of the last

Earl of Devon. Returned home, Carnsew read in Montanus' medical work, *De febre sanguinis*, on fever. He prided himself on his medical skill and was ready to administer potions, kill or cure. Next day he gave Frances a dose of stibium, 'wherewith she was not much molested, but wrought so as she had three vomits, one stool, and amended.' But next day, 'Frances amending, complained of her head and stomach. Mary Roscarrock amended. My brother John Carnsew with me.' Stibium, or 'stibby' as Carnsew familiarly calls it, was black antimony, which powdered was used as a cosmetic to blacken eyebrows and eyelashes; it was used medically as an emetic, and also as a poison. Webster in *The White Devil*: 'I will compound a medicine out of their two heads, stronger than garlic, deadlier than stibium.'

27 February: 'delivered letters to carry to the Lord Treasurer, to the Earl of Hertford, to Edmund Tremayne. Richard and he rode both away, Richard to bring him on his way.' These letters concerned mining prospects in Cornwall. The great Lord Burghley, during his long administration of forty years, did everything he could to develop the country's real resources, not inflationary projects. Next day, '*Wet*: dunged beans in the mead-park. Heard that Mistress Isabel Roscarrock was diseased.' This was followed by a fair day, in which he rode over to visit her, and home again. 'Read the story of the Turks newly set out this year.' 'Giles Creed gave me his bill of reckoning between him and me'—Creed was to become vicar of St Minver. Back to the insufferable Cartwright, who wanted to upset the order of things: 'read the *Admonition* of Cartwright for the new order of discipline, and the slipping of the Church of England.' The *Admonition* was Cartwright's propaganda for Presbyterianism after the dreary Geneva model: the Church of England was only 'slipping' because he could not get his way with it.

In March Carnsew was much concerned with his neighbours at Roscarrock. On the 1st he rode over and dined there; 5 March: 'Thomas Roscarrock dined with me'—he was now head of the family; his brother John came at night. Next day 'I played at cent and won of Thomas Nicoll and John Roscarrock.' On Ash Wednesday, the 7th, 'went with my family to the church, whence John Roscarrock had Richard Carnsew home with him. I determined to write to Nicholas

Roscarrock.' Next day, 'wrote to Nicholas Roscarrock, but yet kept the letters.' A couple of days later 'Thomas Butshed told me of two in the Tower.' 13 March: 'went to Roscarrock, whereat I met Mr Richard Grenville and Mr Arundell Trerice. Lay there.' The day following, 'at Roscarrock all day playing and trifling the time away.' Spending the night there again, he rode off to Tintagel with Grenville. 24 March: 'sent letters to Nicholas Roscarrock, and received answer. 25 March: wrote to him again . . . 26 March, wrote to Nicholas Roscarrock, but he was gone before my letters came to him.' Next day, 'sent my letters to N.R. to be carried to him by young Nance to Oxford from Treharrock.'

Why this concern with Nicholas Roscarrock, the hesitation about writing to him, and then the urgent letters in succession? This younger brother was heading for very serious trouble. An Oxford man and a scholar, he was an uncompromising Catholic and took the youngest brother, Trevennor, along with him. Nicholas had contributed verses, from the Inner Temple, to Boswell's *Works of Armoury*; and in this year 1576 to Gascoigne's well-known *The Steel Glass*, in which Walter Ralegh, of the Middle Temple, made his first appearance as a poet. Roscarrock was a learned antiquarian, whose enormous volume on the Lives of the British Saints has never been published. Next year he was inculpated in Grenville's campaign against the Cornish Catholics, setting the laws at defiance, and Roscarrock was a life-long Recusant. When the Jesuits began their Counter-Reformation campaign in 1580, he made one of the group of well-to-do young men who subscribed to maintain them, aiding and abetting. He was sent to the Tower, where he was racked, but was able to pursue his studies. Released, he eventually found shelter with Lord William Howard at Naworth Castle in Cumberland, where he lived to an immense age, far from the Cornwall of his youth, whence he recalled nostalgically the rites of the old faith and the folklore of the saints.[9]

Evidently nothing that sensible Carnsew could say had any effect on young Roscarrock or could save him from a life of proscription. He had independent means. He and his younger brother steadfastly refused to go to church; they remained unmarried. Their obstinacy had its part in ending the prosperity of the family and bringing it to an end.

To resume Carnsew's daily *train de vie*. 1 March coming back from Roscarrock he rode over to Pencarrow, the farm in Advent which marched with his land at Trecarne: 'Robert Edward had set forth 30 yards to make, and I promised the ground to him for three years; but we agreed not of the rent. Diseased by eating fish.' Some of his bullocks miscarried. 3 March: 'mine ear troubled me more than it did the half-year past.' 6 March: 'talked with Thomas Nicoll for a relief between the Weales brothers, which is Mr Treffry's request.' The Treffrys of Place—the historic house that remains at Fowey—also owned Rooke in St Kew parish for two or three centuries. 9 March, '*Frost*: made an end of tilling oats. No manner of news. Walking. 10 March: rode to the haven, bought fish there. Talked with Honor of William Penkivell.' Honor was his sister—why this conferring? There was trouble in the family; the son, Francis, pushing his mother out of her land. 11 March, 'played at bowls and won 6d. 12 March, Matthew Carnsew delivered my letters to the Earl of Hertford, and had answer.'

Back from Tintagel, 16 March: 'at home all day. Gave my horse medicine for the botts', i.e. worms. We recall that Petruchio's horse in *The Taming of the Shrew* suffered from the botts, along with much else. 'Chid Richard for his sloth'—the eldest boy was not the clever one of the family: Matthew and William were—the last became a Fellow of All Souls only three years later. Next day, 'rode to Dannon-chapel, had thence three kine and calves. My horse skinned.' This was a bleak spot out on the cliffs in St Teath parish, where the Carnsews shared in the holdings, though William had little success with his farming there. 18 March: 'played at bowls handed with Mr Vicar.'

Most of the month he remained at home, occupied interestingly as usual—nothing dull or vacuous about him. 19 March, 'John Goldsmith came to me and lay here all night, by whom I heard of a Spanish ambassador coming to the Court.' This was the insufferable grandee, Bernardino de Mendoza, who had his hand in plots against the régime, intriguing with Mary Queen of Scots, supporting traitors like Francis Throckmorton, encouraging Catholic irreconcilables to undermine the government. Mendoza, though very grand, was a stupid man, expelled in 1583; it must have given

Walsingham pleasure to give him his *démission*, speaking
Italian, before the assembled Court.

20 March, 'read to Richard Littleton's *Tenures*.' This text-
book of land law was regular reading for a young gentleman
who was to succeed to an estate. 'Read to him and William
Carnsew Vegetius and Whitehorne.' Vegetius' *De re militare*
was held a prime authority on military matters during the
Renaissance. We watch Carnsew taking a hand in the
education of his sons; he was an educated man, and they
read Latin together, but we do not know where the father
was educated. The day following 'Langford grassed', i.e.
sowed grass for pasture after arable. 22 March, 'did nothing,
but read to Richard and saw my hedgers. Wrote to Petherick
Mason and Tynke for going to sea, appointed them to go on
31 of March.' Here we see the Justice of the Peace exercising
authority and giving aid in the community. One of the prime
reasons for resentment against the Catholics, among their
fellow gentry, was that they were opting out of their responsibilities, by not going to church, taking a proper hand in
parish life, etc.

23 March, 'Removed trees, set hops and raisin [currant]
trees. Sold tin to Henry Sexton', a pewterer from St Columb
major. 28 March, 'made an entry at Gear-bury in presence
of William Glyn and William Lobb.' This would be a formal
taking possession of some land at Tregear Rounds. 'Read on
Fulwell's book of the Eight Sciences.' Here William was very
up-to-date, for the book came out only that year; it shows
his alert and wide intellectual interests. He evidently bought
books, though he does not mention his purchases; he
exchanged books with his friends who were similarly awake
mentally. Next day, 'rode to Hamatethy with William Glyn,
and from thence to Trecarne, whereat William Glyn claimed
half the mill-park.' Hamatethy was a large Doomsday manor
up on the slopes of Bodmin moor, across the upper Camel
valley from Bokelly: part of the Hungerford lands, it came
to the improvident Earl of Oxford, a clever extravagant fool
who sold everything and left himself not a stitch of land.
Next, 'Rain: I went to Lanseague and was well wet for my
labour.' This is where his wood was, down in the Allen
valley. We see him abroad in all winds and weathers.

1 April, 'Wet: at home all day. Heard of a new Keeper of
the Great Seal, viz. Mr Solicitor [General], Mr Bromley.'
This was a bit premature, for Lord Keeper Bacon did not
die till some eighteen months later, but it shows how quickly
rumours spread from the centre. Next day, 'gave Henry
Chapman stibby, and myself troubled in my urine. Thomas
Nicoll lay here. 3 March, at home all day. My brother George
Carnsew had of me a tree to make "zylys" ', i.e. ceils or
rafters. George Carnsew farmed Brighter next door, a little
further down the valley. 'William Bond came to me', i.e. the
brother-in-law from Earth near Saltash. Next, 'rode to Henry
Chapman whom I found very well, but I was well wet for
my labour'—a regular phrase from William's lips. 5 April,
'my lambs died downright, and some old sheep. Carried
ashes to the meadow in the fenton'—this would be the spring
that fed the meadow. 'Reckoned with Langford. 6 April,
mended and stopped the well in the fenton. 7–8th, Fair:
divided chains with Collins. Mr Trencreek came hither. Rode
to the haven, bought fish there. 8 April, Henry Thomas told
me that my father levied him a fine for Devis and Treverbyn',
i.e. near Penryn. 'I let Sir John Killigrew a horse, for that
his was tired, to go to the assizes.' Assizes were held at
Launceston then, a long way from Arwenack at Falmouth—
the remains of the big house now happily being restored.
Killigrew was brother of the leading diplomat, Sir Henry,
who was Burghley's brother-in-law. These people in their
remote fastness had their direct lines to Court.

9 April, 'made my gardens, and nothing else, save that I
read the Turks' coming into Hungary annis 1538, 39, 40, 41,
42, 43, 44, and of William Thorpe.' Thorpe was a Lollard
follower of Wyclif, burned for heresy; Carnsew was much
interested in reading about such, usually in Foxe's best-selling
Book of Martyrs. 10 April, 'walked about my ground. Had
my sheep told, young and old. 11th, William Rich told me
news out of France not worth the hearing. My garden was
a-making.' This would be in the sheltered close in front of
the house. 12th, 'Sir John Killigrew here in the morning.
Conceived a bill in writing against Francis Penkivell for with-
holding of evidences and writings.' This is the first notice of
anything of that kind: Carnsew seems to have been exceptional in avoiding law suits—Elizabethans were a litigious

lot—perhaps because he was exceptionally friendly and kindly-given.

13 April, 'Thundered. Rode to Dannonchapel and to Port Isaac. Richard Good here, who showed me that war was open between France and Spain.' This, however, was a mere rumour. 'Met John Cavell at Port Isaac'—over from Treharrock. 'The parson of Tregwethen buried, leaving seven children motherless. Likely to be of the plague.' These simpletons seem to have had no idea of birth control—their large families thus lay open to luck. Two days later, 'took order at the church for the keeping of the parson's children'—Carnsew was quick on the mark in doing his charitable duty. The weather was hot; the day before he had remained indoors reading 'Ridley's end, and Latimer and his friendly farewell. Item, Winchester's sermon before King Edward.' On the 15th he dined at Roscarrock, and noted that Leonard Loveys, of Ogbeare Hall in North Tamerton—the fine Tudor hall there remains—was buried. His brass inscription remains in his parish church at North Tamerton, telling us that he died on 14 April 1576, 'General Receiver to the Queen's Majesty of all her revenues in the counties of Devon and Cornwall.' It was this that enabled him to build his tall hall with impressive roof and gallery. Four days later Carnsew's wife rode to Ogbeare on a visit of condolence.

Meanwhile at home William was reading bishop Gardiner's sermon and his end. 'I counselled Bennet's wife how to use her sickness. 17th, John Nicoll of Bodwin, in St Teath, with me for wood, to whom I assigned some in the wood at Lanseague to make stakes. Received letters from Matthew, but not the first he sent me. 18th, delivered John Nicoll a load of stakes. Met Hawse the Receiver's man. 19th, *Rain much*: tarried at home within doors all day. 20th, *Windy*, cold: Good Friday, went to the church. Treated with my cousin Carnsew and the constables for scolding matters. Jane Penkivell paid me £3. Poled some hops. My wife came home. Sexton the pewterer came to me with pewter; looked on our reckoning. Paid for my tithing corn 26s 8d.'

On Easter day, 22nd, he communicated, according to the statute. 23rd, St George's day: 'gave medicine to the Vicar Goldsmith, which wrought well. 24th: dined at Stytson's.

Wrote to parson Grenville for his lambs.' This was the old vicar of Kilkhampton, who sensibly held on to his living through all the chops and changes of Henry VIII, Edward VI, Mary I, Elizabeth I, and was to die in 1580 full of years and kin. 'Met Ford the preacher, to whom I delivered the book *Discipline*'; perhaps that is the person he got it from—one of the unbeneficed Puritans who went about the country stirring up trouble. 25 April, 'St Mark's day: put my oxen to leas [i.e. pasture]. Langford did set some ground to till at Dannonchapel. Read a lease made by Thomas Martin to Thomas Nicoll of Upton. 26th, went to the Vicar, who was extremely sick. Promised my rinds [i.e. bark of trees] to J. Edwards the tanner. 27th, sent my cattle to the Moor, viz. of mine own 33; a horse, heifer and her calf of Morgan's. 5 young cattle of Widow Dangerd's, besides mares and colts.'

28 April, 'Robert Goldsmith our Vicar died. 29th, saw him ripped. Thomas Nicoll sent me £10 for sheep promised him. 30th, dined at Treharrock at the marriage of Calmady and Elizabeth, John Cavell's second daughter: whereat I met Digory Chamond. Read Henry Bullinger's work against the Pope's Bull.' This was a defence of the Queen and Church against the absurd Bull of excommunication and 'deposition' emitted by St Pius V, which created a hopeless dilemma for Catholics.

1 May, 'came late to the church. 2nd, our Vicar Goldsmith was buried; wrote to Mr Trevanion [of the Caerhays family] for the widow. Wrote to Matthew Carnsew and Doctor Kenall.' John Kenall was archdeacon of Oxford, but enjoyed several benefices in Cornwall, including the rich living of St Columb major, where he sometimes resided. Carew wrote that in him 'the principal love and knowledge of the Cornish language lived, and with him lieth buried.' We cannot forgive him for not writing it down: he was one of those who do not get their books written. The Puritans said that 'his conversation is most in hounds'; for once we share their disapproval.

3 May, 'my servants rooted and trimmed the meadow at Lanseague. 4th, *Cold*: I rode westward.' He wrote to parson Crane, acting for the archdeacon of Cornwall, on behalf of Giles Creed, a Fellow of Exeter College, Oxford, who was after the living of St Minver. At Coswarth near Newquay—

the old house used to have a Jacobite portrait belonging to the Vyvyans on the staircase—he met Mr Arundell, his old friend Blanche St Aubyn, Colan Blewett and Kempthorne, of the family whose Tudor house of Tonacombe remains near Morwenstow, all on a diminutive scale but perfect, little hall with gallery and all.

Carnsew went with Arundell to hospitable Trerice for the next two nights, where he heard of the extenting of John Cosgarne's land—a levy upon it of £10—'of Thomas Coswarth £5 and mine £5', probably on account of mineral rights, for both were involved in mining. Creed called on him. 6 May, 'Francis Godolphin and his wife *cum multis aliis* [with many others] dined at Trerice', in the new hall lit by its fine big window. 'Talked with Francis Godolphin of tin and tin works'—he was the leading authority on the subject, the fortunes of that most famous of Cornish families made by the minerals on their land.

7th, 'paid Thomas Coswarth £10'—he was Receiver General of the Duchy. 'Dined at Colan Blewett's'—interesting that he should be called after the patron saint of the parish; the Colan Blewetts were a branch of the Somerset family seated at Holcombe Rogus, where their splendid Tudor house still exists. At Trerice Carnsew met Charles Tredeneck, head of the family at St Breock. He was to die in May two years later: we have his slate monument there, an excellent example of the local school of slate workers, arms, quarterings, lively putti, a long roll of verses:

> You children which on earth remain,
> Behold of man the brittle state:
> Know this of truth, judge all things vain,
> What in this world God did create,
> But that we see right every day:
> Each thing to change and pass away . . .

I cite them as so characteristic of the age: a humble variation on the theme of Spenser's canto on Mutability.

On the 7th William returned home, when his wife rode next day to Boscastle in company with John Kempthorne and his wife up along the coast road. 'Had home some of my furze'—for firewood. Next day, 'walked about my ground; sorted my leases; had masons, sadlers, and young Calmady to supper and his wife: to whom I gave instructions for Richard and Lord Mountjoy.' The sixth Lord Mountjoy lived at Bere Ferrers near Plymouth, in the peninsula between Tamar and Tavy, a metalliferous area where was a silver mine in the middle ages. Hence the extraordinary wealth of ornament and beauty in the church, defaced by the Reformation and subsequently, and of which only pathetic remnants have survived. Burghley encouraged Mountjoy's mineral interests in alum and copperas.

10th, 'rode to St Merryn to speak with parson Nicoll for the presentation to St Tudy. Played at bowls and lost; won at tables', i.e. backgammon. 'Lay at Charles Tredeneck's.' 11th, '*Much rain*: came home, brought a Foxe with me [the book, not the animal]. Mr Erisey came to me'—all the way from the Lizard, where something of their ancient house with forecourt and piers survives. He was a cousin of the Grenvilles, with whom Carnsew concluded a piece of business, but parson Nicoll was 'not concluded.' Evidently he was not giving up the presentation to the living of St Tudy. 12th, 'rode with Erisey to parson Nicoll, who said his son had answered him that he would keep it, since God had provided it for him. And was I bobbed [taken in] and mocked!' Richard Foote arrived with his book of accounts.

Sunday, 13th, 'went to the church and there showed a sequestration to John Nicoll and William Goldsmith. Dreamed that John Goldsmith had the benefice of St Kew. Creed came home not desperate. 14th, had home my furze this day and the next. Thomas Nicoll somewhat sick. 15th, *Fair*: went to St Kew to Lanow mill; had £5 of John Inch upon wool. 16th, *Misty, windy*: rode to Dannonchapel to see my corn and other things there; conveyed thither horse, oxen, colts and kine', evidently for summer pasture on that high ground. 'The corn failed much there.' Next day he went down to Tretawne, which Francis Carnsew farmed with Brighter, 'to treat between William Goldsmith and Crome.' Carnsew reckoned up that he had forty-three wethers. 'Read Thomas Wolsey's, the Cardinal's, story in Foxe. 18th, Mr Kestle came to me and offered to abide Mr Charles Tredeneck's order between him and Crome: which I said should be at Killibury on 28 May.' It is interesting that these ancient encampments continued as the traditional venue of

hundred courts and such—as Kit Hill, visible on the skyline
all over the lower Tamar valley, was the meeting place of the
Stannary parliaments.

19th, 'within all day; caused my men to make a head [? to
plough] in the culverhouse park'—from which we see that
Bokelly had a dovecot. 20th, 'wrote to Matthew by John
Roscarrock, who supped here. 21st, set workmen to skim
the lane. 22nd, Matthew came home'—Carnsew frequently
writes Mathy, as the name was pronounced. 'John Goldsmith, obtaining the benefice, came home. Francis Godolphin with me, towards London. 23rd, William Langford
rode to Clowance with my letters. Wrote to meet Charles
Tredeneck. 24th to 26th, *Fair*: went to see widow Goldsmith
being sick. 25th, rode to Brown Willy with William Goldsmith, who put in there three colts. William Langford
returned from Clowance with letters and money from
Carnsew. Stronger beer did me no good. 26th, my sheep
shorn all and sorted. Viewed wood for Paul Tremayne. 27th,
went to church; saw the widow worse than before. 28th,
went to meet Mr Charles Tredeneck at Killibury; played
there at bowls. 29th, Charles Tredeneck came home with
me; played and lost. 31st, *Ascension*: at home all day.'

1 June, 'rode to Dannonchapel. 2nd, did nothing worth
remembrance. Sunday, 3rd, dined at John Lynham's at
Penpont; played at bowls and won'—Carnsew was no
Puritan. 4th, 'dined at Nicholas Webber's at Penpont; played
at bowls and lost. Slept evil. 5th, young Button's wife died
of travail *immodicoque fluxu uteri* [from excessive bleeding
of the womb]. 6th, *Fair*: Petroc's Fair [i.e. at Bodmin]. News
brought me secretly that Mary Roscarrock was frantic. 7th,
Misty: I wrote to Roscarrock for his sister, who sent me
word that she was amended, *quod non credo* [which I do not
believe]. Velling [i.e. cutting turf for burning] in Dannonchapel.' One should observe that, in the so much harsher
conditions of life then, everything was turned to use. 8th,
'*Rain*: read with Matthew in Orontio', probably Oronce
Finé who wrote on geometry and astronomy. 'Began to make
my sandridge', a compost heap of sea-sand, manure, etc. to
spread on the fields as a fertiliser. 9th, 'at home, not best at
ease.'

The whole of Whitsun week was fair and hot. 10th, 'Whitsunday: Grace [his daughter] was very evil at ease, of whom I mistrusted. 11th, she amended. My wife rideth to Ogbeare. Thornbury and I shoot [? plover]. Spent 4d at the Clarks' in ale. Nicholas Rush came home from Dorsetshire. 12th, at home all day, not very well at ease. Mrs Butshed with me. 13th, washed my wools and set it to dry in my green lane. A horse brought me of Mr Arundell's of Tolverne'—this was the branch of the family that lived above King Harry Ferry, overlooking the Fal. 14th, 'Mr Butshed dined with me'—he had expected John Cavell and Calmady's son, but 'these came not, and I supped at Mr Butshed's. 15th, cut the grass in my gardens. Matthew came home from his mother, being at Ogbeare. 16th, John Inch paid me fully for my wool, viz. £6 17s. Richard Dangerd netted some of my woods. Wheat sold for 10s 4d in Bodmin. 17th, sent Matthew to serve a subpoena [a writ] to Francis Penkivell, but he missed him. William Pearce died and his wife extremely sick. John Dagge's wife dead also. 18th, began to carry dung, 30 load a day to my sandridge. Francis Penkivell took the subpoena. Mary Roscarrock buried *ex melancholico humore* [i.e. of depression]. Wrote my remedy for Bath's son. Harvey and others with me for wood. 19th. William Pearce's wife dead; sent Richard thither to fetch me two heriots'—the customary payment of the best beast to the landlord on the expiry of a 'life' in a leasehold—'Began to burn [i.e. turf] at Dannonchapel. Sold wood to Mr Butshed. Read Bonner's Deprivation', i.e. in Foxe.

20th, 'my wife came home. I sent John Palmer for a still, and fish; he brought both. 21st, *Thunder, rain*: had eleven burners at Dannonchapel', i.e. to make ash for cultivation. 'William Bond of Earth was buried; Katherine Fitz, my wife's sister, having five children. 22nd, wrote to Sir John Killigrew; had no answer. Charles Tredeneck with me, homewards from Exeter: no news. Made conserve of roses for Grace and Anne Wills'—his sister had married a Wills of Saltash. 'Richard Carnsew fetched home another heriot. 23rd, set my still in the garden; had in my garden hay; began to distil rose water. Wrote to the under-sheriff for John Cosgarne's matter. Anne Tremayne and two of her daughters lay here.' Anne was the widow of Roger Tremayne of

Collacombe. 24th, '*St John's day, Rain in the morning*: Philip
Stitson and many others dined with me. My brother John,
going to London, made means to me for moneys. (Lady
Catherine Mountjoy died this day). 25th, wrote letters to
Lord and Lady Mountjoy [not having heard of her death yet:
the previous entry being an interpolation]; to John Cosgarne,
to Sydrach Rich', and others, including his brother John, to
whom he sent money. 'Gave Thomas Roscarrock my great
elm at Lanseague'—today all the elms dead or dying of the
Dutch elm disease.

26th, '*Much rain*: my folks threshed. Creed rode to the
bishop. I wrought upon a medicine. Gave leave to John
Collins to fetch the ox at Dannonchapel, which Richard
Carnsew brought home for the third heriot. 27th, walked
about my ground; found beans not full ripe. 28th, *Showery*:
much diseased by rheums, eating milk and cream. 29th, troubled somewhat in my back. Wrote three libels to Doctor
Tremayne'—official letters on church business. 'Mr Arundell
Trerice's wife with me homewards. 30th, at Visitation'—his
business with Tremayne probably related to this. 'I played
in Bodmin and won.'

Thus ended June.

1 July was Trinity Sunday, '*Cloudy*: at church, talked of
divers things. Walter Roger with me to have the farm of
my tin in Trebell [in Lanivet]. Received letters that Doctor
Tremayne would come no nigher. 2nd, wrote a testification
for the matter between Crome and Goldsmith. Troubled
with the stone. Thomas Martin of Upton [in St Kew] buried.
3rd, my folks cut my meadow above. My wife rode to Earth.
4th, sheared my lambs this day. 5th, made some cheer to
John Cavell and Thomas Butshed; young Michell and
William Mathew dined with me. 6th, *Dark weather*: made
my hay up into cocks in the mead park. Rode to Dannonchapel and went down under the cliff to see the quarry; was
well wet for my labour. One taken stealing an ox in Trelill.
Bargained for 672 [? pegs] to pay 6s, and for 6000 nails
[?] 8d to Richard Geffrey. 7th, *Fair at Camelford*, wrote
reckonings between my brother [-in-law] and me. 8th, mine
ear molested me somewhat. 9th, received letters from John

Cosgarne, little to my contentment. Went to the Smiths. My hay cut down.

10th, *Rain*: received letters from my brother, John Carnsew, of Lady Mountjoy's death. 11th, Erisey came to look at Hawke [near Camelford] with me. 12th, I played at bowls and shove-groat with him. He departed hence. 13th, lay at Port Eliot, met not John Eliot at home. 14th, rode to Newton Ferrers'—where Bishop Bradbridge was farming to his loss. 'At Lanrake met with Anthony Wills; at Saltash with my sister [-in-law] Mary Wills. At the bishop's with Ralph Callard and divers greedy gulls gaping for Egloshayle benefice. Lay at Spriddleston. Mr Fortescue used me contumeliously. 15th, came through Plymouth. Dined at Saltash, whereat I met with Mr Dauntsy, parson of St Keyne. Lay at Earth; talked with Catherine Bond; saw her will and other matters in good order. Rode to my sister [-in-law] Mary's; met Kemp there which shall marry her daughter Joan. Saw Mary Langford, like a fool. Rode to St Germans; met not there with John Eliot.

17th, *Misty and dark weather*: dined at a husbandman's house in St Germans parish. Met there Robert Smyth; played at bowls with him, at cent, and quoiting with even hand. Jane Penkivell was betrothed. Met my brother [-in-law] Eliot at home, and John Langford. I told Grace Eliot and John Langford that my conjecture failed me if John Eliot lived three months to an end. *Laborat orthopnoea.* [He suffers from asthma.] 15th, broke my fast at Robert Smyth's, and so came home. Robin left me at Morval. Richard bought a colt of William Calway. Received letter from Mr Mohun to be at Bodmin on 29 July.

19th, sent Inch to the Fair for keeves [tubs], wheels, and to make money of an ox and a horse.' We observe that little enough money was in circulation—the Elizabethans suffered from the reverse of inflation, and were often hard put to it for ready cash. 'Bennet agreed with me, for the third heriot, to pay me 30s at St Lawrence's day. 20th, *Hot and dry*: rode to Roscarrock where I lost 6s to H. Roscarrock. Missed Thomas Roscarrock. Inch sold an ox and a horse at Fair, bought two keeves and two pair of wheels. 21st, one had away Reskymer's horse. Sent money to Ralph Michell and to my brother John Carnsew. Read 2nd Epistle of Paul to

Corinthians. 22nd, my brother John Carnsew and his wife
dined with me; talked of sundry things with him. He
delivered me mine obligations, but not my father's grant to
him nor Worthyvale's, or the other lease of Pendavy [in
Egloshayle parish]; George Thomas's he delivered unto me.
   23rd, rode forth, met Lord Stourton, after whom I came
to Lanherne: dined, played at bowls there, and supped; but
lay at Trerice.' The Stourtons were Catholics; Sir John Arundell had married Stourton's mother, when widowed by her
husband's being hanged for manslaughter in Mary's reign—
with a silken cord, because he was a peer. It is observable
that, though Carnsew was friendly with the Lanherne people,
he did not stay with them. 24th, 'rode by St Perran-in-the-
Sands. Lay at Clowance. Spoke with no person in the way.
25th, lay at Trewothack [in St Anthony-in-Meneage]. John
Tregose troubled with an issue in his leg. Wrote to Tregantallon with letters John sent him from Carnsew that he should
come to me speedily. 26th and 27th, *Much Rain*: talked with
John Tregose for marriages, who promised me that his son
should come hither.' Tregose was a cousin; William was
evidently hoping that his son might marry one of his daughters. 'Lay at Trencreek's. Ended sanding. 27th, came home;
by the way met Thomas Coswarth, who promised me money
when his other business were ended.
   28th, borrowed of Creed 20s, of George Carnsew, 40s.
29th, I am written to to meet Mr Mohun at Bodmin plays.'
These were probably the miracle plays still being performed
into Elizabeth's reign, though perhaps not in Cornish as far
east as Bodmin. 'Spent there 12s, whereof I gave wrestlers
5s. Dined at Kellygreen [down in the Allen valley], whereat
Toy's daughter was married. 30th, dined there again, played
at bowls there'—the wedding festivities continuing several
days, as usual. 31st, 'walked to Lanseague; saw my meadows
cut, my oats almost ripe, my wheat thin, thin. Read upon the
Commentaries of Luther to Galatians, in English, translated
incognito authori.'
   Thus ended July.

1 August, 'at home, did little; walked over my ground, saw
my oats ripe; took medicine to mine ears. 2nd, was at the
making up of my hay in Lanseague. Heard talk of Mrs Smyth

before Mr Mohun [probably as J.P.] by John Kempthorne. The bridegroom and his wife with others with me', i.e. from Kellygreen. 3rd, '*Rain*: sent to Launceston for keeves and wheels; began to make a say [assay] furnace in my chapel. A horse hurt Edward Cavell's son. 4th, *Vehement winds*: sent to Hills for Creed and had a flout for my labour. Had some wheels and keeves from Launceston. 5th, great harm done to the corn by winds. Report that the manor of Colquite is set to sale', in the next parish of St Mabyn. 'Sir Arthur Basset commissioner to sell it. 6th, began to malt my oats, which was razed more than was sowed in the ground. Met Mrs Coswarth riding to London and three of her sons. John Specott came hither [a Devonshire cousin of the Grenvilles], Thomas Rich and Mary. 7th, *Great winds*: Charles Tredeneck's wife, Mrs Opie's daughter, John Specott and young Facey departed hence. Changed my calves' leas. 8th, *Fair*: rode to Edward Cavell's with my cousin Jane Penkivell, whereat Edward Cavell's son was upon amendment. From thence to Dannonchapel, where Richard Hambly was reaping. Reckoned with Thomas Michell and we parted. Must build a house at my hall door', i.e. a porch.

9th, 'wrote and sent to Thomas Coswarth for money by Matthew Carnsew. Young Mr Carew here'—this would be Richard Carew, author of the contemporary *Survey*, then aged twenty-one—'George Grenville [Richard's cousin, of beautiful Penheale near Launceston], Digory Tremayne, John Smyth and young Monk, towards the sale of Colquite.' This was Anthony Monk of Potheridge, son of Frances, Lord Lisle's daughter and widow of John Basset. Monk was to be the ancestor of the famous General, deliverer of England from the Puritan nightmare.

10th, St Lawrence's day: 'Rode to the Fair [at Bodmin]. Colquite set to sale. . . . At this fair George Lower hurt William Courtenay.' Ordinary humans could not meet at a fair without a *fracas*. 11th, 'wrote and searched writings and evidences. 12th, Sunday, went to the church, met the new Vicar. 13th, *Showery*: wrote letters westward for money. Inch cut his corn at Dannonchapel. I looked on evidences. 14th, *Dark weather*: Matthew rode westwards to do divers errands and to look for moneys. 15th, *Assumption* [of the Blessed Virgin, though no longer worshipped] minding to ride to Brown Willy I tarried at Trecarne: my brother delivered unto me writings of Pendavy and Camelford. Note that John Thom, George Thom's son, is dead, which was lessee'—of land in St Mabyn. 'Had sadlers whom I set to work; parted with Richard.

16th, *Rain*: to Roscarrock; it rained very much, yet rode thither. 17th, met Sir Arthur Basset at Roscarrock, Mr Grenville and divers others.' This would be Richard Grenville, who is always mentioned with respect at some distance. '18th, sent J. Palmer to Port Eliot with gulls. Matthew came home and brought me moneys. Roger Tregantallon came to speak with me: little to better our profits. 19th, Sunday, communicated, had a day temperate. Read on the Exposition of Luther to the Galatians: Abraham a double father, a begetting father, and a father of faith'—interesting for the kind of mythical nonsense that helped to fill the vacant spaces of their minds. 'A great swine died in the lust of eating poisoned rats, I think.

20th, *Rain*: Henry Chapman with me for Jewell of Davidstow's sheep taken on Hamatethy Moor. Showed me Mr Chamond's precept.' The Chamonds lived at lovely Launcells, near Bude. 21st, '*Rain*: made a precept in Mr Grenville's name for Brewer and walked to the constable's. Citations for the clergy to appear before the bishop, Doctor Tremayne and Henry Crane', who was rector of Withiel, where the little Tudor house of Prior Vivian is still to be seen. 'My harvest folks wrought little or nothing, for wet weather, at home or at Dannonchapel; yet some of them took their wages.' This strikes a familiar modern note.

'23rd, bound up my oats. Much business with Jewell, that served a precept for his sheep taken in Rowtor; but no deliverance made without sureties to return his precept. 24th, *St Bartholomew*: my wife and Jane Penkivell rode to Roscarrock. Variance between Thomas Roscarrock and Humphry Nicoll: much wind wasted between them.' Dear William never wasted his breath on that sort of thing, sensible man. 'Dreamed of mine elder brother. 25th, *Fair*: cut all my wheat at Dannonchapel, which is but sorry corn. Sent to the market by William Packett. 26th, *Rain*: dined at Roscarrock, whereat two Bevils' wives; talked with Hugh Roscarrock for the sheep taken at Rowtor. Thomas Roscarrock wasted wind against Humphry Nicoll.

27th, began to carry corn. 28th, carried corn; some came from Dannonchapel. Reported that William Courtenay was dead. 29th, Calmady and his wife came to me, on wain to Mr Butshed's to help in his corn. 30th, made my oats up; cut all my beans and peas. 31st, rode to Bodmin to buy necessaries. The sickness stayed there'—i.e. plague.

We observe that August was apt to be a wet month in Cornwall, then as today.

The next three days were fair. 1 September, 'inned all my corn at home. Matthew came home. 2nd, rode to the nale [ale-house] at Padstow. 3rd, inned my corn from Dannon-chapel. 4th, took my journey towards Sir John Gilbert's and Berry [Pomeroy]; lay at Port Eliot.' The Gilberts lived at Greenway on the Dart and Compton Castle near Torquay; Berry Pomeroy was the fine home of the Seymours, now a ruin. 5th, 'passed Saltash, Plympton and Dittisham. Lay at Greenway, found neither Sir John Gilbert or his lady at home. It was night when I came thither. 6th, went to Adrian Gilbert's house, found him not at home; his wife used me most friendly, showed me her husband's gardens and grass-ings.' Adrian Gilbert is the most elusive of the three brothers: interested in science, medicine, and mineral affairs, he was to attend Ralegh's wife after the birth of his unknown son, which lost Ralegh the Queen's favour.[10]

7th, 'lay at Berry Lodge. Met my Lord Edward Seymour, with whom I tarried more than two days. He gave me venison. Adrian Gilbert came to me there, 8th, and lay with me.' It was regular Elizabethan habit to share a bed. Berry Lodge was the name of the Elizabethan building erected within the walls of the medieval castle. Seymour, Protector Somerset's son and Earl of Hertford, had been downgraded and sent to the Tower for his marriage with Lady Catherine Grey, of Tudor royal blood. He was now living quietly in the country, awaiting rehabilitation. 'Met Mr George Cary of Cockington [near Torquay, where much of their abbey buildings are still to be seen]. 'Came from Berry with venison and my Lord's good language.

9th, lay at Polston's. Went to Newton Ferrers, dined there with the bishop, who told me that he swore both the patron and his clerk for Egloshayle. Came to Earth. Item, the bishop told me that that our Queen went not a progress because of the Flushingers, who made no restitution of the Londoners' goods. Assizes at Exeter. 10th, *Marriages*: passed the water [i.e. the Tamar]; went to Sheviock church, where Jane Penkivell was married to John Smyth [of Tregunnick in St Germans], whereat was good cheer . . . lay at Port Eliot and all my children. Heard of 400 marks offered and fine for 32 acres land in Landrake to Robert Smyth. 11th, returned to the wedding, after that I had seen Mrs Becket at Robert Smyth's, but lay there that night. Wrote a diet and order for bathing.' The Beckets of Cartuther in Menheniot were Catholics, winkled out by Grenville in his campaign next year; Cartuther was ultimately lost to them by their obduracy.

12th, 'wrote to Adrian Gilbert for congratulating my lord of Berry, wherein I wrote of betony to be applied to his nose, and thanks to Sir John Gilbert.' Sir John was the least interesting of the Gilberts; but of Adrian John Aubrey tells us that he was 'an excellent chemist, and a great favourite of Mary, Countess of Pembroke [Philip Sidney's sister], with whom he lived and was her operator. He was a man of great parts, but the greatest buffoon in England—cared not what he said to man or woman of what quality soever. [In that like his half-brother Ralegh]. Some curious ladies of our country have rare receipts of his.'[11] These interests were what Carnsew had in common with him. 'Came home; my men were at the sand-ridge.

13th, *Rain*: at home all day. 14th, rode to Brown Willy, whereat I found a sick bullock and missed my stoned [gelded] colt there. 15th, Erisey lay here, with whom I played and won at bowls and cards. 16th, William Flamank, Roger Flamank and Anthony lay here.' This family of Boscarne near Bodmin produced Thomas Flamank, a leader in the Rebellion of 1497 against Henry VII's taxation. '17th, *Fair*: Assizes at Launceston. Thomas Roche came from Wales and brought me Sir Edward Stradling's letters.' Stradling was Carnsew's scholarly uncle, of antiquarian interests: I suspect that William got his intellectual turn of mind from that quarter. 'Gathered hops. Richard and Matthew went a-hunting.

18th, *Misting* . . . wrought that I sweat much. 19th,
Robert Horsewell's wife and son lay here and sought my
good will for the son being vicar of Egloshayle. Report
made of a schoolmaster called Rawe executed for treason at
Launceston, whereof inquire more. 20th, Thomas Roscarrock lay here from the assizes, with whom I talked for Henry
Thomas of Carnsew; caused Richard Carnsew to forbid him
the occupying of Tremough', the chief property there. '21st,
heard of seven executed and seven others had their books',
i.e. reprieved through reading their neck-verses. 'The schoolmaster judged to lose his ears, and six months' imprisonment
for repining against the sacrament. 22nd, gave Annis Wells
stibby, and myself also: wrought well with me, more with
her. Mr Thomas [Roscarrock] showed me that Lord
Mountjoy would have Charles Tredeneck and me with him
upon Monday next. Whereof I wrote to Charles Tredeneck
forthwith, who sent me letters of his mind.

23rd, *Fair*: Richard Prideaux and his wife lay at John
Nicoll's towards the marriage of Nicholas Prideaux. 24th,
rode to William Vyell's, whereat marriages were and great
feastings. Lay at Charles Tredeneck's.' Sir Nicholas Prideaux
of Soldon, Devon, was the ancestor of the Prideaux-Brunes
of beautiful Place at Padstow by his first wife. His second,
Christian Vyell of Trevorder, was a co-heiress of William
Vyell, whom we see with his wife on the elaborate slate
monument in St Breock church, where the wedding took
place. 'talked with the Receiver for Cosgarne. 25th, returned
to the wedding. Talked with William Vyell, John Carminow
and Charles Tredeneck for Francis Penkivell's commission
whereto there is silence. Came home; met my cousin Jane
Penkivell here.

26th, received Creed's letters. Read Woolton's book,
which I left with Lord Mountjoy, called *An Armour of
Proof*.' This was another work of profitless theology, though
profitable to the author, for, a canon of Exeter, it won him
the bishopric in succession to poor bishop Bradbridge. As
such he was to signalise himself by his persecution of the
Family of Love, a distinguished undoctrinal freemasonry,
precursors of the later Society of Friends. '27th, rode forth
with Charles Tredeneck, lay at Beals Mill', on their way east
to the Tamar. '28th, rode over Horse Bridge. Lay at Bere

Ferrers parsonage. 29th, Charles Tredeneck rode into Somer-
setshire. I tarried with Lord Mountjoy; slept evil; read Sir
Humphry Gilbert's book.' This was his important *Discourse*
advocating the North-West Passage to Cathay. Once more
we find this remote Cornish squire surprisingly up-to-date
in his reading, for it was published only that year. '30th,
conferred with Lord Mountjoy for Rolles, Rush and Jewell.
Had *Arbatel Magiae* of Lord Mountjoy, wherein I read.'
This was a work of Cornelius Agrippa, sceptic, occultist and
follower of hermetic nonsense. 'Lord Mountjoy told me of
Doctor Julio and how he fled into France.' Dr Julio had
been Mountjoy's aide in his mineral and alchemical exper-
iments, and then inculpated himself in some midnight
intrusion into the Swedish Lady Northampton's chamber at
Court. We see our William relishing titbits of Court gossip
from his grand friends.

'1 October, *Much Rain*: lay at Port Eliot, played and won.
Great floods. Heard that the Londoners' ships were restored
by the Prince of Orange and that Flanders was yielded wholly
to him.' Unfortunately this was not so: the war continued.
2nd, '*Tempestuous*: spoke with the sheriff who used me
contumeliously. Came home to plough at Dannonchapel.
3rd, walked about my ground; Rolles brought me letters
from Lord Mountjoy. 4th, rode to Trecarne; saw Anne sick;
spoke with my brother John. Sent to warn the court at
Carnsew. 5th, Rolles returned from Mr Arundell Trerice.
Charles Tredeneck came homeward, lay here. A great fray at
Truro between Carmynow and Killigrew'—two gentlemanly
fools at it again.

'6th, *Cold*: gathered in my quinces, which were more than
300 upon one tree. Robert Edwards brought home my colt.
7th, *Eclipse*: Francis Penkivell served me with a subpoena,
returnable *crastino Martini* [the morrow of St Martin's day,
11 November]. The moon eclipsed from nine till after one
in Aries, showing clearly. 8th, rode to Dannonchapel, saw
my ground in tilling. 9th, rode to Lostwithiel, lay there. Met
Mr Jones, Sir John Danvers' servant.' Sir John was the father
of Sir Charles and Sir Henry, friends of Southampton and
followers of Essex, who had such adventurous lives.[12]
'Reported for truth that the Prince is possessed of Flanders.
10th, order taken by Mr Coswarth and me for to content

the under-sheriff with £10; if Cosgarne discharge us not, then it is so lost already. 11th, Humphry Nicoll moved me to consent that the matter might be answered by commission between Francis Penkivell and me; whereto I disagreed.

12th, *Fair, cloudy*: my brother, J. Carnsew and Calmady broke their fast with me. I sent Richard and Langford to Penryn; to Lanherne with quinces. Andrew Cavell with me. 13th, *Great rain*: a court holden at Carnsew, where Henry [Thomas] was presented for waste, felling five trees and rooting some of them up. 14th, my brother came home. 15th, *Fair*: William Langford paid me moneys, and reckoned with me, but not thoroughly for Carnsew receipts. Thomas Roscarrock made above £1000 fines of £10 rent in Delabole manor.' The Cornish preferred the gamble of low rents and high fines on renewal, rather than the certainty of high rents and low fines. The slate quarries of Delabole made this manor particularly valuable. 16th, 'missed Mr Basset at Roscarrock. 17th, *Rain*: at Roscarrock met Mr Basset, Mr Grenville, Mr Monk and Mr Alexander Arundell.' He was a Protestant Arundell of Ley, cousin of Grenville's; the Lanherne Arundells, Catholics, held themselves aloof, and Grenville was to fix them next year. The gentlemen rode off together; Giles Creed to Fowey.

18th, 'my brother Carnsew, William Langford and many others with me at dinner. All my sheep delivered to Chapman, which I had sold him. 19th, Lord Mountjoy's letters for Matthew. Rode to the haven [Port Isaac]. 20th, *Wind*: Matthew departed towards Lord Mountjoy with weeping tears. The wind south-east. 21st, *Windy*: Flamank, John Barrett [of Tregarden], Stitson, their wives dined with me. 22nd, Margaret Inch [of Trewigget] married to Thomas Morland's son. 23rd, *Cold, dry*: had workmen, carpenters, etc to make a planching [ceiling] in my stable. Devised medicine for Richard's toothache. 24th, *Rain*: Mr Butshed, my brother John Carnsew, Calmady here with me at dinner; Ralf Callerd also with me. Doleful Chapman with me for my heriots. My brother took on him to answer Jewell in London for his precept matters. 25th, *Tempestuous*: made up the planching in my stable. My dream of Winchester's box strange. 26th, ended my tilling of wheat. 27th, George Denys' son came to me for money. 28th, *Fair*: paid him £13, and £3 remained for an anticipation of his rent. 29th, *Rain morning*: Matthew Carnsew came home. Talk between two brethren, J. and William Wells, at St Kew; John Cavell, Thomas Butshed arbiters. I was there and played at tables. 30th, the Vicar Goldsmith lay here with me. Lapper sent me his roan horse, for the which I must pay him £10 the same day twelve month. Herring drawn for 2s 4d a 1000. 31st, sent Palmer to Bodmin; Magor to the herrings, had but ½ a thousand. Read on Marcilius Ficinus *de triplici vita: lectum dignissime,*' (most worthy the reading). This again bespeaks Carnsew's interests of mind, for this work of the Renaissance Platonist deals with medicine and astrology.

1 November, All Saints day, '*Stormy*: communicated, and at great Communion at church talked with Mr Butshed of the communion plate to be more commodiously made.' This seems to have been put into effect, since the chalice cover was adapted for a paten, and a new communion cup purchased about this time. '2nd, wrote to John Kenall for a horse for Matthew, but none came. 3rd, Kenall dined with me and would have William ride to Oxford with. Men hanged a new gate at the high gate. Much troubled by phlegm eating an egg pie. Read Haddon's Answer to Osorius added by Foxe.' Osorio was the Portuguese bishop of Faro who attacked the Elizabethan religious settlement and controverted Haddon. Essex' reply to this later was to carry off the bishop's library on returning from Cadiz, and present the books to the Bodleian at Oxford. '4th, *Fair, dark*: John Kenall with me for to have William go to Oxford, and lent me a nag; promised to write his letters for placing of him. Antwerp burned and spoiled.

5th, *North winds*: a bottle of wine sent me to have my censure [opinion] when time is to go to sea, by Soere of Padstow. 6th, went to the haven, bought fish there, 35 hakes for 11s 4d. 7th, *Close cold*: Matthew and William went away towards Oxford. 8th, *Tempestuous*: at home walking about my ground. Read upon Marcilius Ficinus and Frith', i.e. the Protestant martyr. For the next week he notes '*Snow* and *Frost*: 9th, not much about for cold. 10th, rode to Botusfleming [near Saltash], came thither in the night. 11th, Joan Wills married to Kemp. 12th, lay at St Germans, John Eliot sick. 13th, lay at Glyn; Nicholas Glyn demanded of me 26s 8d for arrearages in Trecarne rent. Sir Richard Grenville buyeth the manor of Stratton of Mr Danvers.' Grenville had been knighted in October, at Windsor.

'14th, came home; Jane Penkivell sealed a licence to work tin at Hernest [in Stithians]. 15th, rode to Port Isaac, Martin Davy with me and Jacob. Read on the Acts of the Council of Basel, that the Church is greater than the Pope. 16th, rode to Dannonchapel; there saw 15 kine, 5 calves, 8 steers, a mare, and 6 colts but not all of an age. 17th, Queen Elizabeth hath reigned full 18 years, God preserve her. Grieved in my tongue synantly [apparently] which were . . . by diet. *Inedia* [fasting]. 18th, *Clear, fair*: Nicholas Rush brought me stibby, found at Pendogget last week.' Antimony occurs in those parts, later to be mined at Portquin. '19th, dined at John Thom's in Trevisquite, whereat I ate something not answerable to my complexion. 20th, had a lask [diarrhoea], and slept evil, molested with a lask. 21st, *Rain*: heard that Creed should have St Minver benefice. Ralph Callerd came hither and offered it to my wife for him. Dined at Roscarrock.

22nd, *Fair*: William Langford rode west with my letters to George Denys for money. I talked with Ralph Callerd, who showed me forth his resignation and bills of debt, and promised to prefer Creed with Mr Treffry's letters to Henry Killigrew for the benefice of Minver, so as I would give my word that Webber should be restored to his money: which I did.' Killigrew, being Burghley's brother-in-law, could put in a word at Court. '23rd, *Stormy*: set the berries in the higher hedge and the garden behind the stable. 24th, at home did little, but talked with Callerd for the benefice of Minver. Creed rode to Bodmin, brought me home news of the plague in William Flamank's house. 25th, at Barrett's feast, met T. Roscarrock, his mother and one of his brethren, Nicholas Roscarrock. 26th, at Thomas's marriage at Amble. Creed rode towards London for a benefice and Matthew Webber with my letters. 27th, dined at our Vicar's at William Goldsmith's marriage, whereat I met Treglygh and played with him all night: lost £3. 28th, *Fair*: dined at vicarage. Came home, saw my calves, and masons at work on my new stile at the high gate. Heard of much wreck.

29th, *Stormy*: met Twigges, Mr Arundell's man, who told

me of Sir Arthur Basset coming to Trerice, and of Mrs Arundell's delivery on 22 of this month.' The child was the son
and heir, only three at his father's death three years
later—and was to become celebrated for holding Pendennis
Castle in a five-months' siege at the end of the Civil War.
The war however impoverished the Trerice Arundells, as it
did many Cornish families. '30th, Mr Basset lay at Roscarrock. Read upon Marcilius Ficinus and *de usu Astrologicae*
by Volfius.' This book, by Jerome Wolfe, had been published
in 1558. Carnsew's interest in astrology was characteristic of
the time—far more common than an interest, say, in poetry
or pure literature. 'This month Antwerp was sacked and
burnt by the Spaniards. Much shipwrecks, viz. at St Ies
[the original name of St Ives, the intrusive 'v' coming from
Huntingdonshire] and others at St Merryn, with wine:
Frenchmen. Three at Widemouth, hulks; one at Treledrock,
a Frenchman from Guinea: all between the 23 and 26 this
November.

1 December, *Stormy*: some of my house blown away. 2nd,
dined at vicarage, where I read of the sinking of Temar
[Temesvar] in Hungary. 3rd, about my masons at home;
rode to Trecarne, met my brother Carnsew.' The next four
days were '*Fair, frosty*: 4th, at home all day, talked of the
burning of Antwerp. 5th, J. Kernick paid me 40s in full
contentation of £4 for his fine, and Glanfield paid me 47s in
anticipation for his rent. Wrote for William Baldwin. A new
stile made up at the gate. 6th, up in the morning, sent to the
Fair, reckoned with my servants, paid them wages; and so
to bed again, when I left but 2s 6d in my purse. 7th, had a
shepherd to overlook my sheep. 8th, rode to Dannonchapel;
met Nicholas Dagge with whom I promised to meet on
Tuesday at Pendogget, to view the place where stibby was
found.'

9th, '*Thawed without rain, dry weather*' for the next week:
'at church, inquired for our constable Dagge being evil at
ease. 10th, rode to Tregellist; talked with Levett May and
young May's wife. Rode to Colquite. Made William Baldwin
a suppository of soup, whereby he had a stool. 11th, dined
at Mr Butshed's; played there, came home after supper. 12th,
rode to Penheale.' This historic house, much beautified by
the next generation, remains to us, exemplarily cared for in

our day. The estate belonged to the improvident Earl of
Huntingdon, and was bought by the ambitious Grenvilles.
'Met Mr Edgcumbe there'—this was Piers Edgcumbe,
Carnsew's partner in mining enterprise—'with whom I
charged Mr Richard Grenville for the sheriff-wick of
Cornwall. Mr George Grenville was sworn commissioner of
the peace. Obtained the bailiwick for Richard Archer [of St
Kew. A bailiff was the sheriff's officer.] Read news of France
and Flanders.

13th, walked abroad at home, saw fagots in the fentongo
[the close with a spring]. John Nance's son was buried in
Oxford. 14th, John Teague of St Mabyn came to move me
for marriages for young Hill. But secretly I must write to
Mr Grenville for a bailiwick for him. 15th, walked abroad
at home. 16th, letters from Oxford [i.e. from Matthew and
William, then at Broadgates Hall]. 17th, *Misty*: wrote to Mr
Sheriff for a bailiwick for Teague. Set trees. 18th, rode to
Port Isaac, bought a little fish there; met Humphry Nicoll
as I rode out. 19th, walked about my ground. Dreamed of
Creed's coming home and how he had not the benefice of St
Minver but was promised to have it shortly. 20th, walked
about my ground. Giles Creed came home with letters patent
for St Minver, and Ralph Callerd with him. Diseased with
eating bread and broth. 20th, *Rain, misty*: read the destruction of Antwerp and other occurrents. Ralph Callerd rode
away and promised to come again at night.

22nd, bishop at Bodmin. Received of William Glyn £10
on mine obligation with Trecarne rent, which was ¼ unpaid.
Obtained Ford's letters for Giles Creed to the bishop. Talked
with Robin the Frenchman for his naughtiness. 23rd at
Trefreak [in St Endellion] was delivered me by Calmady a
subpoena against Francis Penkivell to receive, and a
commission to take mine answer. Dined at Trefreak. Agreed
not with R. Callerd, who would now have Sandys to answer
Webbe at a day, whereat he was contented with my promise
there. 24th, home afore noon; afternoon went to the church,
whereat I spoke with Ralph Callerd for Minver. 25th,
communicated. Read on the book of Calvin's Epistles, specially that written to the Duke of Somerset.' This was Calvin's
impertinent Advice on how things should be ordered in the
Church of England. '26th, tarried at home. All day read

Calvin's Life and the conflicts he had with many, and
Servetus.' Everybody was out of step except the egregious
Calvin; he had Servetus—an original mind, who suggested
the pulmonary circulation of the blood—burned outside
Geneva to publicise his own theological orthodoxy. The
Catholics would equally have burned him if they could have
got him into their hands.

27th, 'nothing worth remembering; at home all day. 28th,
rode to Roscarrock, played there and won. Gave Francis
Penkivell a subpoena to rejoin. 29th, at home all day; played
at cards with Christopher Hockin; wrote to George Grenville
for Sloggett. 30th, Ralph Callerd communed with me for
Creed, and used no small policy. Sloggett brought his
answer. 31st, planted pear trees, and wrote to Anstis and
Bligh the under-sheriff. Read upon Calvin's Epistles, *precipue*
[chiefly] his life.'

'1 January 1577, at home all day, the worse for play. 2nd,
Wind north: walked abroad; many guests came to me. 3rd,
played with J. Bath and George Langford at a little game,
lost £4 3s . . .d. 4th, continued playing all night and felt
myself not much the worse for it. 5th, *Wet*: played at cent
with Thomas Nicoll and lost at evenhand. 6th, many folks
with me: George Grenville, Richard Carew [of Antony];
Richard Champernowne there by chance', from Modbury in
Devon. Thus, mainly at home, with much hospitality and
card play, Carnsew passed the Christmas holidays, which
extended then from Christmas eve to Twelfth night.

7th, 'offered my horse upon certain conditions to Mr
Carew. William Creed's letter came to me for his sealing in
the agreement. 8th, *Sharp rain*: Ralph Callerd with me, Jane
Glyn and others with Calway. 9th, my wife lay at Roscarrock; came home. 10th, began to make up mine answer to
Francis Penkivell—11th, which I ended this day with mine
own hand. 12th, rode to Trevorder, where I was sworn on
mine answer, which was sealed and delivered to William
Vyell for Francis Yarman. 13th, heard of Robert Becket's
answer to the bishop of London'—a preliminary rumble of
the wrath to come for Cornish Catholics, and especially for
Robert Becket, an obstinate man. 'Dined at Tremeer', in St
Tudy, with the Lowers, an interesting family. '14th, *Much*

rain: Harvey with me, and Patchcott—wrote for Patchcott. 15th, at home, walked about my ground.

16th, rode to Tredeneck's; met with Bevil there; played with him, won 8d; lay there. 17th, Mr Arundell Tolverne [i.e. of Tolverne], Thomas Lower, George Lower at Charles Tredeneck's. He told me of Francis Penkivell's behaviour before the Commission. Came home; Mr Dynham with me. 18th, walked about my ground. Mr Sheriff [Grenville] with me, who rode to William Vyell's to make a marriage for George Grenville with Jill Vyell.' This was a promising match, for Vyell's six daughters were co-heiresses to his property. '19th, rode to Camelford with the Sheriff; met George Grenville there. The Queen's or Council's letters we considered there. Many rode to Trevorder. John Langford with me. 20th, *Afternoon mist*: many people dined with me. 21st, *Fair*: at Trevorder met Mr Arundell Trerice, Mr Carew, George Grenville who promised to marry Gill Vyell. Carew gave me his bill for £100.[13] William Vyell and I took widow Glyn's answer. Roche began to plough in the Fentongo. Came home; met Roche, who told me evil news of Cosgarne. 22nd, John Langford rode away westward. Young Cosgarne lay here. Roche agreed with the other brother for £13 5s 8d to be paid at days . . . 24th, overlooked my workmen who delved in the Fentongo mead.

25th, *Fair, windy*: rode to Trecarne; met Morris Hill there, who lay here . . . 26th, young Hill rode away early in the morning.' This young man was of Heligan in St Mabyn: little could they have foreseen that it would be his wife Margaret, John Carnsew's daughter at Trecarne, who would become the ultimate beneficiary of Carnsew's estate. '27th, tarried at home; wrote my letters to Matthew Carnsew and William Carnsew, and to Lord Mountjoy. Ploughed up the Fentongo. 28th, rode in the morning to Trecarne, delivered my books to Carnsew my brother's letters. Met young Hill there and Calmady, J. Carew. 29th sent to Ralph Michell by Roche . . . Many strangers with me and Mr Coswarth, the Receiver [of the Duchy of Cornwall]. 30th, sent to Padstow for peason [peas and beans]. 31st, husbanded [tilled or dressed] my meadow in the Fentongo.

1 February, at home and church. 2nd, at Roscarrock. 3rd, came home. Played and ate there, *nihil aliud* [nothing else];

saw and talked to Thomas Roscarrock for Francis Penkivell. 4th, *Fair*: at home, did little or nothing. 5th and 6th, *Fair*: Ralph Michell's wife and son with Tubb's wife with me; talked with Ralph Michell for marriages, which he took well at worth. 7th, *Misting*. 8th, about my hedge in the Whitstone park. 9th, mostly within doors. 10th, at home all day. 11th, this day about my ground; my wife caused beans to be set. 12th, *Great winds*: rode to Tintagel: met young Hender and Jane Vyell.' The Henders of Boscastle were keepers of Tintagel Castle. 'Mr Basset with me homewards.

13th, *Fair*: talked to Richard Cock for our vicar's duty of the tithe wood in Tretawne. My men at plough. Talked with Landry for the alders. 14th, all day within. A strange dream. Mr Jones came hither, communed with him for Trenant, wherein he offered me friendship', i.e. a farm in St Minver which Carnsew had his eye on. 15th, 'Richard and he rode to Whitstone. Mr Butshed came to me. 16th, Richard and Jones rode to Lanherne. Jones promised me friendship for Trenant. I sent to Padstow for him. 17th, Reynold came home and told me that Jones to the seas . . . carried before day . . . he had a merry wind. 18th, *Rain*: at home all day. 19th, *Fair*: and this also. 20th, went to church; talked for having away the rood loft.' We may regard this as the most disagreeable entry in the Diary. After the crisis of 1569–72 was resolved, it was evident that there would be no going back on the Protestant settlement of religion. Vestments, which some parishes and colleges had stowed away in case of a change, were sold; pre-Reformation wall-paintings whitewashed over, as by John Shakespeare over the chancel-arch in the Gild Chapel at Stratford; the rood lofts destroyed; the images of the saints had gone before. The destruction of the fair works of men's hands in deference to the nonsense they mostly think is to be deplored by all cultivated persons.

21st, 'treated between Mr Kestle and our vicar for the tithe wood in Tretawne; by the aid of Mr Tredeneck and John Barrett we made an end. Set trees in Langford's garden at Lanseague. 22nd, rode to Portquin and Port Isaac; supped at Poltreworgy'—where the Bevils lived. '23rd, saw hunters; talked with Richard and Thomas Roscarrock. 24th, met Tristram Gorges at church.' Gorges lived at Budockside near Plymouth, which was pronounced Butshed, like

Carnsew's neighbour who belonged to that family. Gorges himself was of the distinguished West Country lot that produced Arthur Gorges, poet and translator, and Sir Ferdinando Gorges, governor of Plymouth and founder of the State of Maine. Though this was Quadragesima Sunday, Carnsew 'played at bowls and won. 25th, at home about my business; set trees in William Langford's garden. 26th, And this day also. 27th, rode to Port Isaac; bought a little fish there, where of there was plenty. 28th, received letters from Francis Worthyvale and from Jones.'

And so the Diary abruptly ends. There is no knowing whether Carnsew went on with it; this is all there is left, though other papers and documents have silted up among the State Papers, including the rarity of a little diary Matthew and William kept at Oxford.[14] One gets the impression that their father rather tired of keeping his going: the entries for the last month, February 1577, are briefer and less interesting than those before.

One letter of Carnsew's from his correspondence with the Stradlings has survived, both corroborative and informative. William was writing to his uncle from Bokelly, 18 May 1582: 'of late I talked with my neighbour and kinsman, Thomas Roscarrock, that we both might have a convenient time to make a long-pretended [i.e. intended] voyage to see your St Donat's.'[15] Meanwhile, Carnsew had been pressed to write on behalf of Richard Vivian, 'otherwise—by reason of the house he was born—called Trenowth . . . He is an honest travailer in the trade of merchandise by the seas.' He had been having his ship repaired at Neath, 'which he accounted to do with less charges there than here in our county Cornwall, by reason of the good store of timber there, which is not so plentiful here.' At the end of his business Vivian had been arrested for debt and other quarrels made him, 'only to poll him and to get bribes of him to his heavy loss.'

Carnsew testified to his honesty and worth, 'naturally descended of an honest race, and that is to be cherished in our happy and prosperous estate.' He sought Sir Edward's help in seeing that justice was done,

whereby your neighbours, coming into this angle, shall be assured to find the more humanity, and yourself the sooner and longer remembered in the devout prayers of such as escape wrongful oppressing hands. I received your letters how the two stones, after much trouble of the carriers, were landed for you, which I wished had been better for you. If you lack any such or other things whatsoever lying in mine ability, command; and then see whether I fail you.

Almighty God preserve you with his continual grace and make you to enjoy for ever the joys which the Saviour of the world, Christ Jesus, hath provided for them which love and put their trust and confidence only in him.

This was no empty formula: Carnsew was evidently a man of principle and firm religious belief, and a helper of others. It is also evident that he had mineral dealings with Stradling, for the Cornish ores were carried across the Bristol Channel to Neath to be smelted.

In the State Papers there has survived a considerable amount of Carnsew's mining correspondence:[16] I do not propose to go into it, since here my concern is with the personal. It contains, however, tributes to Carnsew as a person, both to his expertise in mineral matters and to his kindliness as a man. A leading London capitalist, the well known Customer Smyth, wrote to him, 'I find that your opinion carrieth knowledge and skill with experience of the things you write of.' Smyth and his partners made Carnsew their man of trust in their mining ventures, forwarding through him the moneys they were willing to invest. This was in the 1580s. But we know from the Diary that Carnsew was already interested in mining, beginning with lead and silver at Treworthen in Perranzabuloe, and going on to tin and copper further west, at Binnerton in partnership with John St Aubyn, at Penrose and St Just. By 1584 he had some twenty-one men working at St Just, eight at Penrose, seven at St Eval, a couple at Zennor. The find of a vein of antimony at Pendoggett was corroborated, when in the nineteenth century a large mine was worked at Doyden Point on the cliffs by Portquin.

We have seen from the Diary how kindly and hospitable Carnsew was. This too is corroborated from the mining correspondence. The German mining expert employed by the company, Ulrich Frose, was rather *temperamentvoll* and liable to dejection at the difficulties he encountered from water in the works, overburden falling in, etc. Carnsew did not flinch from going down the mine and along the foul adit with him, any more than from descending the cliff at Dannonchapel into the quarry. On 2 December 1583 Ulrich writes from Perran Sands, 'your worship doth invite me to come over to you and to tarry with you until Christmas be past.' Then, 'I was very sorry to hear that your worship was so sore troubled with the stone or colic . . . it is my duty to pray for you because you are all the comfort I have of in this country.' Several times we have mention of Carnsew's disability gaining upon him. He does not seem to have allowed it to cramp his activity: we find that Customer Smyth entertained him in London, and we learn of his contemplating a journey to South Wales, where smelting the ore from Cornwall was carried on, and where he would stay with his Stradling uncle who survived him. For Carnsew was not old when he died, and was buried in his church at St Kew on 26 February 1588. He thus missed the excitements of Armada year. Carew, the young Mr Carew of the Diary, writes of him: 'a gentleman of good quality, discretion and learning, and well experienced in these mineral causes.' He cites him as having been an eye-witness of a Stannary charter which had disappeared from 'one of the church steeples within those tithings'—Blackmore: this, according to ancient tradition, was the church-tower of Luxulyan.

Carew also pays tribute to the kindly family life at Bokelly, which he knew from experience, and to the help he had received from the intelligent young William in compiling his *Survey*. Of the three sons and two daughters,

those brought up in learning and experience abroad, these in virtue and modesty at home, the fruits whereof they taste and express in a no less praiseworthy than rare-continuing concord: having (not through any constraining necessity or constraintive vow) but on a voluntary choice, made their elder brother's mansion a college of single living and kind entertaining. Among whom I may not omit the youngest brother, whose well qualified and sweet pleasing sufficiency draweth him out from this cloister to converse with and assist his friends, and to whose sounder judgment I owe the thankful acknowledgment of many corrected slippings in these my Notes. . . .

This was no less true than generous: no sign of disharmony

in the household at Bokelly. A consequence was that, though
Carnsew did his duty in helping forward the marriages of his
young neighbours, his own children were reluctant to leave
the nest. Matthew, Frances and Grace never married. William
eventually married John Arundell of Trerice's daughter,
Anne, but not until 1 December 1610 at her parish church,
along the lanes thence to Newlyn East. Richard was even
later in marrying—not until 24 September 1619—the widow
of Richard Barrett of neighbouring Tregarden. The result
was that none of them had any children: the family at Bokelly
came to an end.

We have only a few scraps of the life lived there outside
the Diary. In May 1569, before it opens, Thomas Roscarrock
was sending Carnsew £10, the balance of his bill; another
was due at Allhallow-tide. In May 1584 William is writing
to Anthony Rouse of Halton (step-father of John Pym)
affirming that he has 'just cause to praise your love to me,
which I am bound to requite', but press of business, evidently
with the mines at that time, forced him to defer a visit to
Tamarside. We find young William attending the Parliament
of 1597–8 as member for Camelford.

Richard, the heir, was not the most intelligent of William's
sons. In 1607 we find him engaged in a squabble with William
Cavell of Treharrock, who had erected larger pews than his
in St Kew church. This was a fairly common subject of
dispute, but Richard has an angry, self-justificatory note
quite unlike his father—perhaps it came from the tempera-
mental (and legal) Fitzes. Mr Cavell's erection constituted

a prejudice to me, blemish to my ancestors, disgrace to my posterity
[he had none] and to the confusion of many parishioners. I have two
brothers, one a Master of Arts twenty-four years old [he meant
standing], the other a Bachelor of Laws of sixteen, two sisters, and a
family [i.e. household] of thirty, and no seats for ten persons. These
pews would interfere with the monuments of fourteen of my ancestors.

Altogether up-state; and we can only conclude, rather
extravagant. He had been cited before the Consistory Court
at Exeter for failing to contribute to the repairs of the church
and pay his rates. This was his reply: he was rated at £15 in
the Subsidy, none higher except the J.P.s.

In 1613 Richard has a spot of trouble, financial again,

about a small payment out of the county stock to a soldier maimed in Ireland. He remonstrates against the charge, claiming that he was already £3 in advance. In 1615 William writes to his brother from St Anthony that his wife would take pains to restore the old house at Carnsew, if she can have the neighbouring close to make it worthwhile. A few years later Thomas Stephens' sister requires of him the money to pay her husband's large legacies to Oxford: £100 to the poor students of Exeter College, £100 to the Bodleian Library, £100 to St Michael's church where his son lies buried and £20 for a scaffold for scholars in the church.

Richard took some part in local affairs according to his station—at one point treasurer for the eastern division of the county, at another a commissioner to levy the fine for the Prince in 1621. Richard was knighted at Greenwich in November 1619, when under James I there was an inflation in such things. He seems to have had a house in London; for, when in 1623 a writ of outlawry for a debt of £40 was sued out against him, he is described as 'formerly of London, now of Bokelly.' Perhaps he had retired to the country to draw in his horns; he certainly lived above his means. Six years later he was dead: buried at St Kew on 13 May 1629 with his ancestors, where not one of their monuments remains: all cleared out by the Victorians.

Grace and Frances had been the first to go, the latter in May 1605; then Matthew in September 1613, William in July 1627, whose Arundell widow survived him many years, to see the ruin of the Civil War and the losses to her family, dying in 1656 when Cromwell still had two years to go.

To return to the Diary: reading it generates an affection for William Carnsew, he was such a good man; studying it is even more rewarding. For the historian, as for the poet— William Blake insists—the life is in the particular, not in the general: the historian's generalisations should arise from the particulars, not be imposed as a thesis upon them. Carnsew was an exceptionally intelligent and well educated man; though we do not know, he went probably to Oxford as his sons did—he reads Latin easily, and frequently drops into a Latin phrase. In his Diary the life of the time awakes for us; we are lucky to have a full year in which to follow his farming operations, the seasons and the agricultural sequence.

Students of climate and weather will find him useful. He was
out in the saddle almost every day, attending to business,
overseeing his workmen about the house, in the fields; on
the cliffs at Dannonchapel, or up on the Moor towards
Brown Willy and Rowtor. We watch him visiting his friends,
doing good turns for his neighbours, helping forward the
young folk, consoling the sick and old. He must have been
a familiar figure along those endearing lanes between Bokelly
and his parish church at St Kew, where his dust rests with
his people.

Notes

1. G. M. Trevelyan, *English Social History: a Survey of Six Centuries
   from Chaucer to Queen Victoria* (Longmans & Co., 1942) pp. viii–ix.
2. State Papers Supplementary: SP 46.
3. In *Journal of the Royal Institution of Cornwall* (1978).
4. *The Itinerary of John Leland*, ed. L. T. Smith, 5 Vols. (George Bell &
   Sons, 1906–10) Vol. I., p. 178.
5. She was allowed no legal defence; her memorial stands in London, up
   from St Martin-in-the-Fields.
6. We shall find Carnsew spelling this name as it was pronounced,
   Butshead.
7. His name is omitted from the records.
8. Cf. A. C. Bizley, *The Slate Figures of Cornwall*, (Mrs. A. C. Bizley,
   1965) pp. 158–61.
9. Cf. my 'Nicholas Roscarrock and the Lives of the Saints', in *Studies
   in Social History: A Tribute to G. M. Trevelyan*, ed. J. H. Plumb,
   (Longmans, Green & Co., 1955) where a portrait of Roscarrock is
   reproduced. Reprinted in paperback, in *The Little Land of Cornwall*.
10. Cf. my *Ralegh and the Throckmortons, op. cit.*, p. 161.
11. *Aubrey's Brief Lives*, ed. A. Clark, 2 Vols. (Clarendon Press, 1898)
    Vol. I, p. 262.
12. See my *Shakespeare's Southampton*, Chs. 6, 8 and 9.
13. So large a sum probably indicates a mining investment.
14. See my *Tudor Cornwall, op. cit.*, pp. 430–3.
15. *Stradling Correspondence*, ed. J. M. Traherne (1840), pp. 271–3.
16. *Ibid.*, pp. 55–9.

5

The Truth about Topcliffe

The English do not take kindly to persecutors, and Topcliffe has had a uniformly bad press; but there is always something to be said on the other side. It so happens that a copy of Girolamo Pollini's *Historia Ecclesiastica della Rivoluzion d'Inghilterra* in my possession has its margins covered with Topcliffe's comments on his Catholic opponents abroad and at home, signed at several places with his beautiful signature. Besides answering the charges in this scandalous book, he gives us a good deal of new information about these opponents of the régime, on whom he was an acknowledged expert, along with some on the circumstances of the Henrician Reformation, and a good deal on himself and his family. His marginalia give us an intimate insight into his own mind and point of view, hitherto reported on only by his enemies.

With the publication of the latest volume of State Papers Foreign[1] we can now see the serious view taken by the Elizabethan government at the publication of this book, and its diplomatic protest. On 26 October 1592 Thomas, Lord Darcy,[2] reported to Burghley that a couple of days before his coming to Florence a book had been published there 'against the Queen, her father, and her brother.'[3] It had been written by Pollini, a Dominican friar of Santa Maria Novella, who had received 'most of his instructions from Cardinal Allen, to whom the book was dedicated.' With the help of Lorenzo Guicciardini, Commissary General of the militia, Darcy had been able to stop publication and round up copies in circulation. The Queen should thank Lorenzo, for it was 'a most mischievous and spiteful libel.' The friar was much

aggrieved and appealed to Cardinal Allen, who complained
to the Spanish ambassador at Rome.

On 27 December Darcy reported that Allen had written
'very violently to require the Duke [of Tuscany] to punish
Lorenzo for being so hot in stopping the book'; he stood in
some danger of excommunication unless the Duke 'resolutely
avowed his doings, or else bribed the Inquisitor.'[4] The Queen
wrote her personal thanks to Darcy for obtaining 'the
suppression of the lewd book against her state'—Burghley
added, 'and the memory and renown of her father, King
Henry VIII', thought better of it, and then crossed it out.
She also wrote to the Duke demanding 'exemplary correction'
of the author. Florence was a friendly state; the request was
apparently complied with, the friar deprived and expelled the
country.

In her official letter to the Duke[5]—of which the draft
was much corrected by Burghley—the Queen defended her
government, her father and brother, and her mother, 'a lady
by blood of the principal noble houses of the realm, yea, of
them that were descended of the former kings of the realm'
(i.e. through the Howards), and pointed to the success and
prosperity of her government as manifesting God's blessing.

This diplomatic *démarche* did not stop the publication of
the book in Rome, where it appeared fully licensed with a
motu proprio by Clement VIII from the Quirinal in June
1594 and a long dedicatory letter to Cardinal Allen. Published
by Ruffinelli, the book came into Topcliffe's hands, a solid
quarto of 766pp. with a full index—plenty of room for his
numerous comments, and evidently he read Italian easily. He
himself wrote a modern Italian hand, with many finger-
pointers sketched to significant points, with occasionally a
gibbet beside someone whom he considered to merit it.

Before going into all this information, much of it new,
some of it as scandalous as the book he is answering, we
must place him in his historical perspective.

Richard Topcliffe was a kind of Elizabethan Inquisitor-
General. We may regard him as an opposite number to the
Inquisitor General in Spain or in Rome, though the term is
not exact; for it was not Topcliffe's business to inquire into
the faith of those he rounded up, but in their external behaviour, their defiance and breach of the laws, their danger to

the state, their 'treasons' as he frequently described them. And, though mainly concerned with those who defied the Elizabethan religious settlement—the best consensus that could be arrived at in 16th century circumstances—the government employed him in other matters too, secular affairs not concerned with religion. His main task, however, was to pursue Catholics who defied the law, refusing to attend church, sending their children abroad to be educated and trained up hostile to the settlement in England, many of them returning as seminary priests or Jesuits to undermine or overthrow it.

We must recognise that uniformity in general was, in the 16th-century, the only way to keep order in the nursery. In this regard Northern Europe was more tolerant than Southern. In Spain and Italy the Inquisition burned out all vestige of Protestant deviation. In England a considerable Catholic minority survived; but throughout the Catholic community Topcliffe's was a name of opprobrium as a persecutor. They, understandably, hated him; he, equally, hated them: he regarded their undermining the religious settlement as dangerous to the state, their aid to Spain and Rome in time of war as treason. On the other hand, the Protestants never recognised what they owed to him. His was a most unpopular job, not without its dangers; he had a host of enemies and has always been written about by them. In consequence he has been traduced; nobody has explained his point of view or tried to estimate his personality and work fairly. It is the business of the historian to attempt both.

Consider the circumstances. The Reformation was followed by the Counter-Reformation, far more vindictive and cruel, indelibly marked by the assassination of Protestant leaders—the great William the Silent, founder of Holland (most tolerant of nations); Mary Stuart's half-brother, the Regent Murray in Scotland; Admiral Coligny in France, then both kings Henri III and Henri IV, though the first was a Catholic, and the second had become one—both murdered by religious fanatics. The age was signalised by such appalling massacres of Protestants as that of St Bartholomew in France, Alba's executions of some ten or fifteen thousand in the

Netherlands, followed by the Spanish Fury in Antwerp which killed more thousands in 1576.

Rome launched its attack on the Elizabethan settlement with its Bull of Deposition of the Queen, releasing Catholics from their allegiance—which was naturally regarded by the government as sanctifying treason—and followed up by supporting the Northern Rebellion and Mary Stuart's plots to overthrow Elizabeth. In 1580 the first Jesuit mission arrived to carry on the work. They argued that their purpose was wholly religious, but it was not *wholly* so: Father Parsons, their leader and inspiration, was indefeasibly political, doing everything he could to subvert Elizabeth's rule. It was only to be expected that the English government should defend itself and reply in kind. Even if the campaign were dominantly religious, hundreds of seminary priests and Jesuits were trained up abroad and infiltrated into the country; if they had been permitted to carry on their work unhindered, it would have produced grave dissensions in the country and undermined order. Let the extremists on both sides, Catholics and Puritans, have their head—and there would have been civil war, as in the Netherlands and France.

The government was determined to maintain the settlement arrived at with Elizabeth I in 1559. With open war with Spain in the 1580s the struggle became more acute; the majority of Catholics within the country were loyal enough, but the scores, in the end some hundreds, of seminary priests and exiles coming in from abroad constituted a fifth-column in time of war. The government treated them as such. It needed instruments to watch their activities, gather information as to their whereabouts, their doings and supporters, to hunt them down and bring them to book. All over the country, in the Armada years, the J.P.s were instructed to keep a look-out and put the laws into execution. Richard Topcliffe became a specialist in the job: a convinced and aggressive Protestant he hated convinced and aggressive Catholics quite as much as they did him. In circumstances of war and religious conflict his was a necessary, if thankless, task; he got nothing out of it. He was a man of fierce conviction.

He has, of course, been much misrepresented, though his dedication to his job not so. He has been described as 'the rackmaster of the Tower'—which he was not; as a low-class 'monster of iniquity', which was typical abuse of him. He was, in fact, not lower-class, but an aristocrat, a member of the governing class: this was what put him on terms with the Talbot Earl of Shrewsbury, with Leicester and Burghley, and gave him the open door to the Queen. The Topcliffes were an ancient medieval family, going back to Topcliffe in the North Riding of Yorkshire. When one goes there one sees a superb 14th century brass, of probably Flemish workmanship, to Thomas Topcliffe. At some point the large estate came to the Percy Earls of Northumberland—Topcliffe was descended from them. It was his great-great-grandfather, the 1st Lord Burgh, who married a daughter and co-heiress of Sir Henry Percy. He was also descended from the Nevilles, Earls of Westmorland. Both these were Catholic families. Though proud of his descent it shamed him, he said, that they should have engaged in rebellion in 1569. He was connected by marriage with the Fitzherberts of Derbyshire and Staffordshire who could not be made to obey the laws, sent their sons abroad to become Jesuits, and used their wealth to support the infiltrating priests. Topcliffe had a vendetta against the Fitzherberts, and they against him. They were not without means of getting back at him and, in spite of everything, managed to hold on to their large estates of Norbury and Swynnerton. (Protestants would not have been allowed to survive, let alone retain large estates, in Spain or Italy.)

The Heralds' Visitations for Lincolnshire show the Topcliffes going back for six generations, to at least 1400, in that county, before our subject. A grandfather, John Topcliffe of Somerby, was a merchant of the Staple in the early sixteenth century.

Topcliffe gives us valuable information about himself and others, in his annotations to Pollini's book, which was based, Topcliffe tells us, on what had been written by Dr Nicholas Harpsfield, with the aid of Bishop Bonner, Sir Thomas Fitzherbert and Dr Sanders, 'who did compile together the English history which I have extant, when they together all were prisoners in the Fleet and in the Marshalsea, anno 1 and 2 Elizabeth.' Bonner and Harpsfield had recently under Mary been prime burners of Protestants, who naturally detested them. Their book was full of scurrilities against Henry VIII and Queen Anne Boleyn: it even alleged that Anne was Henry's daughter by Lady Boleyn. This, and the like, infuriated Topcliffe, whose grandfather, Lord Burgh, had been Queen Anne's Chamberlain and knew that she was innocent of the charges brought against her. Protestants regarded her execution as a frame-up—as it was.

Topcliffe writes against this passage of defamation:

> Thomas Lord Burgh, my grandfather, being Lord Chamberlain, did openly pronounce him [Henry VIII] a villain in the Court, when his Queen was sent to the Tower, and did cast down his glove among such gentlemen and noblemen as did for popery speak against her fame. And for the same he was threatened to be sent to the Tower of London— which infamy was to like effect spoken of that godly Queen Anne, as here is printed.

Then Topcliffe bursts out—one sees something of his temper: 'O rabble of traitors', and he names Harpsfield, Bonner, Sanders and Sir Thomas Fitzherbert as the compilers of the original book.

Topcliffe was an educated man, reading Italian easily, an insatiable collector of information about all these people whom he regarded as enemies of the state; and when one checks his information from other sources it is confirmed. He was indeed the grandson of Lord Burgh, whose daughter Margaret was his mother; he married a lady of family, Jane, daughter of Sir Edward Willoughby of Wollaton, which was being rebuilt into a palace at the time. His father was Robert Topcliffe of Somerby in Lincolnshire, to which the son and heir succeeded. He gives us an interesting piece of Lincolnshire information about the Pilgrimage of Grace:

> I lived at this time and divers of them were my kinsmen, and I remember their treasons were barbarous and unkind, and shame to their kindred and posterity. And for my own part, I thank Almighty God that the Lord Thomas Burgh, my grandfather, and my own father, Robert Topcliffe of Somerby, were the two only gentlemen of blood in Lincolnshire who did go and serve their sovereign, King Henry VIII, under the noble George, the Earl of Shrewsbury, against those traitorous rebels of the North, being their own kinsmen.

We see that Topcliffe had a vehement way of writing and speaking—but he was a North Countryman himself, rough

and aggressive, liable to outbursts of rudeness, always ready
to stand up for his own rights, persistent and tenacious. But
it was the regular thing for Elizabethan judges—Attorney
General Coke, for example—to bully their prisoners. Torture
was applied in cases of treason against the state; our own age
can hardly regard itself as any better when we remember
Auschwitz and Dachau and Belsen, or the atrocities of Stalin.

What is historically significant is that Topcliffe belonged
hereditarily to the Protestant party that stood by Queen
Anne Boleyn—with Catholics nothing was too bad to say
against her. This naturally recommended him to Anne
Boleyn's daughter, who would have known that her mother
had been framed. He had the *entrée* to the Queen, as we see
from an angry letter to Robert Cecil in 1601 about a libel
defaming her.[6] The old lady said that she took no notice of
such low insinuations; then, as to one clown's defaming
speeches, she suggested to Topcliffe, 'apprehend him
discreetly.' Topcliffe asked for a warrant under the Council's
seal, 'as I had in Lord Burghley's time'—then he would be
armed against this monster in the Peak. Evidently a Fitzherbert, for in his parish were a hundred persons none of whom
was known to be christened, all born since 1558, in the
Queen's reign: thus defying the laws.

Catholic landlords defended themselves by restricting
leases of their farms to Catholic tenants and, though they
belonged to the governing class, they opted out of their
duties as such; they formed little enclaves, neglecting their
parish church, which in one or two instances in East Anglia,
fell down in consequence. It was deplorable enough, and
Topcliffe considered dangerous—this particular family had
harboured numerous seminary priests. Her Majesty has
bound Topcliffe with her good opinion of his endeavours,
'in the desperate times I have lived in, who have seen six
rebellions.'

There we have the man in his letters. He felt that his
was an uphill struggle, as it was—particularly in Catholic
enclaves, or in London where seminaries and Jesuits had
many to harbour them, could go disguised, and often enough
escaped from prison, even from the Tower. Nicholas Fitzherbert of Padley, Derbyshire made himself conspicuous by
joining rich George Gilbert's group of young men, who

raised money to support Parsons and Campion on the first
Jesuit mission of 1580, which 'reconciled' so many people as
to alarm the government. This Fitzherbert, one of several
émigrés, became Secretary to Cardinal Allen in Rome, though
he was an opponent of Father Parsons there.

Another association which connected Topcliffe with Anne
Boleyn's circle was this: opposite a reference to Henry's last
Queen, Topcliffe has written, 'This lady Katherine Parr was
first wife to Edward Burgh, my uncle, son and heir of the
Lord Burgh who was Lord Chamberlain to the godly Queen
Anne, and whose virtues I have heard this lady, Katherine
Parr, commend wonderfully.' The relationship was as
Topcliffe stated; he was sixteen when she died—old enough
to have registered.

His indignation against Cardinal Allen knew no bounds,
for he had founded the first of the seminaries—a number
of others followed in Spain, Italy, France, Flanders—which
brought up hundreds of students contrary to their country's
laws and priests sent to England to subvert them. To North-
Country Topcliffe Allen was 'Carnal Allen'; he draws a neat
gibbet against his name, on which he would like to see him
suspended, for he was by any reckoning a traitor, supporting
the Spanish Armada with all his might. Topcliffe records
twice over a piece of information about him, which occurs
nowhere else. 'I have heard it reported by gentlemen of good
worship'—elsewhere he says 'a popish knight and a popish
gentleman'—'that catholic Dr William Allen, after Cardinal
at Rome, or his father, was begotten and was the bastard of
the Abbot of Dieulacres in Staffordshire, of the body of one
Nan or Bess Bradshaw, when she was the wife of one Allen;
which Allen was the bailiff of husbandry, or storer, of that
Abbot, who was godfather of his own son.'

Topcliffe was careful of his facts and scrupulous both times
to say that the Cardinal was either the son, or the son's son,
of the Abbot. But what of it? That other Cardinal, Wolsey,
had had two bastards, one an archdeacon, the other a nun.
Protestants were apt to bring up this kind of thing against
Catholics, since they preferred the state of holy matrimony
to a queasy celibacy, which they unreasonably regarded as
unnatural.

Catholics retorted, with ludicrous credulity, about Anne

Boleyn's physical deformities, that she had six fingers, etc.
Topcliffe annotates: 'This is known to be a monstrous fable',
and 'Dr Sanders was ever known to be' [a liar]. That was
true enough. Topcliffe says of the rebel earls of 1569, 'I
thank God I am descended of both the noble families of
Westmorland and Northumberland, and of the best of the
kin and gentlemen that were rebels. But I am ashamed of the
rebels who, I know, had been so particularly bound, the one
Earl for gifts, the other for his life before the Rebellion in
the North.' He asserts again that 'it is well known that Queen
Elizabeth did once give to that Earl his life for a treason.'
This may refer to Northumberland's attempt to take Mary
Queen of Scots out of the proper custody of the Deputy
Warden of the Marches without warrant, in 1568. That gave
umbrage at Court, when he was reported to Cecil as 'dangerously obstinate in religion.' Topcliffe may have had some
other information; one notes merely that Topcliffe itself was
the Earl's favourite place of residence.

Topcliffe had a number of relations among the recusants.
The Catholics said that Robert Dymoke of Scrivelsby died
in confinement, but Topcliffe glosses, 'O mighty God, what
favour did I know that he, being my cousin and countryman
[i.e. Lincolnshireman], was suffered to live most part at
liberty, I know well.' Of Thomas Mettam: 'My kinsman,
but a very disobedient man, and his wife Dr Pallin's niece,
both froward . . .', unfortunately here the margin is shaved,
but the meaning is clear: they were obstinately Catholic.

Some of Topcliffe's information is new to us—about
Campion, for instance.

Edmund Campion was a foundling and for that reason to be reputed as
filius populi, and was brought up in an hospital in the city of London.[7]
He being an excellent scholar and orator in Oxford, he disdained that
the Earl of Leicester, then Chancellor of Oxford, did esteem better of
the now Bishop of Durham, Toby Mathew, than of him. So as Edmund
Campion, being then known to be a Protestant, grew thereat a malcontent and went into Ireland. And he did write a history of the description
of Ireland . . . but after his return he did envy the fortune of others so
much that desperatio fecit Jesuitum.' (Despair made him a Jesuit.)

As for Parsons, I can prove Father Robert Parsons to be
a traitor, under and by his own hand extant, by the ancient

laws of England in force since William Conqueror's days and before.' Actually the Statute of Treason under which Campion was condemned was that of Edward III, giving aid and comfort to the enemy. Of Alexander Bryant, condemned at the same time: 'I did see him die a traitor by our temporal old laws'—Topcliffe means the political Statute, and holds rigidly to it that their offence was treasonable.

Elizabethans rejoiced at the kidnapping of Dr John Story; for this Oxford civil lawyer, chancellor to the burning Bishop Bonner, had been one of the most active persecutors of the Protestants under Mary, Queen's proctor for the trial of Archbishop Cranmer, and had actually dared in a speech in Parliament to suggest laying the axe to the root of heresy, i.e. Princess Elizabeth. This was never forgiven him. Though he took the oath against foreign, i.e. papal, jurisdiction at her accession, he opposed Elizabeth's religious settlement in Parliament. Arrested in 1563, he escaped to Flanders, where he had some part in establishing the Inquisition in Antwerp. The persecuting Alba gave him a commission to search ships entering harbour for English books. One July day in 1570, when he was below on an English ship sniffing out heresy, the hatches were closed on him and he was conveyed back to England to answer the charges against him. It was in the middle of the chief crisis of Elizabeth's reign: the Northern Rebellion, the conspiracy of Mary Queen of Scots and the Duke of Norfolk, the Ridolphi Plot with the support of Rome and Alba. Dr Story was arraigned with Christopher and Francis Norton and Christopher Neville—three of them kinsmen of Topcliffe's—for inciting the Rebellion of 1569, Story through his influence with Alba. Story was hanged at Tyburn in 1571, and beatified in 1886.

Opposite this event as recounted by Pollini, Topcliffe gives us his version.

Here he beginneth to make mention of the stinking martyrs, and for the proto-martyr he setteth down Dr John Story, who in a Parliament in Queen Mary's time in an eloquent speech . . . did openly wish that the wisdom of the higher and lower House would lay the axe to the tree root of heresy, and to strike at the top and at the head of heresy, which and whom he named falsely to be the Lady Elizabeth, then prisoner in the Tower.

Topcliffe adds, 'I myself did see this [Story's] execution and did hear Dr John Story speak, a viperous traitor, at his death.' He emphasised that the Doctor was condemned as a traitor and rebel, 'as good cause by law and nature was proved. He hanged upon new-fashioned gallows like his three-squared cap triangled'—the triangular gibbet provided for more expeditious hanging. The proto-martyr of the seminarists was Cuthbert Mayne, 'another viperous traitor, who did come to Trudgeon of Cornwall.' This poor seminary priest was much less to blame than the obstinate Francis Tregian who brought him in—Topcliffe spells him Trudgeon, which is the correct Cornish pronunciation. Mayne's skull is still venerated at the convent of Lanherne in Cornwall. On a passage in the Italian text about the credulous Northerners venerating the blood of his kinsman, the Earl of Northumberland, Topcliffe has a gloss on his reasons for taking arms, with the crisp comment, 'and did run away like a coward.' He had indeed fled into Scotland.

Topcliffe has two informative accounts of the taking of William Carter, printer and publisher, who circulated large numbers of Catholic books damaging to the régime. He tells us that Carter was Dr Nicholas Harpsfield's boy (others say, amanuensis), 'who did bring him up with old Cawood, printer. He became skilful in the art of printing and was learned in the tongues: he did print many traitorous books, as *The Treatise of Schism*, unto which Gregory Martin[8] did subscribe his hand and name, and so did Dr Allen. . . . That written book I have under Harpsfield's or Carter's own hand extant, by the Queen's Majesty's commandment to keep.' Under this Topcliffe has subscribed his own elaborate signature. He was proud of having apprehended Carter and tracked down his secret press; among the books was Harpsfield's, of which he sold manuscript copies for £20 a copy—a large sum in those days; 'out of one of those written copies, sent to the traitor Cardinal Allen, this false and traitorous History was written. And that same original written book I did find in this William Carter's custody: which the Queen's Majesty did see and hath read of and her highness did command me to keep, which I have extant still for her Majesty's service.' Again there follows a proud signature with its fine flourishes.

Actually the passage for which Carter received a death-sentence was interpreted as an incitement to her ladies in waiting to kill the Queen: Judith was commended for killing Holofernes, and 'if our Catholic gentlewomen would follow, they might destroy Holofernes, the master heretic and amaze his retinue.'

An autobiographical passage goes back to Topcliffe's childhood at the time of the Dissolution of the monasteries. 'I myself was at this time of the age of four or five years'—this was correct, for he was born in 1532—'and I did see great abomination in an abbey to which my father did send me for refuge in this first rebellion.' This means the Pilgrimage of Grace in 1536. 'And I did assuredly hear of the heads and bodies of dead children that were found buried in the floors of chambers of nuns.' This was regular Protestant scandal, though there was nothing improbable in it, human nature being what it is:

> And I can prove that there was great abomination used in those monasteries, as that a vicar of a town called Stixwould in Lincolnshire did get three nuns with child in a short time; for the which offences both those three nuns and that vicar were punished. As the Chapter books at the suppression of three abbeys did make mention, and I myself had seen that vicar of Stixwould, who could not deny it to be true.

At Stixwould nothing of the priory remains today, except some of the coffin lids of the nuns.

Such were Topcliffe's comments on this ultramontane book, compiled from opposition sources, then put into Italian and published at Rome to slander England and the English Reformation. Topcliffe, who was easily roused to anger, was infuriated by its libels and lies. It provides an authentic and vivid revelation of the temper of the time on both sides. They were at war, and his was a war mentality.

It is not known if Topcliffe was a Cambridge man, though his aggressive Protestantism was in keeping.[9] Cambridge was more Protestant (and even Puritan) than Oxford, while most of the eminent Catholics who attracted his powder and shot so far were Oxford men. Like so many sons of the country gentry he went up to an inn of court—Gray's Inn, the leading one at the time, with its Protestant inflexion, nurse of the

Cecils and Bacons. He was always close to Lord Burghley, both Lincolnshire men, engaged in the same battle to preserve and defend the Elizabethan settlement. An early notice of their relations is a bond between the two, in September 1573, for the payment of £50.[10] This was not a transaction of any importance, and Topcliffe does not seem to have got anything in the way of grants—as regular government servants did. His was an irregular job, which he performed out of an overriding sense of duty; as the war with Spain approached he became more and more obsessed with it, spurred on by the sense of danger.

Topcliffe first comes to notice in the crisis of the Northern Rebellion of 1569, in which he served against the rebels, as his father and grandfather had done before. He made suit for the lands of old Richard Norton, a foremost figure in it— and a kinsman.[11] He did not get them. Indeed he spent himself on government service and impoverished his estate, so that his son and heir, Charles, did not succeed him there— he was in and out of prison for debt, and the Topcliffes came to an end at Somerby.

Richard Topcliffe, however, enjoyed the personal confidence of the great, for the Queen sent him with a message to Leicester in January 1570. Leicester writes back to her from Kenilworth: 'your old eyes [her name for him, as Burghley was her 'Spirit'] are in your old ill lodging here, very well and much the better for the great comfort I have lately received by Mr Topcliffe of your healthful estate.'[12] Topcliffe had come to Leicester's brother Warwick at the crisis, 'with thirty horse and men, all well appointed at his own charge and so continued all the time, without either requiring or receiving wages for himself or them.' This must have cost him a large sum—just the way to impoverish one's estate, and quite unlike average Elizabethans, who regularly clamoured for more than they gave in service. This was not wise of him—but Richard Topcliffe was not an average Elizabethan.

He served, as M.P. for Beverley,[13] in the aggressively Prot- estant Parliament of 1572, which brought the great crisis of the reign to an end with the attainder of Norfolk and wished to bring Mary Stuart to book too. No doubt this was Topcliffe's view, for one of his marginal comments à propos of the eventually executed Mary was, 'Queen Elizabeth did defend her overlong.' In the Parliaments of 1584 and 1586 he sat for Old Sarum. Already in 1573 he is officially described as the Queen's servant, when his house was burgled.[14]

The next notices of him show him on friendly terms with those grandees, the Earls of Shrewsbury and Rutland. Friendship with Shrewsbury was hereditary, for Topcliffe's father and grandfather had served against the Pilgrimage of Grace under the Earl's father. On his way homeward from attending on Shrewsbury at Kenilworth, Topcliffe sent news of the Queen's progress and enthusiastic reception in East Anglia.[15] Unfortunately she had been ill-advised to honour with her presence the Rookwoods at Euston. These were leading Catholics, and her stay under that roof had given offence in an overwhelmingly Protestant area. While there, search had been made and an image of our Lady found hidden in a hayrick. Elizabeth had commanded it to the fire.

It is a pity aesthetically that images and sculpture should have suffered such losses, for being perhaps mistakenly venerated. Elizabeth herself had not wanted the roods taken down in the churches, but she must have been irritated with the Rookwoods (in the next generation they were involved in Gunpowder Plot). Such fanatics were irrepressible, though Topcliffe—a fanatic on the other side—did his best to repress them. He was often frustrated or defeated, and this maddened him. The Queen had told him, evidently on the progress, of 'sundry lewd Popish beasts'—his language, not hers—resorting to Buxton. There were more opponents of her policy in the North: she trusted that Shrewsbury would keep an eye on them. He did.

This was in the summer of 1578. Next February Topcliffe was writing from the house of Gilbert Talbot, Shrewsbury's son and heir, commending the work of Mr Clarentius in the roof of the chamber beside the gallery—evidently a decorative plasterer. Topcliffe considered it to 'exceed in rareness and beauty'—so he evidently had some aesthetic appreciation, provided the objects were not popish.[16] Most of these long letters report news to Shrewsbury, detained in the northern Midlands by his duty to watch over Mary Queen of Scots. In March 1580 Topcliffe was sending him the news from

Portugal—critical for England, for Philip was going to take over Portugal with its ocean-going navy, which would enable him to form his Armada against the heretic country. Topcliffe had got his news from Dr Lopez, 'now chief physician to my Lord Leicester, a very honest person and zealous.'[17] After Leicester's death Lopez became Elizabeth's physician; Essex ran him to death as an intelligence agent.

Topcliffe sympathised with Shrewsbury in the prolonged struggle he had with his tough tenants of Glossopdale: 'your bad tenants of Glossop want coals to their irons.'[18] The Queen's sympathies were with the poorer classes, and she did not like lords being on bad terms with their tenantry. We see that Topcliffe was in favour of reducing them to order, hot coals for them no less than for other recalcitrants. Later on we find him encouraging Shrewsbury's drive against the recusants in Derbyshire, where a good many Catholics flourished owing to the open stand of leading families like the Fitzherberts. Topcliffe could not reduce them to order, and this made him furious with frustration. Shrewsbury found two seminary priests residing in Sir Thomas Fitzherbert's house at Padley, Topcliffe's kinsman, which made him all the more angry.

On a more sociable note, we find him writing to his neighbours, the Rutlands, for a buck from Sherwood Forest, or sending them news of Lincolnshire folk.

In 1580 the Jesuit campaign began, with Parsons and Campion in the country and at work in spite of all the government's efforts. One must remember how inefficient government was—no police or standing army; it was difficult to provide surveillance for a country so much larger in those days, when communications inland were by horse, the country more varied with forest, moorland and waste. Places, houses were more remote; people could be hidden, especially in London. The houses of ambassadors and peers were not open to search, and were honeycombed with hiding places.

Catholic peers were not interfered with for their religion, provided it did not lead them into treasonable activities, as with several it did—St Philip Howard, Earl of Arundel, for instance. Many persons were crypto-Catholics, who conformed outwardly, while their womenfolk were recalcitrant and maintained priests. The government needed a dedi-

cated agent in its service; Topcliffe dedicated himself to it,
and from the 1580s came into his own. He was often met
with invincible resistance. Here is a report on the Fortescues,
close relations of Sir John Fortescue who grew rich as Chancellor of the Exchequer. 'Great celerity must be used in
search of John Fortescue's house, there be many places of
secret conveyance in it. All secret passages towards the water
must be looked to. Fortescue has many provisions, upon
many warnings given to him and Sir John Fortescue by
Topcliffe and others.'[19]

All to no avail. When examined, Mrs Fortescue stoutly
held to it that she had been a recusant since her infancy, 'and
so purposeth to continue.' Her daughter Catherine, aged
sixteen, 'never came to church, neither intendeth to come to
church; she will do as her father and mother do and, though
her father and mother should go to church, yet she will not,
for she hath been otherwise brought up.' Daughter Elizabeth,
aged fourteen, 'never came to church, neither intendeth to
come. If the Romish religion should come, she knoweth not
whether she would go to church or no.' What was to be done
with such people? One knows what would have happened to
recalcitrants in Spain: they would have been burned alive. The
English government was more civilised and more patient. In
a generation or so the Fortescues came to church—so what
had been the point of refusing, after all?

Then there was the nonsense about exorcism. The
infiltrating priests had a ploy that they could exorcise evil
spirits, and this they used to convert the credulous, especially
women. Samuel Harsnet exposed several such cases in his
book, *A Declaration of egregious Popish Impostures*, from
which Shakespeare took the names of the spirits in *King
Lear*.[20] Topcliffe pursued a convert called Robert Barnes,
who had written out a manuscript on this nonsense, and was
made to confess: 'I, being newly a Catholic, wrote a copy
thereof at the request of a friend and, utterly misliking
thereof, never kept any copy for myself, neither was I at
the exorcism.'[21] Nevertheless, such credulity was a means to
conversion—Topcliffe could never catch up with it, try as
hard as he could.

Often there were escapes. In January 1599 Bishop
Bancroft, Thomas Gerrard, Richard Martin and Topcliffe—

all very respectable persons—had to examine Robert
Wiseman, of the family that held on and on until they produced the Victorian Cardinal Wiseman.[22] The Elizabethan gent
had been concerned in the escape of the seminary priests,
Lister and Fletcher, out of the Marshalsea. In June that same
year Father Watson escaped, when his man left him alone in
a garden; 'some of his keeper's servants were not so true to
their master as they ought to be, for within this fortnight
Dexter also escaped.' So Father Watson lived on to fabricate
the Bye Plot against James I in 1603. Actually the Jesuits
informed against him for, as a secular priest, he was their
opponent. Hanged at Winchester, he was thought to be half-
crazy anyway.

A sensational escape was that of the Jesuit, Father Gerard,
from the Tower in 1597—he was the Jesuit who tipped the
government off about Father Watson. While in the Tower a
friendly keeper supplied him with a rope along which Gerard
swarmed across the Tower moat. Father Gerard's autobiography has aroused sympathy for its account of the torture
he endured hanging up by the wrists, etc.[23] This has a topical
interest for our time, which has witnessed far worse tortures
in Germany and Russia, everywhere in Europe in the course
of resistance to the Germans, and of course all over the
uncivilised globe. But this is four hundred years after the
benighted Elizabethans.

It was regrettable enough for the Elizabethans to have to
inflict torture against the obdurate—even so, the permission
of the Privy Council had to be obtained. Nevertheless Father
Gerard was able to continue his underground work for
several years, until the Gunpowder Plot forced him to leave
the country. He survived to a good old age, rector of the
seminary at Louvain, then at Liège, and ultimately of the
English College at Rome, where he died well on in Charles
I's reign, in 1637.

Topcliffe first reports on him as a young man of nineteen,
when he and Richard Blount left the country without licence
in 1583.[24] Blount belonged to the enduringly Catholic
family—it is pronounced and is the same name as Blunt—that
produced an Essex conspirator in Sir Christopher Blount, and
he converted Sir John Davies to Catholicism as well as to
conspiracy. Gerard became a Jesuit at Rome in Armada year

1588, and then joined the Jesuit mission in England. At such a time, in these war years, they needed a Topcliffe to keep an eye on them. Priests were infiltrated into the prisons to make converts—Ben Jonson was converted by a priest while in prison and remained a Catholic for a decade. A considerable number of gentlemen of leading families were brought over by the proselytisers at this very time, the war with Spain impending. The government brought in severer penalties for refusing to attend church, for receiving and maintaining seminarists and Jesuits, for saying and hearing mass, being reconciled to Rome, sending children abroad to be educated against the laws of the country, etc. All these activities were reported on by Topcliffe and receive vivid illustration in his correspondence.

In 1582 he received information about priests saying mass in the Fleet, where the obstinate Francis Tregian was confined: his unecumenical stand ruined that Cornish family. Topcliffe had good sources of information, a regular one being Benjamin Beard alias Tichborne, a Catholic who regularly betrayed his co-religionists. Masses were being said in the Fleet before Lord Vaux, Sir Thomas Tresham and the Tregians, who lived in some comfort there; masses too at Lady Vaux's at St Mary Overy's, i.e. in Southwark.[25] The Vauxes and the Treshams were leading Northamptonshire families; their recusancy meant their abstention from taking their part in the government of their county. Lady Vaux of Harrowden was a very stiff-necked woman; the Treshams, whom the Jesuits had brought over in 1580, went obstinately on through imprisonment and fines into the folly of Gunpowder Plot and the ruin of their family.

Topcliffe's opinion was that the Jesuits and seminary priests were 'among the most traitorous and bloody-minded wits among the fugitives.' Elizabethans meant brains by 'wit'—not much wit in laymen like Sir Francis Englefield in Spain or the stupid Earl of Westmorland in Flanders, led by the nose by his fanatic wife. It was the priests, Topcliffe considered, who had the influence upon the discontented in England. If banished, they were good intelligencers and spies for Spain; in case of invasion, they were good guides for the enemy. What then to do with them? The conclusion was obvious: he did not need to state it. In examining the infiltrators one crucial question was put to them: in case of invasion, would they side with the enemy? Some of them even said or implied that they would—they were then for it; the sensible recanted. With refractory cases we find Topcliffe and Richard Young occasionally given warrant, 'if necessary to apply such torture as is usual for the better understanding of the truth of matters against her Majesty and the state', i.e. where treason was involved or suspected.

In most official examinations we find Topcliffe associated with important colleagues: sometimes the Attorney General or Serjeant Drewe, the bishop of London or London J.P.s like Richard Martin or, most often, Richard Young, who was a specialist in these cases. Sometimes we find him associated with Francis Bacon. In June 1587 the Privy Council appoints Topcliffe with Mr Barker to consider the points with which Jesuits and seminaries may be charged—process against them had to be in accordance with the laws—since they were 'acquainted with such persons and causes', in the prisons about London, if the prisoners 'will not yield to conformity.'[26] Some did, some would not—and the Armada was threatening. While it was in the North Sea in August 1588 Sir Owen Hopton, Lieutenant of the Tower, Mr Francis Bacon and Topcliffe had orders to bring out the recusants from the London prisons and examine them, especially to find out 'which are Jesuits or seminaries.'[27]

So Topcliffe operated under orders, along with other respected persons, though he—as a specialist in a subject which he made his own—got the odium. He does not seem to have received much in the way of thanks for his ardent service. Nor were these his only services. In 1586 an Admiralty case was submitted to the Master of Requests and Richard Topcliffe, esquire, for their opinions—he was clearly equipped with the requisite legal knowledge.

In 1597 he was concerned in the well-known affair over the play *The Isle of Dogs*, which involved Nashe, Ben Jonson, and the player Gabriel Spencer. Next year Jonson killed Spencer; but the year before, Spencer had killed a man. It was a rough age—we must remember that when estimating Topcliffe. In August the Privy Council instructed Topcliffe, Thomas Fowler and Richard Skevington, esquires, to examine the matter of the 'lewd play performed in the theatre on Bankside and those players who had been imprisoned, whereof one of them was not only an actor but a maker of part of the said play.'[28] This was Ben Jonson. Those players in prison 'whose names are known to you, Mr Topcliffe', he was to examine as to the rest 'that had part in devising of that seditious matter', what copies were given out and to whom; 'we pray you also to peruse such papers as were found in Nashe's lodgings.'

Apparently the 'seditious matter' in the play related to the Emperor of Russia and might cause trouble in foreign relations. Nashe was also thought to have satirised some nobleman. He himself claimed that he had written only the Induction and the first Act; the other four Acts 'without my consent, or the least guess of my drift or scope, by the players were supplied, which bred both their trouble and mine too.' He thereupon decamped to Yarmouth, out of the way. Ben Jonson, Gabriel Spencer and Robert Shaw were held in the Marshalsea until October; meanwhile the Council ordered Burbage's Theatre and Curtain to be plucked down and no plays to be performed in any public place that summer.

For years Topcliffe conducted a struggle with a much more powerful neighbour, Sir Christopher Wray, Lord Chief Justice, who made a large fortune out of the practice of the law. This was the man who presided at the trials of Campion and Lord Vaux; the conspirators against the Queen's life, John Somerville and William Parry; and the sanctified Philip, Earl of Arundel. Like Topcliffe, Wray was of Yorkshire descent, living in Lincolnshire; even closer kinsmen of his were involved in the Northern Rebellion, his brother and his nephew both requiring pardons. He and Topcliffe were in dispute over the lease of lands of the prebend of Corringham and Stow, which had belonged to Lincoln cathedral. This would be for the rectorial tithe of those parishes, which had been appropriated. Topcliffe put in his claim in a petition to the Queen in 1584, and this was referred to the Privy Council.

Topcliffe engaged in a law-suit for stay of corn-threshing on the land, and wrote a brisk letter to the Lord Chief Justice for attempting to try the cause in which he was a party. Topcliffe cited his family's antiquity, 'when his lordship's grandfather served the Lord Conyers as a morrow-mass priest', i.e. a mere chantry priest.[29] It is a characteristic touch, the point of which is that the Lord Chief Justice was thought to be of illegitimate descent. Topcliffe had sixteen quarterings on his coat of arms, which Lord Burghley had depicted on his walls with those of other Lincolnshire worthies.

This did not help him in his struggle with the Lord Chief Justice, as tenacious as himself and a rich man. A relatively poor gentleman, Topcliffe was not giving up. He pressed his suit, the Privy Council was harassed, until three years later it appointed a Lincolnshire commission to investigate and arbitrate. Another three years passed; the dispute continued and the Council wrote down to the Dean of Lincoln and the Archdeacon to consult the records with regard to the impropriation of the prebend. This meant that during the Reformation one of the numerous prebends attached to the cathedral had been suppressed, and the tithes which had supported it were thrown on the market for secular investment. The question was who was the legal impropriator. In July the Council sensibly ordered that, pending a legal decision, Sir Christopher Wray was to enjoy the tithes of Corringham, Topcliffe those of Stow; elaborate provisions surrounded the compromise, but Topcliffe was not having the decision made by the Lord Chief Justice in his own court.

In September 1588 a sad case came before the Lieutenant of the Tower, Richard Young and Topcliffe. An Englishman had been taken on board Don Pedro de Valdez' ship, which Drake captured from the Armada. In these circumstances the Council gave them warrant to put the fellow on the rack to screw out of him what information they could. This Englishman turned out to be a Cornishman, Tristram Winslade, whose life had been ruined by the folly of his father as a leader of the Prayer Book Rebellion in 1549, by which he forfeited his estate in Cornwall and the son was driven into exile.

In February 1590 Winslade was set at liberty, as he had been often examined by Sir George Carew, Ralegh, Sir Richard Grenville, the Attorney General and others, and 'hath been also upon the rack to draw from him his knowledge of the intended invasion.'[30] What was found from reports of others on board the ship was that Winslade was 'brought hither against his will.' So he was discharged upon bond, and passes out of history. He led a wandering life; his name was really William Winslade—he had been the heir to charming Tregarrick near Looe. Richard Carew tells us that he led 'a walking life with his harp, to gentlemen's houses, wherethrough, and by his other active qualities, he was entitled Sir Tristram; neither wanted he (as some say) a "belle Isoult", the more aptly to resemble his pattern.'[31] Anyhow, the poor fellow survived.

In this same year Topcliffe had a small victory when one of the recusants he had committed to the Gatehouse in Westminster repented. In April 1590 a seminary priest had sent a recusant's child to be educated abroad, 'withdrawn in his young years from the loyalty and allegiance which he ought to bear to his natural prince and obedience to her Highness' laws.' The father was to repair to Richard Topcliffe, esquire, 'one of her Majesty's servants', who was to take order for the son to be educated at Hornchurch and pay £15 a year for the same—evidently a gentleman's son.[32]

This was small beer compared with the rich clan of the Fitzherberts with members of their family abroad, in Spain and Italy and Flanders, the seminaries and Jesuits they regularly maintained in their remote houses. In May 1590 Topcliffe was 'purposely sent down' to his old acquaintance, the Earl of Shrewsbury; they were to resort to Norbury to investigate Sir Thomas Fitzherbert regarding matters concerning her Majesty and the state.[33] Topcliffe was acquainted with the causes and the interrogatories the Council wished to be put; the commission was to proceed on the basis of his information. Naturally Sir Thomas had contacts with his family abroad, and naturally he was imprisoned for his defiance of the laws.

Topcliffe urged that the Queen take advantage of Fitzherbert's treasons to acquire near £1000 a year land, which should fall to the Crown, 'if she will take the benefit of her laws.' Topcliffe recited their record: there was Nicholas at Rome; then Francis a friar, George a Jesuit, and Anthony at home were all brothers to Thomas in Spain, all heirs by entail. 'I am threatened by these confederates with deadly revenge. At my solitary Somerby.' But Queen Elizabeth dragged her feet: she did not wish to ruin a leading family, merely bring them to due obedience. She never succeeded with the Fitzherberts.

They were powerful enough to hit back and heap all the odium on Topcliffe. Anthony Fitzherbert charged him with searching Norbury without warrant. Topcliffe wrote an aggrieved letter to Sir Robert Cecil that he never searched a man's house unless he had beforehand evidence to charge him directly with treason. Many would have complained to Queen or Council if he had stumbled in this, but now in his seventieth year (in 1601) and after forty-four years of service, it was only traitorous papists that wronged him. He brought up the Fitzherberts' letters 'from the dear cousin, and the brother that served the King of Spain in his fleet in the intended invasion in 1588.'³⁴ Topcliffe's blood boiled to think of it, and to find himself now sued by the Fitzherberts!

Shrewsbury hardly needed prodding: a confirmed Protestant himself he cooperated as best he could in rounding up Derbyshire Catholics. In December he died. At once Topcliffe wrote to his old acquaintance, Gilbert Talbot, congratulating him on succeeding to the seat of his noble ancestors. 'I, that was entangled by many obligations not long since unto Leicester and Warwick—never for that lucre which was the lure to many followers—now am I a free man. . . . You are a prince in two counties in the heart of England more dangerously infected than the worst of England to my knowledge.'³⁵ An earlier report on Derbyshire had mentioned priests meeting the Catholic gentry at Buxton—Constables, Dormers, the kinsmen and connexions of Lord Montagu and Lord Windsor. Topcliffe rounded up one of the Northern priests this year, one Boost—appropriately named, for he argued the extreme Catholic position: if the Pope proceeds against Queen Elizabeth as a heretic, he cannot err; nor can the Church, and Catholics must obey the Church. This man had accompanied Ballard, who had obtained the Pope's sanction for the Babington Plot against Elizabeth's life.

Above all were the Fitzherberts, with their three houses in which to stow away priests. Unfortunately Gilbert Shrewsbury had not the conviction or the energy of his father, and he was under the thumb of his wife—Bess of Hardwick's daughter—who was a Catholic convert and put

everything to risk years later by her support of Arabella
Stuart, with her claim to the throne, and her attempt to spirit
her abroad. So she too fetched up in the Tower, where
Arabella ended, under her cousin James I.

In the 1590s the products of the seminaries abroad were
coming in in greater numbers than ever; Father Parsons
expressed the belief that England would be won by the
priests. Some of them were men of distinction and learning,
like the Jesuits Campion and Parsons, Henry Walpole and
Robert Southwell. The Privy Council left it to Topcliffe to
submit regular articles upon which they were examined; if
they would not confess or give information, he was given
authority for them 'to be put to the manacles and such other
tortures in Bridewell.' These were war years, each side fought
with no holds barred; Catholics were now placed in the
appalling situation of being enemies of their country, as even
the tolerant Shakespeare called them in Sonnet 124:

> the fools of time,
> Which die for goodness, who have lived for crime.

In July 1592 the Privy Council instructed Topcliffe to
deliver the Jesuit Robert Southwell to the Tower; there was
to be no access to him except such as Topcliffe appoints as his
keeper, for they considered him 'a most lewd and dangerous
person.'[36] Southwell was an important catch. For some years
he acted as chaplain of Philip, Earl of Arundel, whose actions
and intentions at the time of the Armada were treasonable.
This Jesuit was a successful proselytiser and, gifted as a poet,
he wrote a number of prose tracts to sustain the faithful in
their resistance to the laws. He openly defended the Jesuit
doctrine of equivocation, which brought such opprobrium
upon his colleague Garnet at the time of the Gunpowder
Plot. He was in the habit of visiting the Bellamys at Uxenden
Hall near Harrow, a well-known family of recusants, one of
whose members had been executed for his part in the
Babington Plot. Of a son of that house Topcliffe had better
hopes. Old Mrs Bellamy, 'that hatched those chickens', was
incorrigible: she should be sent with her two daughters to
the Gatehouse at Westminster, 'let them feel a day or two's
imprisonment.'[37] But the son might be sent to St Katherine's,

to set a good example thereabouts. He was willing to conform, 'and will then play the part of a true man, with charity in the end, to the honour of the state.'

Topcliffe caught Southwell at old Mrs Bellamy's: 'I never did take so weighty a man, if he be rightly used.' He was the most distinguished Jesuit in the country, of much influence; this meant that he had a store of information to be extracted. He was examined some thirteen times by members of the Council; though he admitted that he was not racked, he was subjected to other tortures. Little could be got out of him. The government kept him there for some three years, until they decided to make an example of him in 1595. His hanging at Tyburn was horribly mangled; this won popular sympathy for him, as it had done for Campion—neither of whom was a politico, as Parsons was to his fingertips. The odium was placed on Topcliffe's shoulders, for he had caught Southwell. The government tempered itself to the wind by putting Topcliffe under arrest; this may be regarded as rather unfair, to make him take all the blame. He was not responsible for the decision to execute Southwell, though of course he would agree with it. He was shortly let out. In May 1595 Richard Verstegan *alias* Rowlands reported the news from England: Father Henry Walpole had been executed at York and Topcliffe released, 'so that Barabbas is freed and Christ delivered to be crucified.'

Robert Southwell was the only man of genius of them all— except for William Byrd. Nothing happened to Byrd, though he was a recusant; for he did not challenge the régime, he served it, writing his splendid music for the English liturgy as well as for the Roman rite, sensible man.

Henry Walpole had been an enemy of, and a danger to, the state: this was the distinction the government drew in the punishments it meted out. Walpole had begun with a eulogy of Campion, harmless enough; he then went to Rome to join the Jesuits, was ordained and became a chaplain in the Spanish army in Flanders in the Armada years. There he translated one of Parsons' many attacks on the régime in England and went to Spain to serve Parsons' purposes there. Parsons sent him to England in 1593; it was unlikely that the government would let off this emissary if caught—and he was immediately caught, landing at Flamborough. Topcliffe was sent up to York to examine him.

He reported to the Lord Keeper that Walpole's companions, his young brother and Edward Lingen, had both been soldiers under the traitor, Sir William Stanley, who had betrayed Deventer to the Spaniards.[38] The Lord President's chaplain, 'a very mild divine, Dr Favour,[39] prevailed with young Walpole, an amiable youth, to confess everything.' At Flamborough, they had buried over a score of letters to disloyal men and women about London and in the country. Father Walpole and Lingen would reveal nothing, though they carried messages and tokens: they must be dealt with more sharply.

Taken to the Tower, Walpole was examined by the Attorney General, Serjeant Drewe and Topcliffe, and yielded a good deal of information. There were forty young English scholars in the seminary in Seville, three in San Lucar, forty more in Valladolid, where Walpole had seconded Parsons—all in enemy territory. In Brussels he had had conference with the rebel Westmorland, and the traitor Hugh Owen. There could be no doubt about Walpole's fate under the laws; there was no delay in his case, as there was in Southwell's for years. Walpole was taken back to Yorkshire, where he had entered the country, for public trial and execution.

Verstegan, who relayed the information abroad, was a distinguished antiquary. He had gone abroad to Antwerp and thence to Paris, where he published tracts against Elizabeth's régime and was imprisoned. He made his living by circulating information among the émigrés, and sending books up and down—for Cardinal Allen, the Jesuits Parsons and Holt, Spain's agent Hugh Owen—in Flanders and in England. However, gradually the government was winning its battle against the underground. It took a long time, and a Catholic minority survived—as also did the Puritans on the other wing.

The last phase of the long and exhausting war was marked by the brilliant exploit of the capture of Cadiz in 1596, which resounded through Europe and discouraged Spain, especially with the disasters to two more Armadas, in that year and the next. No more hope of 'universal monarchy', though Spain was still to remain the first country of Europe for the next half-century.

All the bright young sparks were anxious to share in the Cadiz adventure—and the loot. Among them was Topcliffe's son and heir, Charles, who was involved with Sir Anthony Ashley in appropriating what was rightly the Queen's, to go towards the heavy expense of the expedition. On his return he was investigated along with others by Robert Cecil—Topcliffe himself desiring to see the questions to be put to his unsatisfactory son.

Charles replied like any other Elizabethan, trying to conceal as much as he could.[40] He stated that in the castle at Cadiz was found only £2450, no gold; he and Sir George Carew had delivered to Sir Arthur Savage £1700. He claimed that he had carried only iron armour to his ship, not treasure, and had given all his individual loot to the General, Essex, for love. Essex was now putting a hard construction on his doings: the treasure given to him by the Corregidor (Governor), his lady and the Seville merchants was his own by right; what belonged to the King of Spain was Queen Elizabeth's right. Five bags and a chest were carried to Sir Gelly Mèyrick's ship, no gold.

Robert Cecil got him to admit that the silver handed over by the Corregidor's wife was the Queen's due. Then, retorted Charles, how about the deal coffer with the King of Spain's arms on it, which he had sent to Sir Arthur Savage's lodgings, with not less than £550 in it? And Sir Anthony Ashley could deliver to the Queen 5 or 7000 ducats, which the Corregidor confessed he had taken out of the trunk before it was presented by his lady to Topcliffe. Sir Anthony Ashley was a royal official, a personal servant of the Queen: he tried to get away with a lot, was disgraced and sent to prison. It does not appear that Charles got into trouble, but he was made to cough up.

Evidently he was a disappointment: he had his father's vehement temper without his devotion to the state. The year before Cadiz he had been arrested in King's Bench in Westminster Hall for some outburst in court. Later on, he was in and out of prison for debt. We know that his father made no money whatever for his lifetime of service, when others made fortunes. When the old man came to die the administration of what he left was directed to the daughter Margaret, not to son Charles. And so the Topcliffes came to an end at Somerby.

Old Topcliffe remained on friendly terms with Robert Cecil, as he had been with his father. In his last years, from New Year 1602, we have a letter from Cecil expressing the complete confidence he and the Queen had in the old servant of the state. She approved of Topcliffe's warrant against some defamer of her. Cecil was overworked with Irish business, and signed himself 'Your very loving friend.'[41]

The Queen herself had no religious prejudice against Catholics who were loyal to the state; but if they were in touch with the enemies of their country, or lent themselves to their purposes, she backed her servants in cracking down on them. Personally, she was tolerant. We even find her occasionally making an exception and suspending the operation of the law for someone or other, especially for personal servants or dependents, like Lady Cornwallis.[42] The Queen remained always on good terms with the unsatisfactory Southampton's charming mother. Southampton was brought up a Catholic and was never in trouble for religion. His grandmother, Lady Montagu's, house was a constant resort of priests. When the Privy Council licensed Topcliffe to search her house for several of them, they specified 'all which persons and their several offences are best known to you, Mr Topcliffe.' The examination was to proceed 'upon such interrogatories as you, Mr Topcliffe, shall set down'; there should be due moderation in the search into Lady Montagu's houses, 'with regard to the quality of the lady.'

All had to be in accordance with the due process of the law, as we have noted Topcliffe recognising. Again, at the time of the capture of Cadiz, he had to report on eight priests in prison. One of them, however, a seminary from Parsons' Valladolid, had been captured at Flushing, and 'therefore was not in danger of death by the Statute 27 anno Elizabeth.'[43] However, he had with him Parsons' Book on the Succession with the pedigree to advance the claim of the Infanta. We know independently that Parsons swore all his priests from the Spanish seminaries to advance her claim—absurdly as the daughter of the country's greatest enemy.

Robert Cecil saw to it—after the suppression of Essex's dangerous challenge to the state—that James I succeeded to Elizabeth's throne in peace and quiet, with general acclaim. The union of the two kingdoms, which had been the aim of English policy for centuries, was achieved the best way by a Scottish Succession. When Queen Anne was travelling south in June 1603, Topcliffe was at Worksop with his old acquaintance, the Shrewsburys, to welcome her. His last letter to Cecil described her showing herself in public to the crowd, and taking up Cecil's little son in her arms, kissing him and giving him a jewel.[44] The boy then stepped forward and took out the little Princess to dance a galliard. This was the young Elizabeth, ancestress of our present royal house.

Next year, the old servant of the state, his battles over, was dead.

Notes

1. *Lists and Analysis of State Papers Foreign Series*, Vol. III, ed. R. B. Wernham, 1980.
2. This was the Protestant Lord Darcy of Chiche, not the Catholic Lord Darcy of the North.
3. *Ibid.*, No. 802.
4. *Ibid.*, No. 813.
5. No. 836.
6. *Salisbury Mss, Hist. Mss. Com.* XI. sig-20.
7. Actually, Christ's Hospital.
8. Principal translator of the Douai version of the Bible.
9. J. A. Venn, *Alumni Cantabrigienses*, makes clear that the Richard Topcliffe of Magdalene College, 1565–9,—wrongly identified by Cooper and others—was not our man. Indeed the dates make that clear.
10. *Cal. S. P. Dom., 1547–1580*, 467.
11. *Ibid.*, 400.
12. *Cal. S. P. Dom., Addenda, 1566–79*, 199.
13. *Return of M.P.s*, Pt.1, 412, 416, 420.
14. *Acts of the Privy Council, 1571–1575*, 213.
15. E. Lodge, *Illustrations of British History, Biography and Manners in the Reigns of Henry VIII, Edward VI, Mary, Elizabeth and James I* 3 Vols. (G. Nicol, 1791), Vol. II, p. 119 ff.
16. *Ibid.*, p. 143.
17. *Ibid.*, p. 164.
18. *Cal. Shrewsbury and Talbot Papers, Hist. Mss. Com.*, 108, 146.
19. *Salisbury Mss.*, Vol. VIII, pp. 74–5.

20. Cf. my *The Elizabethan Renaissance. The Life of the Society*, (Macmillan, 1971) pp. 264–72.
21. *Salisbury Mss.*, VIII, 273–4.
22. *Salisbury MSS.*, IX, 9.
23. John Gerard, *The Autobiography of an Elizabethan*. Trans. Philip Caraman. Introduction by Graham Greene, (Longmans, Green, 1951).
24. This corrects the date given in *Dictionary of National Biography*.
25. *Cal. S. P. Dom.*, *1581–90*, 45.
26. *Acts of the Privy Council, (A.P.C.)*, 1587–88, 122.
27. *A.P.C., 1588*, 235.
28. *Ben Jonson*, ed. C. H. Herford and P. Simpson, Vol. I, pp. 217–18.
29. *Cal. S. P. Dom.*, *1581–90*, 207.
30. *A.P.C., 1589–90*, 387.
31. *Carew's Survey of Cornwall*, 1811 edn., p. 309.
32. *A.P.C., 1590*, 88.
33. *Ibid.*, 141–2.
34. *Salisbury MSS. XI. 223–4*.
35. Lodge, *op. cit.*, Vol. II, p. 428.
36. *A.P.C., 1592*, 71.
37. *Cal. S. P. Dom.*, *1591–94*, 277.
38. *Cal. S. P. Dom.*, *1591–94*, 417–18.
39. He was the excellent vicar of Halifax, well known for his good works, v. my *The England of Elizabeth: the Structure of Society* (Cardinal, 1973) pp. 431–3.
40. *Cal. S. P. Dom. 1595–97*, 279–80.
41. *Salisbury MSS*, XII. 2.
42. *Salisbury MSS*. VIII. 541.
43. *Salisbury MSS*. VI. 312.
44. *Salisbury MSS*. XV. 143.

6

The Tragic Career of Henry Cuffe

Henry Cuffe was Secretary to Elizabeth I's favourite, Essex, and something more: he was the Earl's confidential agent, wholly devoted to him whom he loved and followed to the end. He completely identified himself with Essex's interests and fell with him, was executed because of him and the part he had in advising his reckless course—though Cuffe was not in the fatal outbreak into the City on Sunday 8 February 1601, which the Queen described contemptuously as *rebellio unius diei*. Cuffe was opposed to this crazy venture, and advocated a demonstration in force against the Court at Westminster. This would have been no more successful, but it could hardly have been sillier than what Essex did do. Cuffe was hanged at Tyburn a fortnight after his 'dear lord and master' was executed. His fate was held up as an awful warning in the next generation, in Francis Osborne's popular *Advice to a Son*: 'Mingle not your interest with a great one's.'

Because of his tragic fate and the indignity of his death Cuffe was traduced and contemned. Francis Bacon, who knew him, called him 'a base fellow by birth'—which he was not—though he allowed him to be 'a great scholar'. Others described him as 'a serving-man to the Earl of Essex'—which he was not—but allowed that he was 'a great philosopher'.

What was the truth about this evidently controversial personality?

There is no doubt that he was a brilliant scholar—besides Greek (a rarity with Elizabethans) and Latin, he knew Italian—and was a distinguished thinker. He said of one of Bacon's works, the *Temporis Partum Maximum* that 'a fool could not have written it, and a wise man would not.' Cuffe's

211

own work, *The Differences of the Ages of Man's Life: toge-*
ther with the original Causes, Progress and End thereof,
reveals a mind on a level with Bacon's; if Cuffe had not
Bacon's genius he was at least in the same universe of discourse. He had his own originality, based on exceptional reading for an Elizabethan; for, though he was more concerned
to argue with, and sometimes confute, Aristotle he was
acquainted with the pre-Socratic thinkers, which few were at
the time. He was acquainted with Cicero's sceptical work on
the Nature of the Gods, though he was not a sceptic himself;
with Platonists like Marsilio Ficino, and the Renaissance
physician, Jean Fernel, so much admired by the greatest
physiologist of our own time, Sir Charles Sherrington.

Cuffe appears a deist—no mention of Christ or Christian
belief in his book, though he accepted angels as incorporeal,
intellectual spirits. He might be described more exactly as a
pantheist, for though the cosmos for him was created by and
is suffused by God, there is no suggestion of a personal God
interested in the fate of his creatures. He says that 'God is
tied to no place, being in all places to fill them with his
goodness, in no place to be circumscribed by the circumfer-
ence.' This was Marlowe's position, one year Cuffe's
junior—both highly heterodox:

> He that sits on high and never sleeps,
> Nor in one place is circumscriptible,
> But everywhere fills every continent
> With strange infusion of his sacred vigour
> . . . in endless power.

Marlowe and Cuffe were alike in some other ways too: each
had a dash of the Machiavellian about him, a restless spirit
of ambition, each was fascinated by power, driven on by
pursuit of it—one of intellectual power, the other political.
Each was something of a misfit, driven by a daimon; each
came by a sticky end.

Cuffe's book has been curiously neglected—I do not
remember a mention of it; yet it was read in its own day and
had three editions before the Civil War. It makes disquieting
reading today. For it deals with the most disturbing question
to the minds of our physicists—the title hardly gives one an
idea of the subject: the origin of the universe, had it a begin-

ning, will it end, if so how; is it eternal? What is the nature of Time? Can one imagine Time?—'for you can design us no moment or instant before which Time was not, and after which Time shall not remain.' He quotes Scaliger as thinking that 'motion is the measure of time.'

One is on the border of the unimaginable Space-Time of Einstein. If there was a beginning, or if one can conceive of it, 'what is more absurd than to think the World was made by the untended and casual concourse of indivisible substances?' For whence came these substances? 'If you say they came from Everlasting and so were Eternal, can you conceive such chanceable effects to proceed from so certain and necessary causes. . . . There must needs have been a wisdom overruling power which made them concur.'

To judge from so comparable a contemporary book as Sir Bernard Lovell's *In the Centre of Immensities*, scientists are turning away from explanations of the evolution of the cosmos in the terms of physics, which have yet resulted in such astonishing achievements: rocketry, space flights, landing on the moon, nuclear fission which could put an end to all on this planet. (The Stoics thought that the end of the world would come by fire. Perhaps they may prove to have been not far out.)

There are paradoxes in the constitution of the universe which the human mind cannot conceive; and Lovell quotes Wittgenstein: 'What we cannot speak about we must pass over in silence.' Wittgenstein was a religious man; so was Einstein. Lovell tells us that 'the belief in automatic material progress by means of scientific discovery and application has become a tragic myth of our age.' In science 'the majority of new ideas have eventually transpired to be wrong, while philosophical concepts with little observational basis have emerged as correct.' Lovell quotes a foremost astro-physicist: 'the scientific insights of our age shed such glaring light on certain aspects of the experience that they leave the rest in even greater darkness.'

The experience is ours, man's; yet to grasp it transcends the limitations of human thought—as Hinshelwood, our most eminent chemist, put it in a Presidential Address to the British Association. 'Out of all possible universes this is the only one which satisfies the narrow conditions necessary for development of intelligent life.' If it is an experiment, then of What, and to what End? We are back with Cuffe in 1600, before Galileo and Kepler had burst on the scene—Cuffe believed that the heavens had not changed but were capable of future transmutation. Our scientists have come back to 'an unsuspected entwinement of man with the actual existence of the universe and of time and space.' We are no further forward than Cuffe, with his 'mutual co-existence' of man and world: 'now because there is a mutual co-existence of the world and man, as the world is not but for man, so neither is man but in and by the world. . . . For as the world at the beginning was created for man, so with man it shall also be abolished.'

The one step we have made since Cuffe's day is that now man himself is in a position to abolish it—the result of the scientific discoveries that have brought no answer to the mystery. It seems we cannot know, and that is what Wittgenstein thought.

Cuffe writes with proper awe of the power that created and sustains the universe, which he calls God; there is no other indication of religious belief. He cites the beginning of Genesis on a par with the beginning of Ovid's *Metamorphoses*: 'Ante mare et terras, et quod tegit omnia caelum.' He thought that the Hebrews did but trifle in matters of weight, and did not hesitate to find 'Moses' Chronicle' defective. He preferred the Greek intellect, and was well read in Greek philosophy, and—exceptionally for an Elizabethan— in such works as Aristotle's *Physics* and Plato's *Timaeus*. He had been through the Oxford discipline of the medieval Schoolmen and was an acute logician. He makes a sensible attempt to reduce to reason the ludicrous longevity of the Patriarchs recorded in the Bible, suggesting that the years varied in different ancient countries, in some equivalent only to a month. This was a problem which was to give Sir Walter Ralegh a headache in the Tower, in writing his *History of the World*.

We are only at the beginning of Cuffe's book—impossible to resume its argument here—it should be republished, edited by some competent hand. It is written in excellent clear prose, like Bacon's—no Elizabethan elaborations like Hooker or Donne, long-winding parenthetical sentences like

Sidney, or inspired divagations like Nashe. The book was written in 1600, the last year of Cuffe's life, and was published from his manuscript in 1607, with a Preface by R.M. (I do not know who that was.) It was reprinted in 1633 and 1640. To Cuffe is attributed some translation from the Greek; he assisted Columbanus at Florence in 1598 with his edition of Longus' pastoral *Daphnis and Chloe*, so influential in Renaissance literature. He was the H.C. who contributed the Greek elegiacs that preface Camden's *Britannia*.

It is only at the end of his book that Cuffe comes down from his lofty argument about the cosmos to the nature of man, his temperament and passions. (Another member of the Essex circle, the Catholic Thomas Wright wrote *The Passions of the Mind*.) Man is a microcosm of the universe; he is subject to decay and death. Why? And how? It is only here that the title of the book—which may well have not been Cuffe's—has its point, with its discussion of temperament, physical well-being, what is proper to different ages. Cuffe comes down in favour of the Aristotelian doctrine of Moderation in everything.

He did not show it in the conduct of his own life—another all too recognisable paradox among clever men.

His birth was not base, as everybody said, simply because he fell from grace. He was the youngest son of an armigerous Somerset yeoman, Robert Cuffe of Donyat, where their substantial Tudor farmhouse still remains. The father also leased the rectory, i.e. the bigger tithes of Creech St Michael and a tenth of the twelve mills of the bishop of Winchester in his large hundred of Taunton, chief jewel of the see. Two of the Somerset Cuffes made their fortune in Ireland and became ancestors of two Irish peerages, the Earls of Desart and the Lords Tyrawley. Henry Cuffe made himself a competence and was financially independent before his death—which was exceptional for a mere don in Elizabethan days. He was an ambitious don.

He had his schooling at the grammar school at Hinton St George and, a clever boy, was pushed forward to Oxford by the favour of Lady Paulet of the big house there—whose historic possessions have been sold off and dispersed only in our own ruinous time. He became a scholar of Trinity

College at fifteen in 1578, and early attracted attention. By
1582 he was already corresponding (in Latin, of course) with
Jean Hotman, then in Leicester's service. This was the
brother of the famous François Hotman, a leading Huguenot
writer whose *Franco-Gallia* was a landmark in political
theory: it put forward very advanced ideas of elective
monarchy and representative government. These may have
had some influence later in the Essex circle; they could have
directed the young Oxford scholar's mind towards politics.
It looks more and more like Christopher Marlowe. But Cuffe
was no poet: in his book he jokes about Anacreon, 'I know
not how credible a witness, being a poet.'

Cuffe was elected a Fellow of Trinity at twenty in 1583,
but shortly was made to resign for a joke he made against the
pious founder, Sir Thomas Pope, who had been a Catholic.
Perhaps this was an omen—too sharp a tongue. But his
scholarship had already attracted the attention of the learned
Henry Savile, who became Warden of Merton in 1585, and
next year Cuffe was one of the first Fellows of Savile's election. Savile made a most able Warden, and it was always held
to his credit that he made choice of promising men for
Fellows. He was some thirteen years older than Cuffe, but
they became firm friends, Savile encouraging the brilliant
young scholar's Greek studies. In 1590 he was made
professor of Greek, and in 1592 was chosen out of the university to address the Queen in a Latin oration on her state visit.

She was attended by both Essex and the young
Southampton, who proceeded or was made Master of Arts.
He was probably attended by his poet, who shortly after-
wards used the term in *Love's Labour's Lost*, a skit on the
Southampton circle:

> Proceeded well, to stop all good proceeding!

And next year, in *A Midsummer Night's Dream*, presented
for Southampton's mother's second marriage, he described
just such an academic scene in the Queen's presence:

> Where I have come, great clerks have purposèd
> To greet me with premeditated welcomes;
> Where I have seen them shiver and look pale,
> Make periods in the midst of sentences,

Throttle their practised accents in their fears,
And on conclusion dumbly have broke off.

It is unlikely that the professor of Greek would have shivered
and looked pale, or dumbly have broke off: too bold and
audacious a spirit, his trouble was that he had too much to
say. Moreover, the occasion gave Cuffe a chance of being
presented to the Queen—and to Essex and Southampton,
whom he was to come to know intimately; for after the
academic disputation the Warden and Fellows of Merton
entertained Queen and courtiers to a banquet in Hall.

A few notices still remain of Cuffe's academic life. He
took full part in the affairs of the college, as principal of the
postmasters (or scholars) in 1593, and bursar in 1594 and
1595. More significant than these chores are the Questions
that he put forward for dispute: that the four elements are
the first principles of natural things; that the law should be
superior to every magistrate. A further theme carries a tone
of irony, when one considers the course his life would take:
that man is born for contemplation only, not for the life of
politics. The subject of disputation before the Queen was
even more pointed: whether civil dissensions are useful to
the state.

Academic life, however, was not for Cuffe, any more than
it had been for the aspiring spirit of Marlowe; after serving
his turn as junior proctor in 1594 he shortly was taken into
the service of Essex and moved to London. He retained his
Fellowship, being unmarried, and his room in college; he
continued to be professor until 1597, when he went abroad
to perfect his modern languages, and acquire information
and foreign contacts for Essex—as Anthony Bacon had done
before him, of whom Cuffe became a colleague even closer
in Essex's counsels.

It is likely that Cuffe owed his recommendation to Essex
to his mentor Savile, who, a gentleman of family, was on
friendly terms with the Earl. In 1595 Savile was lobbying
Essex to get him the Provostship of Eton. When Essex failed,
Savile turned unblushing to Robert Cecil: 'the man that may
do most good in this matter is your father [Burghley], from
whom one commendation in cold blood and seeming to
proceed of judgment, shall more prevail with the Queen than

all the affectionate speech that my lord of Essex can use.' He
added that he was willing to bestow 300 angels at Cecil's
appointment, and this was but a small portion of that he had
been ready to bestow another way.

Savile got the job. It was the Elizabethan way, and it
should be added that Savile made a notable Provost of Eton,
a strong disciplinarian. His brilliant protégé, however,
involved him in some trouble at the time of the Essex Rebellion. This was a disillusioning experience for Savile, who
remained on close terms with Cuffe up to the outbreak. No
doubt it was owing to this chastening event that Savile would
say, in later years, when a scholar was recommended to him
for a good wit, (i.e. cleverness), 'Out upon him . . . give me
the plodding student. If I would look for wits, I would go
to Newgate: there be the wits.'

Cuffe was warmly welcomed by the circle at Essex House
overlooking the Thames, where he was regarded not only as
'a great philosopher', but also because he could 'suit the wise
observations of ancient authors to the transactions of modern
times.' Essex had several secretaries, Edward Reynolds and
William Temple to deal with personal business; the highly
intelligent Anthony Bacon dealt with the foreign and political
correspondence, but he was ailing, often crippled with gout
in hands and legs. Evidently Cuffe was recruited to fill in
here and perhaps eventually to take his place. They were
united in admiration for their lord and master, as generous
as he was chivalrous, intelligent and eloquent:

> The courtier's, soldier's, scholar's, eye, tongue, sword;
> The expectancy and rose of the fair state . . .
> The observed of all observers . . .

(He had other Hamlet-like qualities too, which would in the
end pull him down.) Essex was grooming himself to take
over the government on Burghley's death, which would be
soon; the Queen and Burghley, the old Polonius, were
grooming Robert Cecil for the purpose.

The group of young men were amused, irritated and at
length bored by the fantastic Antonio Pérez, Philip II's ex-
Secretary of State, who was at first found useful by the
English government and then, so like exiles, became a liability

and a bore. At Essex House from 1593 to 1595, he was caricatured all too recognisably as Don Armado in *Love's Labour's Lost*. Departing to France in July 1595, he was back again in April 1596. Anthony Bacon found him wearisome and expressed himself as such; so did Cuffe when he encountered him again in Paris in 1598. The young men themselves—and Essex was the leader of the younger generation—were knit together by bonds of warm friendship. One sees from Cuffe's letters that he had an affectionate nature, utterly devoted to his master.

In the spring of 1596 the expedition to Cadiz, which Essex had urged upon the reluctant Queen, was on: all the young men were on tiptoe to go. In the event the capture of Cadiz formed the most signal exploit of the long war (suppose if the Spaniards had captured Plymouth!), and Essex reaped the whole glory of it. This was excessive, for others deserved as much, Ralegh notably; but he did not garner it, for Essex had the gift of popularity, which he carefully cultivated, Ralegh not. So the laureate of the age was able to describe Essex House thus:

> Yet therein now doth lodge a noble peer,
> Great England's glory and the world's wide wonder,
> Whose dreadful name late through all Spain did thunder,
> And Hercules' two pillars standing near
> Did make to quake and fear:
> Fair branch of honour, flower of chivalry,
> That fillest England with thy triumph's fame . . .

And so on.

Cuffe was in personal attendance on Essex in the flagship, the *Due Repulse*, from which he wrote to the Earl's gentleman of the horse, William Downhall:

You have no friends who ever since our first acquaintance more esteemed either your devoted and affectionate mind towards him whom we all honour, or your kindness towards those whom you know heartily addicted to his service. As for my fellow, Ed. Reynolds, I have been so impudent for him as I durst not be for myself, for whereas I have delivered commissions without one farthing profit, yet for him I have gotten something.

He sends his commendations to friends in the circle, Lord Mountjoy, Mr Atey (later Sir Arthur), and Mr Pitchford.

The capture of Cadiz made a sensation throughout the Mediterranean, and Essex was the hero of the hour in England. He won praise even in Spain for the chivalry of his conduct in the hour of victory. Anxious to improve the occasion politically he sent Cuffe home ahead of him to write up his version of the story. Ralegh had to write his own account later to put himself in the picture: he had done as well as Essex, but got no credit for it with the mob.

Sir Anthony Ashley, Master of the Queen's Jewel-house, (and ancestor of the factious Whig leader, Shaftesbury) was also hurrying home with the loot that he had personally acquired. The Queen had had all the expense of the expedition and, as usual, anybody who could scrounge from what belonged to the government was bent on doing so. Ashley was shortly caught out and sent to prison. He had got ahead of Cuffe on the road from Plymouth, 'being better horsed than you; but necessity hath no law.' Cuffe fell ill on the way, 'betwixt Portsmouth and Crook, no great journey, but very ill and almost intolerable way, I grew so weary towards night that I could hardly sustain myself on my horse; and besides my weakness am fallen into a distemper and some accidents of a tertian' [fever]. So he sent on to Reynolds the Relation of the voyage which he had written at Essex's dictation, with particular instructions as to how it was to be handled and published.

Essex's orders were that it 'should with the soonest be set in print, both to stop all vagrant humours and to inform those that are well affected of the truth of the whole—yet so that in any case neither his lordship's name, nor mine, nor any other [follower] of my lord be either openly named or so insinuated that any slender guess may be drawn who was the penman.' Cuffe gave detailed instructions as to copying, and a transcript given to a reliable printer; he wondered whether Fulke Greville would mind the first two letters of his name being inscribed to deflect attention, or possibly R.B., which people might interpret as being Robert Beale, (Clerk of the Privy Council).

In other words Cuffe's Relation was a party-document, claiming the whole credit for the great exploit—which in the event he got with the multitude, who have no knowledge or judgment. But the government were not allowing this partisan account to be published—quite understandably, giving offence to numerous people who had done their duty as well as Essex, not only Ralegh but the Howards. Actually Lord Admiral Howard had been the commander-in-chief, Lord Thomas Howard commander of one squadron, Essex and Ralegh of the other two. Cuffe directed Reynolds to have a French translation made and 'to cause it to be sent to some good personages in those parts, always observing the courses before specified.' Manuscript copies were made by Anthony Bacon, and got away to Scotland, the Netherlands and Venice. Later, Essex dispatched an envoy, Dr Henry Hawkins, to Italy who had Cuffe's forbidden Relation translated into Italian and tried to get it inserted into the history Campana was writing, who first agreed and then withdrew, probably upon warning.

All this was, of course, party-politics. But of the great exploit, which was a joint effort, Essex did manage to hog all the glory.

Next year Essex sent Cuffe abroad with a testimonial as his official Secretary; he 'sends him into those parts to make him more fit for negotiations there. . . . A secretary for Italian may be of as good use as for any other language.' This was in cipher, but it was deciphered by Cecil's intelligence service: there was no keeping from him what Essex was up to.

We have a long letter from Cuffe, from Paris 14 June 1597, to Henry Savile reporting his doings in Florence. Cuffe had had an interview with the Grand Duke, 'and laboured to leave in him the best impressions of my Lord's love and devotion. He protested that he much esteemed the affection of so worthy a prince, and would give him all real co-respondence to the utmost of his power.' The Grand Duke had informed him that peace was being negotiated between France and Spain. 'Spain is so distressed that the King and his Council, instead of erecting an universal monarchy, cast for their own security. His fleet is weakened by disaster and want of provisions; the spirits of his subjects are broken. On land he can do nothing against either England or the Low Countries, his most hated enemies.'

The Grand Duke gave interesting information about the Japanese revolt against the infiltration of Christianity and the crucifixion of the Jesuits there—a blow to the Pope and Spain. He expressed the wish that Queen Elizabeth would react more mildly to Henri IV's defection and that she would urge the duc de Bouillon to be more accommodating with the King. As for Cuffe himself,

> Don Pérez hath sent his man to me *alla Spagnuola* to signify that he takes notice of my being here. I excused myself for not having visited him, saying that my apparel was not yet made, and that I was loth to go abroad in my Italian suit. Once, for fashion's sake, I must visit him; but more I will not, without further direction, because I know not on what terms his lordship and he stand.

In October 1597 Cuffe was back in Florence, reporting the Grand Duke's regret that the English had not held on to Cadiz—this fell in with the prejudices of the Essex party: he said, 'in the hearing of some English, that they had very much to answer who were authors of our abandoning that place.' Cuffe had made contact with another of Essex's correspondents, Guicciardini, who forwarded information from Italy. As for Cuffe himself, 'my little knowledge in the Greek tongue hath stood me in very good stead. For one day in a bookseller's shop by occasion of Demetrius Phalereus, which lay thereupon, I fell in talk with a gentleman of this town, one Marcello Adriani, who wrote the story.' The upshot was that Cuffe was made a member of the Academia della Crusca, and became friendly with the Duchess's confessor. For other informants, apparently Anthony Bacon had an English intelligencer. Cuffe hoped 'to conceal my principal design, which I see I am more carefully to do, as well in regard of the Duke's jealousy, [i.e. suspicion] as also for the folly of some of our nation, who have in divers places reported me to be my Lord's secretary.' He ended by expressing his infinite desire for Essex's 'safe and honourable return.'

Essex was away now in 1597 on the Azores expedition, which he had virtually forced upon the Queen. It proved an extravagant and acrimonious fiasco, and she would have no more of such ventures. It made an irretrievable breach between Essex and Ralegh, to whom the Earl behaved unpardonably, and marked the beginning of the decline of his fortunes from the apex of Cadiz.

At New Year 1598 Cuffe was writing a long letter of Italian news to Savile, and forwarding a piece of donnish gossip. 'Signor Montecatino, secretary to the late Duke Alphonso, the author of the treatise on Aristotle's three first books of Politics, is secretly stolen to Rome . . . and fed with hope of a cardinal's hat.' In March Cuffe was still in Florence, reporting Spanish news home to Savile: that the Spanish forces in Brittany were in distress, from the Adelantado's failure to waft home the treasure fleet from the Indies. Spain was bankrupt, the peace with France—which Robert Cecil had been dispatched to Henri IV to prevent—was about to be made. The Grand Duke wished that the Queen would employ her utmost forces to impeach the peace—then Spain would be reduced to complete distress and 'be at the discretion of the Queen and her allies.' We recognise that this was the line of the war party, which Essex led, in England. One day at a Council meeting when he was urging still more campaigns, old Burghley took out his prayer-book and pointed to the verse in Psalm LV: 'The blood-thirsty and deceitful men shall not live out half their days.'

By July Cuffe was back in London, writing an amusing letter to Sir Charles Danvers, which shows both the man and the terms they were on. Essex's mother was anxious to find a husband for her niece, Lettice Knollys—her own name before she married Essex's father, then Leicester, then Sir Christopher Blount (i.e. Blunt). Sir Charles and Sir Henry Danvers were particular friends of Southampton, who had sheltered them and enabled them to get away to Henry of Navarre, after the killing of Henry Long in Wiltshire.[1] Henry was Southampton's boy-friend, and never married; Charles was as yet unmarried—and

my Lord has principally above all others made choice of yourself, and has asked me my knowledge of your inclination to submit your neck to that blessed yoke. . . . It only remains that you send me your resolution whether you can be contented to have your purgatory in this life, or had rather to defer it to another world. In a word, *avisez vous*, and before you take your journey to yonder wicked country [i.e. Ireland] (whither I understand you are bent, and can imagine none other cause

but some sudden devotion to St Patrick's purgatory) I pray you let me
receive some light from you touching this other purgatory, which,
because it is in effect *via universae carnis*, and yourself affect no singu-
larity, I persuade myself you will one day enter.

There we have Cuffe—on intimate terms with the aristocratic young men of the Essex circle. He was not a marrying
type himself; his book quotes without demur Plato's obser-
vation that children and women were most foolish. And I
detect something of a tone of Platonic friendship among the
denizens of Essex House: Anthony and Francis Bacon were
known homosexuals, Antonio Pérez a flagrant one;
Southampton ambivalent, but even after his forced marriage
was given to 'culling' and hugging, in his tent in Ireland, the
soldier Captain Piers Edmonds, whom Essex took abroad
with him in his coach. Sir Charles Danvers was apparently
heterosexual, but he did not put his neck into the noose of
matrimony before the axe fell upon it on Tower Hill.

In September Cuffe was in Paris with Southampton, who
was in trouble over his secret marriage with Elizabeth
Vernon. He had got her with child, and then was reluctant
to marry her; his leader, Essex, made him do so for the girl
was his cousin. She was also one of the Queen's ladies; the
Queen was very sensitive about their 'honour' and took it as
a personal offence when it was breached. Southampton had
detained Cuffe with him for company, or consolation, who
now had to return. The Queen commanded the Earl to come
back; at the end of the month Essex sent Cuffe down to meet
him with the advice 'to solicit kissing of the Queen's hand
by Mr Secretary [Cecil], and to spend some of your first
time in that suit.' It did not avail; but Essex got him off any
worse punishment than a fortnight in the Fleet. And we see
the confidential terms upon which the ambitious don was
with the great—it had gone to his head. We note too the
characteristic swagger of an Elizabethan who had travelled
on the Continent. It was caricatured this very year, by
another who was well acquainted with this circle, in *As You
Like It*: 'Farewell, Monsieur Traveller: look you lisp and
wear strange suits . . . or I will scarce think you have swam
in a gondola.'

There followed the deplorable fiasco of Essex's campaign in

Ireland. In the fastnesses of unreduced Ulster, Hugh O'Neill, last and ablest of the quasi-independent Irish princes, had built up an army which, in 1598, inflicted the worst disaster English arms had ever suffered in Ireland. A strenuous effort was necessary to meet the danger, when the resources of the state were already strained by the long war with Spain.

We cannot here repeat the complex story of Essex's resounding failure. The government did its best for him, and strained every nerve to equip the largest army that had ever been sent across the Irish Channel, some 17,000 men. The people, never aware of the true state of things, expected victory from their hero. The most popular dramatist, himself a friend of Southampton and thus affiliated to the Essex circle, expressed the mood describing the enthusiastic send-off London gave him: in *Henry V*, but in terms of 'the plebeians swarming' to 'fetch their conquering Caesar in' –

> As by a lower but loving likelihood
> Were now the General of our gracious Empress,
> As in good time he may from Ireland coming,
> Bringing rebellion broachèd on his sword,
> How many would the peaceful City quit
> To welcome him!

The gracious Empress, however, had not only her doubts but her suspicions, which were all too well justified. She suspected that Essex meant to build up an independent power in the state, with an army under his command. He proceeded to place his own followers in key posts, to build up his own party; though Essex himself hesitated (like the Hamlet he was), this was what his followers urged upon him. Sir Christopher Blount, for example—married to Essex's designing mother—wrote to him: '*Since needs go you must*, you should arm against all intended mischiefs . . . for since you know who possess the mind of her that rules, I beseech you leave none of your provisions to the pleasure of your enemies.'

This was the inwardness of the struggle with the Queen over the appointment of Southampton. He was Essex's leading supporter; Essex made him, with no military experience to qualify him, second in command as general of horse. This was against the Queen's express wish and, when she ordered him to return, Essex resisted her orders.

Southampton was thereupon commanded by her to return,
and Essex had to give way. Similarly with the young Earl of
Rutland, who had no experience, but was an Essex party-
man, to whom a command was given. The Queen was furious
at the contravention of her orders, still more with her
suspicions of Essex's intentions. His proceedings were
watched by Cecil with 'eagles' eyes', as he said—this in turn
confirmed Essex's suspicions.

The Essex party all thought Robert Cecil was their chief
enemy—not so, the Queen herself was their real opponent.
She and her chief minister saw eye to eye, as she had done
for years with his father, Lord Burghley. Robert Cecil was
quite as clever as his father, with the same concern for the
well-being and safety of the state, under his care. 'Roberto
il diavolo', Pérez used to call him, and many defaming
rhymes were put about against him for, with his brains, he
was never popular: Essex was the people's darling. (This
increased the Queen's difficulties in dealing with him).

> Back like a lute-case,
> Belly like a drum,
> On horse like a Jackanapes
> Rides little Robin Thumb.

How they hated the ablest servant of the state!

Three conspicuous Earls, in command of the only army in
the two kingdoms, were more than the government could
tolerate, and two of them were recalled—to Essex's disgust.
But all the rest of his party rallied to his standard: Lords
Cromwell and Monteagle, Sir Christopher and Sir Charles
Blount, Sir Charles and Sir Henry Danvers, Sir Thomas
Gerard, Sir Charles Percy, Sir Griffin Markham, Sir Robert
Drury—all names to crop up subversively later.

The indispensable Cuffe went as Chief Secretary. On 20
April 1599 he writes to Ned Reynolds, his colleague watching
over Essex's affairs in London: 'In a multitude of business I
cannot write much.' Reynolds had asked for decisions on
various matters. Essex said to Cuffe, 'at present neither you
nor I can do it, because our hands are full.' Ten days later,
in the press of business, Cuffe sends commendations to
Mountjoy, and 'tell his lordship that his honourable favours

towards me, so many and so undeserved, do force me to acknowledge that I must needs live and die an unthankful man. Remember me likewise to Mr Bacon [Anthony], Mr Smyth and—if he be a courtier—to R. Pitchford; not forgetting my lord's true and faithful follower, Mr Crompton.'

Cuffe himself had had no military experience, so we are not surprised when Sir Anthony Standen reported to Reynolds,

Mr Cuffe's brain-pan to be wonderfully shaken by the importunity or, rather, sauciness of the undiscreet martial sort; and yet his purse never the heavier, because you know we never had any more than theory that way. You have so many friends here that my love can but little serve you; yet you may stretch it at your pleasure like an Oxford glove.

No one ever charged Cuffe with being mercenary, or making money out of his position of confidence with Essex. Standen was a Catholic follower of Essex, a double-intelligencer who had reported home the doings of his co-religionists in Italy. He was much impressed by the St George's day ceremonies with which the Lord Deputy had taken up office: they 'passed all the service that I ever saw done to any prince in Christendom. Though all was to her Majesty's honour, yet what malice may hew out of this you know.'

Here was Essex, treated like a prince; here was the atmosphere of suspicion in which he moved.

Cuffe next forwards private information to be given to the Comptroller of the Household, 'to whom only of all the Council his Lordship now writes, and communicate what he tells you to his Lordship's friends.' This was Sir William Knollys, Essex's uncle, by now his only firm friend in the government. And no wonder, for they had no definite news of his making any progress for all the effort they had put into equipping him. Cuffe's very next news was such as to make them doubt Essex's whole course; for Cuffe wrote on 9 May, 'his Lordship being now ready to set foot in stirrup for our journey into Leinster.' But why Leinster? The centre of the resistance was Ulster, and the whole purpose of Essex's having been given a large army was to tackle O'Neill in his fastness. Evidently Cuffe went south with Essex, who hoped that a Fitzgerald who was a good friend of his would be sent over to take the place of the Earl of Kildare, whose death he expected. 'My Lord is much offended with the Low Coun-

tries Commander, and doth no less wonder at the humours
of our Council at home.' They were not to be wondered at,
for Essex was now to consume the whole summer, and his
army, with a pointless drive into Leinster, led on further
even into Munster. By the time he got back the army would
be wasted with disease—largely dysentery—too weak, and
too late in the season, to confront Ulster and O'Neill.

In July Cuffe was able to send encouraging news of
Southampton, before Essex consented to his recall. He had
led a brave cavalry charge to good effect against the rebels.
One sees the defensive purpose of this: it had no effect on
the Queen, who insisted on his return. Essex was concerned
lest Sir Henry Carey and other gentlemen, who took part in
the action but whose names were omitted in the report,
should take umbrage. Cuffe apologised for the omission, 'as
in regard of my exceeding haste and overmuch watching—
for I assure you I wrote it after midnight—well it may be.'
One gets an impression of amateurishness about the whole
course of their proceedings in Ireland.

In August we hear a note of foreboding.

> I am sometimes threatened by his Lordship to be sent into England,
> there to argue and apologise for his virtue and true worth against those
> who so maliciously and sycophant-like detract from his honourable and
> noble endeavours. The times are so bad and the humours surly with
> you there, that I fear rather than wish the journey. Notwithstanding
> *jacta est alea* [i.e. the die is cast]. I would rather lose with him than
> gain with his opposites.

An ominous note, but Cuffe remained true to it, loyal to
Essex, to the end. It was a mistake Francis Bacon did not
make: he deserted in time.

A week later there followed disaster in Connaught. 'Good
Ned, this dispatch is sudden, so as the cause of it was unexpected. In a word Sir Conyers Clifford . . . hath lost himself,
Sir Alexander Ratcliffe, and sundry lieutenants and serjeants,
and of common soldiers to the number of well nigh two
hundred.' Essex had feared the event, but should never have
allowed the dispersal of the effort. 'It is true that things fatal
may well be foreseen and feared, but cannot be avoided. He
[Clifford] hath paid the greatest price he could; and now his

Lordship breatheth nothing but revenge.' It was now too late.

Back in Dublin Cuffe reported to 'honest friend Ned' Essex's explanations and excuses to the Council, and his letters to friends at home, like the devious Lord Henry Howard. The Queen's favourite, Lady Warwick, had taken the trouble to write to Cuffe a letter of advice as to how Essex should conduct himself in the emergency, and he recognised that it was kindly meant. Cuffe himself replied, and wished that Henry Savile would deliver his letter to her, 'because I know he hath a good interest in her favour and I would for mine own excuse it were delivered with some compliment.'

The Council in Dublin had advised Essex against an immediate advance on Ulster on the ground that so large an army could not be provisioned in that wild impassable country. Now, by death, disease and desertion it was down to 4000: there was no hope of success against O'Neill with such a force. Nevertheless, driven on by the reproaches of Queen and Council, Essex set out for the North at the end of August, too late anyway. Meanwhile he sent Cuffe over to the Queen to explain his situation and excuse the course he had taken. He was politely received and listened to, but the Queen sent back a stinging reply, in which one detects the unanswerable advocacy of Cecil, 'finding now by your letters by Cuffe a course more strange, if strange may be. . . . Before your departure, no man's counsel was held sound which persuaded not presently [i.e. immediately] the main prosecution in Ulster; all was nothing without that; and nothing was too much for that.' Now, for the delay—

if sickness of the army be the reason, why was there not the action undertaken when the army was in better state? If winter's approach, why were the summer months of July and August lost? If the spring were too soon and the summer otherwise spent, then surely we must conclude that none of the four quarters of the year will be in season for you and that Council to agree of Tyrone's [O'Neill's] prosecution, for which all our charge is intended.

The sarcasm was sharp, but the argument was unanswerable; the bitterness too was understandable—all the effort, for all the strain upon the country's resources, was lost.

Meanwhile, on the borders of Ulster Essex was having his fatal interview with O'Neill; for, besides arranging a truce— which was equivalent to a victory for O'Neill—he and Essex had secret communication as to the future and what should happen at the Queen's death. It transpired later that Essex had treason at the back of his mind, leading two or three thousand soldiers back to make a *coup d'état*. For the present he excluded this plan—indeed he could resolve upon nothing. For there were other possibilities, make contact with James in Scotland to bring pressure on the Queen to change her government—perhaps even get his party into position to dominate the circumstances of the Succession present in so many minds. Including Elizabeth's—for this was the Ark of the Covenant to her; she could never derogate from her dignity to put her case to the public—that to allow a subject to challenge the authority of the Crown, let alone dictate the succession to it, would be fatal to the state no less than to the monarchy.

When the news of the truce reached her, her worst suspicions were confirmed: Essex could never be trusted, let alone left in office, again. She immediately wrote disavowing his action. She had never doubted that Tyrone would

offer a parley, specially with our supreme general of that kingdom, having often done it with those of subaltern authority. . . . To trust this traitor upon oath is to trust a devil upon his religion; to trust him upon pledges is a mere illusory [illusion]. . . . If we had meant that Ireland, after all the calamities in which they have wrapped it, should still have been abandoned, then it was very superfluous to have sent over such a personage as yourself.

When he received that missive Essex saw that the game was up. With a few followers he deserted his charge to rush back to the Queen and fling himself upon her mercy.

She had her duty to do, and for the next eighteen months an almighty problem on her hands.

Neither Queen nor government knew quite what to do about Essex. At first he was placed under polite house arrest, and then given more freedom, at length liberty. His best friends urged submission upon him, and from time to time he appeared contrite and sought the Queen's favour. When he fell ill she sent her physicians to attend him. But she would never reinstate him. He always had the sympathy of the people who, poor fools, thought he was badly treated and had no idea of what was involved. Moreover, he had a large, if motley, party with him: all the malcontents and oppositionists, those out of office who hoped to get in if there were a change, aristocratic irresponsibles like the young peers and swordsmen who followed him; he had both Puritan and Catholic supporters.

Everything depended on the Queen, more authoritarian than ever, on her life, and the Succession. The subject of Richard II's deposition was much in people's minds; jokes had been made about Richard II between Essex and Cecil when their relations were better. The deposition scene in Shakespeare's *Richard II* was censored until the Queen's death and James was safely on the throne. At this critical time John Hayward produced his account of the Revolution of 1399, the deposition of Richard and accession of Henry IV. It bore a pointed dedication to Essex, which infuriated the Queen, for he must have permitted it and the book, like Essex, was very popular. No less than four issues had been called for in 1599, and the government sent the sanguine author to prison. Elizabeth was convinced that 'some more mischievous person' was behind it. When yet another issue was printed in May 1600 Essex sought to clear himself by sending Cuffe to the Archbishop of Canterbury, who had the charge of suppressing the book.

Essex's party was divided into two wings: those who urged him to back down and make his peace with the Queen— which he appeared to do. But this meant giving up, and letting down his party-following. The others, closer to him, were activists who urged him on. This wing was led by Southampton, and to it Cuffe belonged. The cleverest, like Francis Bacon, saw the red light and began working his passage to the other side. From his fascinating Apology one can read the sullen resolution gradually forming in Essex's wavering mind not to give in. On the Queen's side one can read her wish not to ruin him but to reduce him to submission. Hence the collision. Bacon saw a good deal of the Queen this year over law business. She had appointed Mountjoy, the right man, to succeed Essex in Ireland. Bacon happened to say, 'if you mean to employ my Lord of Essex thither again, your Majesty cannot make a better choice.' Elizabeth interrupted him with passion: 'Essex! whensoever I send Essex back again into Ireland, I will marry you. Claim it of me!' It shows her in a vivid light—downright, like Margaret Thatcher speaking.

At the end of July Sir Henry Bromley wrote to Cuffe, having Essex's innermost confidence:

> My dear brother, I may not omit this opportunity to urge you to let me hear what is done or what hope there is of doing good for our lord. It were good in my poor opinion that an end of his expectations were urged. I expect but direction, for I am wholly his that you are. Let us not lose the start that we have gotten, but rethink of some means either to be winners or savers. I doubt of the forbearing hand by former experience, for vile natures will ascribe that patience to pusillanimity that the noble would to contempt. I am ready to undergo what he doth . . . I pray you lose no time to perform those offices that you have undertaken and I have promised.

In other words, they were committed to action.

In August Sir Gelly Meyrick, Cuffe's colleague as Essex's steward, was writing to Cuffe about a farm that he was selling—raising cash, to what purpose?

> My Lord had a purpose when I came from London to have had some bedding and hangings, which we bought of the Earl of Northumberland, to be sent by sea from Milford to London. I spake to my brother to provide a bark for that purpose, but I willed him not to send it away until he heard again from me. Let my Lord, I pray you, be moved in it, because his lordship may be altered.

One did not buy bedding and hangings from the Earl of Northumberland at Milford Haven—this referred to a consignment of arms. And Essex was recruiting to his cause such younger captains as Sir Ferdinando Gorges, in a keypost as governor of the citadel at Plymouth.

The atmosphere within the party we may judge from Meyrick, who continues: 'Then I hear some of our own family are very malicious against us both, but especially against me. I am very sorry that some of them professing religion can be so malicious. We have envy and malice besides, to have it plotted and practised by those that my

Lord useth so near him.' As we have said, Essex's supporters included both Puritans and Catholics—anything to be out of step.

The position taken up by Essex's party was that there was something wrong with the state, and they were out to change it. One sees that there was little likelihood of its amendment from people in that state of mind, with Essex at the top. William Shakespeare, who was also observing from close at hand, saw that.

Little is heard of Cuffe during this year of suspense: evidently, with Essex out of office and under some restraint, the Secretary was at leisure to write his book.

Negotiations of dangerous import followed in which Cuffe was employed. Mountjoy had been close to Essex and sympathised with him; but he was now Lord Deputy himself, beginning well on the arduous task of reducing Ulster and O'Neill. At one point Essex wished him to send an army across to England to his support, and then saw that this was not feasible. Mountjoy did go so far as to make representations to King James on Essex's behalf, and both Essex and James wished to advance the date of his accession. Preparing her funerals before she was in her tomb, the Queen called it. Cuffe was involved in the Scottish negotiation, and he and Meyrick prevailed on Mountjoy to change his Secretary—one can see why.

That autumn Essex's monopoly of the import of sweet wine, his chief source of income, lapsed. When he sued yet again for a return to favour, Elizabeth said she perceived that it was but a matter of sweet wine. With his extravagance and the expenses his course and following incurred, he was virtually bankrupt. Early in the New Year the summons went out for his supporters, armed, to gather in London, while at the same time James's ambassadors were to move south. Before they could arrive Essex received a sudden summons before the Council—the government was on the alert, and beforehand. Early on Sunday morning, 8 February, a deputation from the Council was sent to Essex House. This precipitated the outbreak into the City. Essex House and precincts were filled with armed supporters. The Earl's

Puritan preachers had led him to believe that the City would
rise in his support.

Cuffe never believed it. In all the discussions as to the
course they should pursue he unwaveringly urged that the
best plan was to make a sudden descent upon the Court itself
at Whitehall. It might not have succeeded, but it offered
more chance of success than Essex's unorganised *sortie* into
the City, where he found no support whatever. When he
turned back down Ludgate with a confused idea of making
for Whitehall, it was too late: the way was barred by government forces under the command of Cecil's brother, Burghley.
All through that day of fatal fiasco Cuffe took no part in the
outbreak, but remained at Essex House. It did not save him,
nor did he ever expect to save himself, for he was up to his
neck in the conspiracy—and his neck was now forfeit.

It is difficult for anyone of political judgment to do justice
to Essex, for he had little. He had other qualities, which
made people fall for him and become devoted to him—he
was a good deal of an Antony pitted against an Octavius,
bound to lose. Women were devoted to him, and he had
many; he had good looks, plenty of sex and immense charm
when he chose to exert it. Well-educated, he was eloquent
both in speech and writing. He had the capacity to arouse
the enthusiasm of the mob, the devotion of his followers and
the love of his intimates. Of such men the leaders of the state
are not made, and in the event he ruined his devoted servants.

Shortly the prisoners were rounded up: no less than five
earls—Essex, Southampton, Rutland, Bedford, Sussex; three
barons—Cromwell, Monteagle, Sandys; sixteen knights.
Even a Lady was held prisoner: Essex's restless sister, Lady
Rich—Sidney's 'Stella'—who lived openly with Mountjoy
and bore him a family of children. Many of the gentlemen
were of leading families, some malcontents to appear again
in the Gunpowder Plot: a Percy, Tresham, Catesby,
Lyttelton. Sir Ferdinando Gorges had come up from
Plymouth, Anthony Rouse, I regret to say, from Cornwall.
One sees how widespread the affair was. Soon the whole
story was worried out by extensive examinations of the
participants—in which Francis Bacon took a leading part.
While the examinations proceeded, the leaders tried and
sentenced, James's ambassadors arrived in London. Robert

Cecil neatly stepped into Essex's place to make contact for the day of James's inevitable succession—all in the best interest of the state.

A mass of information as to their previous dealings was extracted from the thorough probes to which they were all subjected. There had been many secret meetings of Meyrick, Cuffe and others at Lord Mountjoy's house in Holborn; Sir Christopher and Sir Edward Blount often lay there. The government wisely turned a blind eye to Mountjoy's doings: they were now dependent on him to bring 'rebellion broachèd on his sword', which in the end he accomplished, where Essex had failed. Cuffe had been sent to Sir Charles Danvers at Oxford to communicate their plans to Mountjoy, which, however, he did not approve. Danvers gave evidence—rather ungallantly for a gentleman of family and a soldier—that he had been rallied to Essex by Cuffe, and was in the conspiracy out of love to Southampton, who had saved his life. This did not save him now. Cuffe had been used to attempt to rally Sir Henry Neville, the ambassador in Paris, and had provided the arguments: that Neville's service in Paris was disparaged, that he had failed over the peace negotiation, and was out of favour at Court. Later, Lady Neville wrote to Cecil that Cuffe could best have told what passed between them, and that he had absolutely cleared the ambassador at his death. This was more gentlemanly than some of the great gentlemen's behaviour about Cuffe.

It transpired that some weeks before the Rising Cuffe had been dismissed by Essex—probably wavering as usual between the two courses to follow. Cuffe had fallen down in a dead faint at this, and made representations to Southampton who got him reinstated. Southampton had much influence with Essex, was virtually his right-hand man, and presided at the meetings at Drury House where he urged on action. 'Shall we then do nothing?' he had protested against the more sober elements.

References to the deposing of Richard II were spread about to put people in the right frame of mind, and a group of the conspirators arranged with Shakespeare's Company at the Globe to have *Richard II* put on the day before the outbreak. His colleague, Augustine Phillips, gave evidence that Lord Monteagle, Sir Charles and Sir Joscelyn Percy and some three

more offered the players 40s more to substitute it for the
play they had intended to perform. To this they had agreed,
not knowing what was in the wind. Sir William Constable
had met with Monteagle, Blount, Sir Charles Percy, Sir John
Davies, Meyrick and Cuffe at Gunter's house over against
Temple Gate (now Bar), where they dined. Afterwards they
had all assembled at the Globe on Bankside, except Cuffe.
'Know ye not that I am Richard II?' stormed the Queen.

At his first examination Cuffe did his best to defend Essex
and to put the best face on his proceedings. In effect the
practised logician was too plausible to convince. Particularly
examined with regard to the political implications of the plot,
he said with regard to the negotiation with King James that
Essex's intention was 'principally that by assuring that Prince
of his good affection—such as might stand with his sovereign
duty to her Majesty, whereof he made special reservation
[!]—he might stay him from irreligious courses in declining
from his religion; next, that he might the better hinder the
designs of the Infanta of Spain.' She was the favourite candidate of the pro-Spanish wing among the Catholic exiles,
inspired by Father Parsons. With regard to Mountjoy, all
that Cuffe said was that Danvers 'found him very affectionate
to the Earl, thinking the public to suffer with his private
[grievances], and consequently that his return to her
Majesty's former grace would turn to the good of thousands.'
As for the outbreak, 'force—so God be my saviour, there
was never intended any to my knowledge; nor any other
countenancing of the cause by the confluence of the
gentlemen his followers but only this—that nothing might
be attempted against him before his access to her Majesty.'
This was too good to be true.

Cuffe's attempted defence of his 'late dearest Lord and
Master' was in sharp contrast with the great man's conduct
at his trial, when he blamed it all on Cuffe. He said that
Cuffe urged 'the injury and dishonour offered me, the misery
of my friends and the country, and the necessity of holding
them together.' The last consideration was the obvious
concern of a party leader, one who aimed at forming an
alternative government, as Essex clearly did. Cecil was to
have been displaced for Sir Henry Neville or Thomas Bodley;
Ralegh replaced as captain of the guard by Sir William

Russell, etc. Essex vehemently declaimed against his devoted
Secretary as 'a principal instigator of the violent courses'
into which he had fallen; he blamed Blount (his mother's
husband), Cuffe and those at Drury House (i.e.
Southampton) for driving him on. He asked to be brought
face to face in Westminster Hall with Cuffe, whom he then
charged: 'Henry Cuffe, call to God for mercy and to the
Queen, and deserve it by declaring truth; for I must prepare
for another world . . . and must needs say that none hath
been a greater instigator of me than yourself to all these
disloyal courses into which I have fallen.'

There was no doubt that Cuffe would be condemned; but
if there had been, this would have sealed his fate. It was the
most caddish thing that the noble Earl ever did.

Cuffe was held for further examination, since he obviously
knew more. After Essex's execution it did him no harm to
admit at last what was obvious: that the action was treason
and Essex a traitor. Cuffe did not incriminate Sir Henry
Neville, but thought that his private visit to Essex at night
was concerned with 'nothing but compliments and foreign
occurrents.' Savile's papers were impounded and himself held
in custody; a woman attendant was examined as to Cuffe's
visits to him. Cuffe knew that King James's last communication to Essex the Earl had carried about on him in a black
purse, but that on his return from the fiasco in the City he
had burned it; this Cuffe regretted. He did say that Scottish
correspondence had been mainly in the hands of Anthony
Bacon: this was not followed up, for Bacon was dying. It
cannot have been pleasant for brother Francis to hear, whose
rôle in the proceedings was generally regarded as little to his
credit.

Cuffe did not cave in at his trial, as other aristocratic
delinquents had done. Southampton was quite as guilty as
he, if not more so, and had urged action on Essex. He was
indeed condemned, but held in the Tower under suspended
sentence. He made a good impression at his trial, relying on
his youthful looks—he was in fact twenty-seven. But he was
an earl, and the Queen was opposed to the extinction of
peerages; the other peers were let off with fines and varying
degrees of imprisonment. Cuffe knew that there was to be
no mercy for him.

The governor of the Tower wrote to Cecil that at last
Cuffe was penitent, and 'grieved that he did not at first
explain all things.' It was reported that at his trial he stood
up to the bullying Attorney General Coke, who was used to
riding rough-shod over prisoners. John Aubrey tells us that
Cuffe 'would dispute with him in syllogisms, till at last one
of Coke's [law-] brethren said, "Prithee, brother, leave off:
thou dost dispute scurvily".' Cuffe was a smart man, and a
great scholar, and baffled him. Said Coke:

"Dominum cognoscite vestrum;"

Cuffe replied, "My lord, you leave out the former part of
the verse, which you should have repeated:

"*Actaeon* ego sum"—

reflecting on his being a cuckold.' Everybody knew that in
marrying a fortune Coke had caught a tartar, who turned
him into a beast with horns, i.e. cuckolded him. Cuffe actually dared to stand up for himself in public and face his
judges.

> The fellow, after he had made some introduction by an artificial [i.e.
> formal] and continued speech and spent some time in sophistical argu-
> ments, descended to these two answers: for his being in Essex House
> the day of the rebellion, they might as well charge a lion within a grate
> as him; and for the consultation at Drury House, it was no more treason
> than the child in the mother's belly is a child.

Cecil reported to Mountjoy the information—no doubt he
took it in his stride—that 'Blount, Meyrick, Davies, Danvers,
Lyttelton and Cuffe are like to die. I grieve for the young
Earl of Southampton, who was drawn in merely for love of
Essex; but as most of the conspiracies were at Drury House
and he always chief, it will be hard to save him; yet I despair
not, he being penitent and the Queen merciful. Sir Henry
Neville is in displeasure for not revealing his acquaintance
with Cuffe.' It is clear that Cecil was going to save
Southampton, who was not so young after all—old enough
to have known better.
Faced with the gallows, Cuffe wrote his last confession to

Cecil with dignity and style. 'It is now high time that he whom public justice hath pronounced the child of death should with the soonest lay aside all cares of this life, reserving himself wholly for that one which the only author of life hath honoured with this testimony, that *unum est necessarium*.' He gave a full recital of the principal points in the projected *coup d'état*, concluding 'thus most humbly beseeching your honour to vouchsafe me your favourable opinion at my last farewell out of this miserable world.'

No one had any favourable opinion of Cuffe—after all he was not an earl—and he elicited no sympathy. The government Declaration, drawn up by Bacon, described him as 'a base fellow by birth, but a great scholar, and indeed a notable traitor by the book, being otherwise of a turbulent and mutinous spirit against all superiors.' No doubt he did mean to rise in this world—but so did everybody else. His former colleague Sir Henry Wotton described him as ambitious—so was *he*, what of it?—but 'smothered under the habit of a scholar, and slubbered over with a certain rude and clownish fashion that had the semblance of integrity.' It was not the semblance only—he had integrity, far more than most; I dare say he had donnish, rather than aristocratic, manners.

A man's will gives a more just portrait of a man's personality. Cuffe left one half of the fine laid out for Bodenham Devereux—evidently land granted to him by Essex for service—a sum of £350 'to be laid out for the best use of my noble Lord and late Master's daughters, the Lady Frances and the Lady Dorothy Devereux, as it shall seem best to my dear Lady and Mistress, the Countess of Essex.' The large sum of £1700 was in Mr William Killigrew's hands, a personal attendant on the Queen, at use and owing interest. Of this Cuffe wished that Sir Henry Neville would accept £500 'from his poor distressed friend, whose exceeding grief it is that he hath, by his late Master's commandment, been an occasion of his trouble, which I pray him most heartily to forgive me.' No one else expressed any such regret, except *pro forma* to the Queen. 'With the like affection I desire that there may be given to my true and dear friend, Sir Henry Savile, £100; and I beseech him to continue the memory of his unfortunate friend, and ever to think charitably of him, however some

endeavour to ruin and deface as well his name as his estate.'
It does not seem that Savile did remember him charitably.

Cuffe desired that £250 be given to Merton College, to
raise £10 a year 'for a commemoration or *dirige* to be always
on Lammas day, betwixt such Fellows as shall be present at
evening prayer that day. . . . To my honest friend, John
Norton the bookseller, £40, as well to discharge the debt I
owe him, as also to give him some recompense for the trouble
which this great tempest, I fear, is like to bring upon him.'
Norton had conveyed Essex's dangerous communications to
Scotland. The debt of £80 from Mr Killigrew, Cuffe wished
him to divide among ten such persons as 'he knew to love
and affect me, his wife and two daughters being comprised
. . . I do likewise pray that £100 may be given to my poor
aged mother, as the last remembrance of my bounden duty.
It remaineth that I only add—O Lord, into thy hands I
commend my spirit, for thou hast redeemed me, O God of
Truth.'

On the 13th of March Cuffe was hanged, along with
Meyrick, on the triangular gallows at Tyburn, their bodies
dangling there together. It is unlikely that his generous will
took effect: the vultures were already gathering. The
Lieutenant of the Tower reported that Cuffe's estate was
'sufficient to pay, and a good deal more, and enough to pay
all her Majesty's charges for him here to good advantage.'
Mr Killigrew had the grant of his lands, and should pay the
Warden of the Fleet, where Cuffe was first imprisoned, for
his charges and also for those at the Tower. There was no
reason why the Queen, having given away the goods, should
have his charges imposed upon her.

Note

1. See my *Shakespeare's Southampton*, Ch. 6.

Sources

Calendar of State Papers Domestic
Historical Manuscripts Commission, *Salisbury Manuscripts*.

J. Spedding, *The Letters and the Life of Francis Bacon*, 7 Vols. (1861–72).
J. Spedding, R. L. Ellis and D. D. Heath (eds.) *The Works of Francis Bacon*, 14 Vols. (Longman & Co., 1857–74).
G. Brodrick, *Memorials of Merton College* (Oxford, 1885).
J. Fletcher, ed., *Registrum Annalium Coll. Merton, 1567–1603* (Oxford Historical Society, 1976).
H. Cuffe, *The Differences of the Ages of Man's Life*, (1640 edn.)
Dictionary of National Biography
G. Ungerer, *A Spaniard in Elizabethan England: The Correspondence of Antonio Perez's Exile*, 2 Vols. (Tamesis, 1974 and 1976).
J. Bruce, ed., *The Correspondence of James VI with Sir Robert Cecil* (Camden Soc., 1861).

7

Richard Carew, Antiquary

By general consent Richard Carew's *Survey of Cornwall* (1602) is the most delightful of such Elizabethan works devoted to separate counties. William Lambarde's *Perambulation of Kent* is fuller and more complete, the work of a legal scholar. Richard Carew was not unscholarly, but a gentleman amateur; his notable advantage was that he was a born writer. His personality comes through his writings, even his translations, and it is a charming one, as appealing as Harington.[1] Nothing ill of him is known in that scuffling, quarrelsome age; but we do know much that is good of him. He had an affectionate family life; he had public spirit and worked unceasingly for the good of his neighbours and his country. Everybody trusted him and liked him. He was intelligent, mainly self-educated and widely read in several languages; quite undemanding and the reverse of assertive, he made his quiet mark. He had a pleasant, joking sense of humour, with a touch of quaintness, appropriate for an antiquary, which makes him endearingly old-fashioned.

The Carews—the name right up to our time, which obliterates all landmarks, was always pronounced Cary—were not an indigenous Cornish stock. They were a widespread Norman clan with possessions mainly in Devon and across the Bristol Channel into South Wales; hence, in the expansive Norman way, extending themselves across the Irish Channel into Ireland. A fifteenth-century marriage to an heiress, Joan Courtenay of Boconnoc, brought the manor of East Antony to the family. She left it to one of her sons, Alexander, who was the great-great-grandfather of Richard Carew. The manor of Antony lies along the south bank of the St Germans

or Lynher river, where it runs into the broad estuary of the
Tamar, the Hamoaze, on the Cornish side from Plymouth.

Carew did not know what Lynher meant, for his knowledge of Cornish was little and faulty: it meant 'long pool'.
And all that delectable Tamarside country is full of tidal
inlets, estuaries, pools, the land broken into by waters
gleaming on every side through trees, beyond meadows,
cornfields and woods. The Antony estate dominates the
northern half of the secluded peninsula running out to Rame
Head and around to Mount Edgcumbe, which dominates
the southern half. Richard's father married a neighbouring
Edgcumbe, great-granddaughter of the famous Sir Richard,
a leading supporter of Henry VII in the West. Thomas Carew
sagely completed his hold on the peninsula by the purchase
of the manor of Sheviock—up to its narrow neck between
river and sea-coast. This had belonged to the Dawnays in the
thirteenth century; in the twentieth century the heir to
Antony has married a Dawnay.

In his own time the antiquary was regularly spoken of as
Richard Carew of Antony, to distinguish him amid that
numerous clan, who proliferated in state and Church,
penetrated the peerage and produced a memorable figure in
rumbustious Sir Peter. Most of them were firm Protestants,
some of them aggressively so, and burned their fingers in
revolt against Queen Mary's Spanish marriage.

Richard Carew never got into trouble—the more remark-
ably for an Elizabethan in that his father died quite young
in 1564, leaving the boy of eight to grow up on his own, to
take early charge of the estates and the responsibilities of the
family. This meant that, unlike so many young gentlemen of
the time, he was never able to make the Continental sojourn
which was frequent for one of his station—and he was so
much better equipped than most of them to profit from it. He
remained at home, teaching himself the modern languages,
Italian, French, Spanish. Latin he acquired in the ordinary
way, from school and tutor, and at Oxford. In the late 1560s
he was at Christ Church, though, like other West Country
gentlemen of means, he resided across the street at Broadgates
Hall. He tells us that, when of three years standing, he was
called on, 'upon a wrongly conceived opinion touching my
sufficiency, to dispute extempore (*impar congressus Achilli*)

with the matchless Sir Philip Sidney, in presence of the earls,
Leicester [Chancellor of the university], Warwick, and divers
other great personages'. We catch a glimpse of the cult the
age accorded to its young hero, dead before his time. Sidney
was at Christ Church from 1568 to 1571; so this was Carew's
time of apprenticeship, and he must already have been well
educated, to be nominated to dispute in public before a
distinguished audience. He never forgot the distinction; it
was the only one that came to him in a lifetime of hard work.

From Oxford he went in the regular course to an inn-of-
court for his legal instruction; at first to Clement's Inn, then
in 1574 to Middle Temple across the street, the inn with
which he had family associations. He was now of age: time
to return to Cornwall and take up his responsibilities as head
of his family. And, shortly, to acquire a wife.

Cornwall's remoteness intensified county life within it.
Even the gentry could not afford many visits to London,
especially if they had an estate to look after; a lawyer's or
merchant's life in London, a career in the Church, in army
or navy, voyaging across strange seas,

To seek new worlds for gold, for praise, for glory—

all that was for younger sons, like the author of those words
himself, Walter Ralegh, a cousin of the Carews. So the resident gentry made the best of it, constantly visiting each
other, snow-balling along as Carew puts it; putting each
other up, bowling, hawking, dining, drinking, not without
the pleasures of discourse, discussing business, county or
family, marriage settlements, lending each other books. One
is surprised at the amount of reading the more intelligent of
them accomplished and more in foreign languages than today.
Naturally, too, they were much related.

Carew describes it: 'this angle which so shutteth them
in hath wrought many interchangeable marriages with each
other's stock, and given beginning to the proverb that all
Cornish gentlemen are cousins. Which endeth in an injurious
consequence—that the king hath there no cousins'. This
meant that there were no peers: no one was rich enough to
support a peerage, for the Duchy of Cornwall, in supporting
monarch or prince, ate up too much surplus-value, in Marxist

phrase. 'They keep liberal, but not costly builded or furnished houses'—no money for that: too much left the poor county one way or another, dues and tolls on tin, its chief source of wealth, for the Duchy, rectories and tithes for bishop, dean and chapter at Exeter. No large Elizabethan house in Cornwall as in richer counties.

However, the gentry made the best of things, 'give kind entertainment to strangers, make even at the year's end with the profits of their living, are reverenced and beloved of their neighbours, live void of factions amongst themselves—at leastwise such as break out into any dangerous excess'. This presents a somewhat idealised picture; but it was still the Elizabethan age, some way off from the horrors of the Civil War, when two of Carew's grandsons were executed. During this blissful interval of sanity, friends 'converse familiarly together, and often visit one another. A gentleman and his wife will ride to make merry with his next neighbour; and after a day or twain those two couples go to a third, in which progress they increase like snowballs, till through their burdensome weight they break again'. We have seen this account of their way of life borne out in minute detail in Carnsew's Diary (See Chapter 4).

In 1577 Carew married Julian Arundell, a girl of fourteen from Trerice, which appears frequently in the Diary. It lies above the ford, which gives it its name, not far but well back from the mess of modern Newquay. The family at Trerice was a junior branch of the 'Great Arundells' of Lanherne, richest of medieval Cornish families now under a cloud for their Catholicism.

The Arundells at Trerice were Protestants, and had just completed their beautiful house—not large, but with elegant decorative gables, fine hall within, the plaster work dated 1572. Upstairs, the great chamber was finished next year, with large coat of arms displaying the now remote connexion of the family with the earls of Arundel. Julian's grandfather had made money as a mercer in London and married into trade. Carew, of an old landed family, is somewhat self-conscious about this, but it had the advantage that Julian was a bit of an heiress.

Equipped with a young wife—who produced nine children before the *Survey* was born, with yet one more to come—

Carew was ready to step out on his career of public duties
and chores proper to his station. Hitherto he has been seen
entirely in the perspective of his one memorable book, by
which he lives; we must try to see his life more fully in the
round, with his book in perspective.

First for his solid basis of land and family. We find him
buying from his uncle Edgcumbe the manor of Drew-
steignton in Devon, site of today's spectacular Castle Drogo.
To raise the cash for it he sold a little manor in the parish of
Lanteglos-by-Fowey to the rich merchant, John Rashleigh,
making a fortune by trade and shipping there; and a small
manor on the steep slopes of Yarcombe Hill, on the Devon-
Somerset border, to Sir Francis Drake who was to build the
house that still exists there. (The money had come from the
Voyage round the World.)

Carew took a hand in the education of his own children.
His eldest son, another Richard, inherited his father's scrib-
bling propensities without his gift. 'My father, from my
childhood, took all the care he could to have me bred up in
learning, well knowing the value thereof by the sweet fruits
he still gathered of his own, which he always increased by
his almost incredible continual labour; for, without a teacher,
he learned the Greek, Dutch, French, Spanish and Italian
tongues'. I suspect that Carew had little Greek and less
Dutch, i.e. German; linguistically he was a modernist, in the
swim of the Elizabethan enthusiasm for Italian. 'He ever
delighted so much in reading; if he had none other hindrance,
going [i.e. walking] or riding he would ever have a book and
be reading'. This is like the great Lord Burghley, who had the
same habit. Thus Carew accumulated a store of miscellaneous
reading; not only the usual classics and the fashionable Ital-
ians, but geographers like Sebastian Münster, Leo Africanus,
Olaus Magnus, or Francisco Leandro; more recondite authorities like Procopius or Zosimus; well-read in the medieval
and Tudor chroniclers, he was also abreast with his contemporaries, Sidney, Spenser, Daniel. He was very much a
reading man; and he made notes of antiquarian objects as he
rode about Cornwall—monoliths, inscribed stones, inscrip-
tions, brasses, people, their stories and their folklore.

He had plenty of opportunity to observe things and pick
up information on his way, either for business or pleasure,

though these—meeting places for J.P.s' sessions and his friends' houses—made some routes familiar, others out of his way, so that some areas of his *Survey* are fuller than others. He became a Justice of the Peace in 1581, and helped on a compromise in the squabble for precedence between Bodmin and Truro with the sensible suggestion that sessions met alternately in either. (It reflected the rivalry between East and West Cornwall, and the conflicting convenience of each.) Riding about Cornwall was a business in itself, the roads no more than tracks, 'uneasy by reason either of the mire or stones'. The one thing Fuller tells us of the Carews is that either the antiquary or his son 'first brought up the use of *gambadoes* [a large boot attached to the saddle], much worn in the West, whereby whilst one rides on horseback his legs are in a coach, clean and warm, in those dirty countries', i.e. counties.

At the end of 1582 Carew was picked sheriff of Cornwall. This was an ungrateful but unavoidable chore. The sheriff's chief job was to supervise the return of taxation, and he was liable for the sums that were in arrears. This demanded the exercise of tact, in which Carew was never wanting—no one supposed that Sir Richard Grenville ever had much tact. No less unpleasant was the job of supervising executions; but Elizabethans took that in their stride.

Evidences of a J.P.'s chores remain from 1584. In August uncle Edgcumbe and Carew were together at Saltash examining Robert Frost who had been in Spain to consult the exile, Sir Francis Englefield. What they found—or what he said—was that he had been sent regarding the purchase of a manor for Sir Walter Ralegh. In October Carew was taking the deposition of Henry Caesar, vicar of Lostwithiel, concerning the appearance of Cardinal Pole after his death, to Sir Walter Mildmay, by conjuration. Henry Caesar seems to have been a High Church ass, and this was the kind of thing people were apt to believe, and which caused trouble.

Religious hysteria was mounting, with plots against the Queen's life, culminating in Babington's plot which ended Mary Stuart's instead, and open war with Spain was approaching. The critical Parliament of 1584–5 met in November, its main concern the safety of the Queen's life, to which end an unprecedented Act of Association was passed,

contrary to her wishes; still more rigorous legislation was
passed against incoming Jesuits and seminary priests, and
home-keeping recusants. Carew served in it as member for
Saltash—with a number of famous newcomers—young
Robert Cecil and Francis Bacon, Sir Francis Drake and Sir
Walter Ralegh; together with a number of prominent Puritans
who pushed forward the legislation and wanted to bring the
Queen of Scots to the block. Elizabeth had great difficulty
in preventing this, as in 1572, as she wrote to Mary in a
warning letter.

From 1585 open war with Spain began. On his return from
London Carew was made a deputy-lieutenant to Ralegh as
Lord Lieutenant, with military duties especially for the
defence of Cawsand Bay, now in the front line, with the
Armada preparing. He also became treasurer of the Cornish
militia. In the stormy summer of '88 he was called upon,
with his fellow deputy-lieutenant, Sir Francis Godolphin, to
raise the cash to recoup John Rashleigh for his expenses in
equipping the *Francis* of Fowey and a pinnace to serve against
the Armada. Of £600, only £100 had been raised; they were
to lay a tax on the towns and hundreds near adjoining to
raise the rest—an unpopular assignment. In October Godolphin and Carew were to investigate the complaint of a
Cornish gentleman against the hard dealing of two Devon
merchants; to call the parties before them and compound the
matter or report to the Council.

All through these years Carew had to take a leading part
in containing the dispute regarding the Plymouth pilchard
fishery in bounds: a complicated matter of which we can give
only the outline.[2] The pilchard fishery was growing rapidly;
so was the export market which took the largest proportion
of the catch. The fishermen were located on the Cornish side,
with their fish-cellars for curing concentrated at Cawsand
and financed by fish-merchants. Against their interest was
arrayed the consumers' interest of the town of Plymouth,
and in the Privy Council's numerous letters and instructions
one can see their overriding concern that the prime fortress
in the war against Spain should not go short. Other factors
entered into the dispute: a conflict between mercantile
monopoly, free enterprise of the fishermen, the demands of
the market at home and for export.

To maintain the Orders approved by the Council six commissioners were appointed: for Devon, Sir John Gilbert, Sir Francis Drake, and Christopher Harris; for Cornwall, Carew, Anthony Rouse, and John Wray. They were to meet alternately at Plymouth and Mount Edgcumbe to see that the orders were observed. This chore was a continuing business which we cannot pursue; conflicts remained, and as soon as external pressure was relaxed the townsmen of Plymouth returned to the charge with a petition to Carew and the commissioners that they would see to exact compliance with the Orders in Council. All very Elizabethan.

No less so was the dispute concerning the Venetian argosy, the *Uggiera Salvagina*, which continued all through 1590 and half of 1591. She had been brought in as prize with a rich cargo of sugars, pepper, spices, and ivory ('elephants' teeth'). The question was whether the cargo did not belong to a state in amity with the Queen. Trial at law decided that the cargo belonged to merchants of Venice and Florence, both of which were friendly states. The cargo was to be restored, Captain Davies now back in Falmouth to be pursued, stayed and searched for goods. Carew was involved in all these proceedings along with his friends, Drake, Gilbert, Edgcumbe, Rouse and the mayor of Plymouth.

Their diligence was commended by the Council in staying the *Tiger* of London, and stowing its captured goods in safe custody; but they had in this instance omitted to inform Sir John Gilbert as Vice-Admiral of Devon; henceforth they were not to proceed without his privity. In July 1591 the French fishing fleet from Newfoundland was brought into Plymouth. These J.P.s were to examine which ships were from ports in obedience to Henri IV and which were under the Catholic League, in revolt against him: they were to 'draw them to accuse one another', League ships to be brought up to London. Drake, Edgcumbe and Carew were to inquire into the petition of Thomas Limbery of Plymouth, who had sustained great losses through employment at sea under Drake, Frobisher and others. He had not been able to recover house and goods wrongfully detained from him for four years, with bonds and bills, by three rich Plymouth men. They were to inquire and, if the claims were substantiated, to set down an order for relief. Even in September 1591 the goods of the Venetian argosy were still held sequestered, for them to see to, in Plymouth and Dartmouth.

Next month the London ships which had set forth to reinforce Lord Thomas Howard in the Azores expedition, in which Grenville lost his life and the *Revenge*, returned with valuable prizes from Spain's Indies and Mexico fleets. Drake, Carew, Rouse and Harris were to see that no mariners came ashore until the cargoes were inventoried, and to examine the prisoners. In December Plymouth was to be further fortified: the question was whether a fort protecting the town on the sea side, or a wall around it would be better. Gilbert, Drake, George and Richard Carew with others were to examine and report. Such was the constant fare of the deputy-lieutenant in these earlier years of the long war. There was not only the pressure of war-work, musters to be seen to and inspected, money to be raised, training to be supervised, beacons seen to, detachments later sent abroad to Ireland and Brittany—but in 1594–5 Carew took the lead in the affair of the conventionary tenures of the Duchy of Cornwall. This was a matter of great importance, for it affected some 10,000 people; Carew raised the matter, organised the protests from the hundreds, led the delegation to London and carried the business through.

The affair affords a precious glimpse—almost unique in its detail, since Carew was a writer and wrote it up—into how great personages, the Queen, Burghley and others, conducted business. We catch them in characteristic attitudes—the wish at the top to do justice, to do the best for everybody, manoeuvring for a practical solution to an imprecise, contingent problem which yet could have wide repercussions and make future trouble.

The issue was this. Within Cornwall lay the seventeen ancient manors of the Duchy; a few more had been added from the monasteries, but these were not involved. The ancient manors spread across Cornwall were called the 'assessionable manors', for the customary tenants therein renewed their tenancy at a formal Assession court every seven years, paying fines for renewal and agreed rents. For all practical purposes they had come to regard their tenancy as inheritable, as if long prescription constituted a right. This was not the view of the Duchy officials, whose duty it was to make the best profit for the Duchy—during Elizabeth's reign in the possession of the Crown—and so regarded the conventionary tenants as not freeholders but tenants at the will of the lord. This latent conflict of interest had long been present, and was to continue; it had been the practice to let sleeping dogs lie, *Quieta non movere*.

An interfering interloper, one Meggs, born in the Isle of Ely but married in Cornwall, brought the matter into the light of day by challenging a number of such conventionary leases in the courts of law. The judge, in spite of his sympathy for the tenants, could not but deliver his view of the law, namely that they were tenants at will. The case brought into question 'all whose estates depended upon the self-same title'; it would be 'the utter undoing of many thousands who had quietly enjoyed the same for many scores of years', as Carew put it. These conventionary tenants were of all classes and standing, from gentry like Sir Francis Godolphin down through substantial and ordinary farmers to poor cottagers. The upsetting of such long-continued custom on so widespread a scale, if it had been allowed to spread, might well have precipitated a rebellion like those in which the Cornish had engaged in 1497 and again in 1549. No wonder Henry Meggs—to the Cornish 'a foreigner'—was mobbed and insulted, his cattle driven off, servants beaten up: earlier in the century he would have been murdered.

Carew took the lead in taking the matter to Westminster, to the Exchequer Court and its Chancellor, to Lord Treasurer Burghley, the Queen herself. He drafted the protests which were circulated to the authorities, organised the tenants according to the hundreds where they dwelt, held meetings of the J.P.s at sessions. It was decided to levy a year's rent from the tenants to meet the charges of a deputation to London. In the event the affair kept them there for seven weeks, consultations, lawyers, searching the records, audiences with the highest in the land.

The ground was well prepared by a series of petitions, written by Carew, to the relevant authorities. To the Queen: 'that it may please your highness of your accustomed bounty to vouchsafe your favourable allowance of those their customary tenures, which under your Majesty and your progenitors they have enjoyed by the space of 300 years, and now lately are sought by certain particular persons to be overthrown . . .'. To the Privy Council: 'This poor shire of Cornwall wherein we live is at present many ways distressed by the enemy's surprising our ships; by fear of their invasions; by stopping of our accustomed trades by dearth of victuals; by decay of the mines and by the late infection of the plague [severe in 1592 and 1593]. Whereunto is adjoined another more harmful plague of such as seek to reap a private profit with the undoing of a great multitude'. The most forceful argument was that the threatened insecurity would affect some 10,000 persons, if allowed to pass. This was urged in petitions also to Lord Burghley, the Earl of Essex, Sir John Fortescue, Chancellor of the Exchequer, Sir Walter Ralegh, Lord Warden of the Stannaries, William Killigrew, Groom of the Privy Chamber, and Lord Chief Justice Anderson, who had had to decide the case against the tenants at the Bodmin Assizes. No stone was left unturned.

Not for nothing was Carew a writer: each petition was nicely tuned to the ear of the recipient. To the Lord Chief Justice: 'That pitiful case which your lordship heard with remorse at our late assizes'. To Ralegh: 'Certain vile disposed persons, nothing discouraged by the ill success which— through your lordship's principal help—hath befallen their fellows' late attempts in sea matters,[3] are now as busily working to bereave us of our possessions over the land'. To William Killigrew: 'there are some greedy persons who have gotten leases under the Great Seal of certain Duchy customary tenements. . . . As it would breed little benefit unto her Majesty, so it would thrust 10,000 her highness' loyal subjects and poor tenants into extreme misery and beggary, and only a few covetous caterpillars should suck the sweet sap both from her Majesty and them'. William Killigrew, fellow-Cornishman, was in daily personal attendance upon the Queen: this was the kind of thing to feed her with. She was always sensitive about the complaints of poor tenantry: had she not rated her 'good old man', the Earl of Shrewsbury, for his ill relations with his tenantry in Glossopdale?[4]

It was not an easy matter to get an agreed course out of so many people, or to hold the deputies together on the way. Carew and Jonathan Trelawny were to lead the delegation, but one of them stole a march on the others, set out before them to curry favour with Sir Walter Ralegh by a typical piece of Elizabethan tale-telling. They set out to arrive in London a week before Easter term, when the courts might be too busy to give them full attention. From Exeter they made for Honiton

and pitched next at Sherborne and made repair to Sir Walter Ralegh. Where they were entertained for some hours by Mr Adrian Gilbert, his half-brother, with viewing the new buildings, and had their access delayed upon pretence of his sickness. But more indeed through a conceit grounded upon a fore-report that they meant either not to visit him at all, or else only to do it for a fashion sake, and not in any sort to rely upon his furtherance.

There is always some fool to make trouble of that sort, and Ralegh too behaved very much in character—though the incident is unknown to any of his biographers.

At last, as they grew amongst themselves into terms of departure, admittance was given. Whom they found lying upon a pallet in his little chamber; received a courteous welcome, and delivered their letters. Which, after he had read, he alleged his indisposition of health, and gave his advice what course was fittest to be taken in following the suit. . . . Not to depend upon the help of many, but principally to solicit the Lord Treasurer, to whom such matters specially appertained. Though his lordship should at first oppose himself with sharp terms, yet were they not to take discouragement, but to persist in their suit, which—the importance thereof once thoroughly conceived—he doubted not would sort to a good effect.

Ralegh knew his Burghley well, but he himself was still in disgrace with the Queen, and was in a difficult mood.

Then the deputies told him what sinister report they heard was made of them and besought his lordship not to credit the same. They withal acknowledged how much in former occasions he had friended their country [i.e. county], and that this properly belonged to his office as high steward of the Duchy: they ought both first to seek him and meant principally to rely upon him. He made a slight answer—that he had not been so informed'.

Before they left Sherborne Castle that evening, he relented and did his best for them with personal letters to the Lord Treasurer, the Chancellor of the Exchequer, Sir Robert Cecil,

and Burghley's Secretary, Mr Maynard. Lodging at Salisbury, they resolved to suspend the offending deputy until he
should explain himself; at Staines each deputy put all his
information at the disposal of the rest. Arrived at London,
4 May 1594, they learned that many poor folk and certain
gentlemen were coming up to follow the suit. Calling upon
the Lord Chief Justice next morning, they asked him to move
the Queen in the matter: to which he gave a No. Referred
to the Lord Treasurer, shrugging his shoulders—in Carew's
Italian phrase—he dismissed them with, 'I will do you any
good I can'.

The next two days were spent in searching the records and
Thence to the Lord Chief Baron of the Exchequer, who
promised his 'lawful favour'. Part of the afternoon was spent
with Sir Henry Killigrew, Burghley's brother-in-law, 'who,
with no less love than great experience [he was a foremost
diplomat], gave directions what course was fittest to be
followed'. They next retained as counsel Sergeants Harris,
Glanville and Hele—all West Countrymen. Next morning
they went down river to the Court at Greenwich, where
William Killigrew took them under his wing, presenting their
letters to the Queen and Burghley, who were particularly
impressed by Sir Francis Godolphin's. It was a great help to
have Killigrew on their side; he accompanied them everywhere to the grandees they had to see, 'advised, argued,
served, and laboured for them'. They felt proud of Cornwall
'in that it bred a gent of so rare a kindness, honesty, and
reputation'.

The next two days were spent in searching the records and
getting copies of the new disturbing leases. They then waited
upon Lord Treasurer Burghley, who teased them for not
coming sooner, for he had news for them. Someone had
handed in a paper to the Queen making various points against
the Duchy tenants, by which she was much deceived in her
revenue. This was very like him, to put all the objections
first for them to answer—which they did. He asked them
for a list of the assessionable manors, and dismissed them
while he conferred with the officers of the Exchequer.

At the formal session next morning, surrounded by these,
Burghley told the twelve deputies called in that no custom
alleged by the tenants could bar the Queen from making her
best profit. They replied that 'those lands thus set yielded

more profit to her Majesty than any other belonging to the Crown'. Their counsel had advised them that 'though they might prescribe for their custom against their Duke, touching her Majesty they chose rather to appeal unto her highness' clemency'. This was wise advice, since she would always be moved by the consideration that 10,000 people might be affected.

Thus the suit went on, arguments of lawyers backwards and forwards, more searching of the Tower records (in the keeping of Carew's antiquarian colleague, William Lambarde). Time passed; their suit was at a stop. Killigrew advised them at their next session with the Lord Treasurer whether they might petition the Queen personally. He replied, 'Yes; I pray you, do so'. Carew penned their humble petition for favour, concluding in courtier-wise, 'in vouch-safing whereof, though your Majesty cannot increase the fame of your own virtues or the bond of our loyal affections, yet' . . . etc. This was the right note. They were to be admitted to the presence of the deity, who however 'disliked, as did all the other greatest personages, that so many came up about it, and forbade their trooping together'.

On Whitsun eve they waited upon Essex 'to use that means of purchasing the more grace with her Majesty'. He asked for a paper of their case for his better information. On Whit Sunday morning they sought him at his lodging in vain, for he had gone up by a privy way to the Queen; meeting him going along to chapel, they delivered their paper, which he read while at service. Killigrew guided them to the place where they should be for delivery of their petition, on the right of the chapel door, and 'by good hap their countryman, Goit, one of the Guard, waited that day and kept them from thrusting'. In the *Survey* Carew pays tribute to 'my friend John Goit' as champion among Cornish wrestlers; 'his clean-made body and active strength extend, with great agility, to whatsoever other exercise of the arm or leg, besides his ability to take charge at sea, either as master or captain. All which good parts he graceth with a good fellow-like, kind and respectful carriage'. Elizabeth liked to have such fine looking fellows about her.

Majesty then came forth from chapel in state, supported by Essex on one side, Lord Admiral Howard on the other.

As she approached, Essex spoke to her on behalf of the
Cornish petitioners. She asked who were they, among the
crowd present. They thereupon knelt down and delivered
their petition. The oracle spoke, very much in character:
'There are many foolish things gotten out against. But it shall
be remedied. I would they were hanged who have been the
doers thereof; for we respect the public more than the
private'. Precisely: playing for popularity as always, sincere
enough—it was her rôle—leaving it to others to carry out
the message. Shortly after, Essex came out again to tell them
that they were now in a good way.

The Queen handed the petitioners over to her favourite,
Lady Warwick, who, meeting Serjeant Harris on his way in
to explain the case to the Queen, expressed her own affection
to the West Country as Bedford's daughter, who had once
borne rule there—and derived large revenues from the estates
of Tavistock abbey, we may add. The deputies were now to
attend the Lord Treasurer's direction, upon her Majesty's
pleasure that the offending leases be revoked and no more
such granted.

To their dejection Burghley handed down an ambivalent
and canny decision, reserving all the rights of the Duchy.
'The dukes of Cornwall have not been bound to any strict
certainty of fines, neither her Majesty may be by any law
restrained to take such fines as shall reasonably by her officers
think convenient. But yet her Majesty mindeth to use them
[the ancient tenants] with all reasonable favour without
exacting any unreasonable fines' . . . etc. Carew comments:
'the word *unreasonable* inserted herein seemed unto them to
be such indeed'. Alarmed as they were, Sir Henry Killigrew
advised them not to make too much stir about it 'lest the
Lord Treasurer, not easily drawn from his once-taken course,
might take some conceit against them'. They went to Burghley's Secretary, who agreed with Killigrew. Here we have
the great man.

There followed several interviews with his officials,
sympathetic enough. 'With the Lord Treasurer they found
less grace'. He somewhat testily told them that they had no
custom, and so their counsel could assure them. The question
of the expenses of one of the new lessees came up; the
deputies did not want to pay the large bill for £240 for

someone who had caused all the trouble. This man, Edwards, threatened a suit at law, which would be a prolonged affair. He kept the deputies waiting while he consulted counsel; Burghley then chided them for keeping him waiting. The old Polonius, after a lifetime of such chores and suits, was querulous and testy. When they all waited on him at Cecil House, Edwards was greeted with a sharp welcome for not coming when he was required, and for procuring the lease, i.e. for being a nuisance.

Then Meggs, the initiator of the trouble, was summoned, who 'met his lordship the next day as he was coming down the stairs. Whereupon, exhibiting a petition, he received the title of a "shifting fellow"!' At a further gathering of them all in Burghley's garden, 'Mr Meggs was again bitterly reproved and one of the deputies . . . with sharp words touching the cause in controversy'. When both parties offered to submit to his decision regarding the expenses of the new lessees forfeiting their leases, Burghley said that he must take time to consider the matter; when 'they offered to follow him he chid them away'. How badgered he must have felt with so much greater problems on hand, the war and the financial strain it was! 'The delay grew alike tedious to both parties. Whereon the deputies offered Edwards 100 marks in consideration of his charges, but that he would not smell unto'.

Lord Burghley was now having to leave Westminster to prepare to entertain Queen and Court at his country palace of Theobalds (in itself a vast expense: it cost precisely ten times Edwards' bill), and he would not be back again that term, which was drawing to an end. 'Whereof one of them [evidently Carew] watched his lordship as he went to his coach and besought his pleasure. He said that he liked not the excess of Edwards' demand. Yet other answer could none begotten, "unless", quoth he, "you can agree amongst yourselves".'

Edwards thereupon approached Burghley's Secretary, Michael Hicks, who 'was that afternoon to follow his lord unto Theobalds, who could in no wise brook to be troubled there with suitors'. It is to Hicks that we owe a charming description of the old man taking his ease in the garden at Theobalds, by one of the canals he had made, reading and

dozing over a book. Hicks suggested writing a letter. While
waiting for a reply they all went to thank Essex for his help
at Leicester House.

From Theobalds—'tomorrow this poor house will be
called the Queen's house'—Burghley wrote three letters with
his instructions. He considered that the request of the deputies was reasonable, and ordered that the tenants should
renew their leases according to the ancient custom, the fine
being 'arbitrary at her Majesty's pleasure'. On the other
hand he thought it reasonable that the tenants should repay
Edwards' charges, since they were 'to taste of her Majesty's
gracious favours'.

Michael Hicks forwarded the letters to Carew, 'which
drew the deputies into a peck of doubts'. They had not
achieved a clear decision as to their tenant-right for the
future. Mr Fanshawe of the Exchequer advised them to hope
for the best. 'Thus far did we wade in our suit and then,
after seven weeks' space, turned our minds and our faces
homewards'. Carew concluded: 'in the meantime all indif-
ferent lookers into the cause, we hope, may find that we
leave the same in better terms than we received it'. Carew
signed his account of their mission with his personal motto,
Chi verace durera (who speaks truth will live), and, with a
sigh of relief, '*Deo gloria, mihi gratia*, 1594 July 9'.

He drew up a detailed paper of pros and cons (as Burghley
regularly did himself). 'We have no decree for us. We must
pay money to our adversaries. We are threatened our fines
shall be altered and so consequently our customs broken'.
On the other hand, 'the alteration of our fines is builded
only upon a perhaps and no near harm', while the new leases
had been certainly put a stop to. When they got home there
was still a peck of trouble in raising the money to meet
Edwards' charges: a few whole manors and some tenants
refused outright to contribute. As late as May 1595 another
letter from the Lord Treasurer was needed, with the threat
that when the time came to renew their leases the recalcitrant
should be barred from renewal.

Carew gave a brief impersonal account of the contest in
the *Survey*; he does not mention the leading part he had
played in it from beginning to end, though his personal
feeling does come through in his reference to the Queen's

'express order for stay of the attempt' against their ancient custom, testifying 'her great dislike of the attempter: since which time this barking dog has been muzzled'. Henry Meggs did not prosper in Cornwall. Carew pays tribute to the help they had received from the cousinage: Ralegh's helpful letters, Sir Henry Killigrew's sound advice, William Killigrew's 'painful soliciting, being the most kind patron of all his country [i.e. county] and countrymen's affairs at Court'.

We turn with relief from these complicated business affairs, with their human obstinacies and perversities, to the simpler delights of literature—as no doubt Carew did. For it was in this same year, 1594, that his first two works to be published appeared. The first was his translation of five cantos of Tasso's *Gerusalemme Liberata* which, though printed in both languages in London, was published by Christopher Hunt of Exeter.

We are left in some uncertainty as to the circumstances of publication, for it was fairly common for Elizabethan gentlemen—as indeed later—to disclaim pushing themselves forward into print. The title page bore only the initials R.C., and Hunt's prefatory epistle, or blurb, may be something of a cover-up. The work came to his hands by 'good hap . . . done, as I was informed, by a gentleman of good sort and quality, and many ways commended unto me for a work of singular worth and excellency . . . At the instance of some of my best friends I determined to send it to the press'. He hoped that his forwardness had not 'forerun the gentleman's good liking', etc. He must have become acquainted with Carew later, for he concludes: 'Whereas I thought you should have had all together, I must pray you to accept of the first five Songs; for it hath pleased the excellent doer of them, for certain causes to himself best known, to command a stay of the rest till summer. From Exeter, the last of February 1594'.

Carew was heavily engaged otherwise for the rest of that year; it would seem that he had completed the translation of the poem, though it never appeared. If so, there was a good reason for that. Edward Fairfax also was translating Tasso, and his complete translation appeared in 1600. It was a far better work, for he was a poet, where Carew was only a versifier. It looks as if this first publication, in somewhat odd circumstances, was a trial run; that it was not a success and not republished. Carew's gift was for prose, not verse.

It is likely enough that Carew had been inspired by Harington's *Orlando Furioso* to follow his example, and Carew similarly writes in ottava rima, regular eight-line stanza. Christopher Hunt—or Hunt writing for Carew— makes it a virtue that the translation is so literal: 'the learned reader shall see how strict a course the translator hath tied himself in the whole work, usurping as little liberty as any whatsoever that ever wrote with any commendations'. But that is precisely the trouble: the verse is so constricted as not to be very readable.

> Sweet roses' colour in that visage fair
> With ivory is spersed and mingellèd,
> > But in her mouth whence breath of love outgoes,
> > Ruddy alone and single blooms the rose.

Or,

> And shall respects of fading honour vain,
> Which like sea waves soon slow, and ebb as far,
> Work more with you than either faith or zeal?

Godfrey of Boulogne, or the Recovery of Jerusalem . . . The First Part, containing Five Cantos, was an abortive work, a sufficient reason for not going on with it. Hunt—or Hunt-Carew—regarded it however as 'the readiest means to draw him to publish some of his many most excellent labours'.

Anyway Carew drew out of his drawer for publication this year, 1594, a prose translation of a famous Spanish book, Juan Huarte's *Examen de Ingenios*, though he rendered it from the Italian translation. This work, a stout octavo of 335 pages, was printed by Adam Islip for Richard Watkins, and was evidently successful, for it received three reprints in Carew's lifetime: in 1596, 1604 and 1616. In this case the trial-run paid off.

For us the charm of the work lies in its dedication to Carew's friend and colleague:

To the right worshipful Sir Francis Godolphin, Knight, one of the

Deputy-Lieutenants of Cornwall. Good sir, your book returneth unto you clad in a Cornish gabardine [coarse woollens] which, if it become him not well, the fault is not in the stuff but in the botching tailor, who never bound prentice to the occupation and, working only for his pastime, could hardly observe the precise rules of measure. But such as it is, yours it is, and yours is the workman, entirely addicted to reverence you for your virtues, to love you for your kindness; and so more ready in desire than able in power to testify the same, do with my dewest remembrance take leave, resting at your disposition, R.C.

We see that these elect spirits in Elizabethan Cornwall were an educated circle—certainly more so than today— reading Italian; for Carew had borrowed the Italian translation from Godolphin. None of Godolphin's books survives there today, though some of Carew's remain at Antony— Spenser and Sidney, Holinshed and the chroniclers.

This solid Renaissance work, based on Aristotle and Plato, was a remarkable attempt to bring psychology into relation with physiology—the latter of course based on Galen. We go through the usual gamut of the four humours—heat, cold, moistness, dryness—and then branch out into the effects of climate, for example, on temperament and mental faculties. It is amusing at that moment of conflict between Northern and Southern Europe, between Reformation and Counter-Reformation, to notice a Spaniard's opinion of Northern Europeans. Those of Northern abode have want of understanding; the wits of Flemish, Germans, French and English are like those of drunkards, 'for which cause they cannot search out nor understand the nature of things'. But those who are seated in the temperate zone, between cold North and torrid South, are of great wisdom. Spain lies in such a zone; hence Spaniards . . . QED.

In more concrete observations, away from the dubiousness of generalisation, Huarte speaks sense. Carew translates, for instance: 'He proveth by an example that, if a child have not the disposition and ability which is requisite for that science whereunto he will addict himself, it is a superfluous labour to be instructed therein by good schoolmasters, to have store of books, and continually to study it'. This piece of common sense, a commonplace of education in the 16th century, is rather lost sight of in the 20th, with its bias in favour of the not very educable.

Carew's next venture into publication—anonymously, without even initials—was a curious work indeed: '*A Herring's Tale: Containing a Poetical fiction of divers matters worthy the reading*. At London. Printed for Matthew Lownes. 1598'. Carew was in London for the Parliament of 1597–8; evidently he arranged for its publication then. It is a comic, mock-heroic poem, a skit on the heroics of *Orlando Furioso*, *The Faerie Queene*, Daniel, Drayton and such, in long, rhymed alexandrines:

> I sing the strange adventures of the hardy snail,
> Who durst (unlikely match) the weathercock assail . . .

I do not find it very comic; it comes rather under the heading of Elizabethan quaintness. We see in it the disadvantage of Carew's living so far away from literary society, though the verse is no worse, say, than that of Arthur Brooke or Thomas Churchyard.

The fact is that the poem is provincial; even its points of interest are provincial. Here as elsewhere Carew uses Cornish dialect words naturally. The snail's house is 'built of a thin strong *cloamy* wall': in Cornwall we still use the word cloam for earthenware.

> Then *clibby* ladder 'gainst his battered flank he rears:

the word means sticky. It is probable that the numerous words in Cornish dialect beginning with 'cl' represent the original inflected 'll' of Welsh, as Carew mentions in the *Survey*. He has the practising farmer's eye for detail:

> Even as the steal-corn pismire [ant] tugs and hales his load,
> Till winter store in keep of cob[5] safely stowed.

His chief literary admirations are glanced at:

> Who list such know, let him Muses' dispenser [Spenser] read,
> Or thee whom England sole did since the Conquest breed
> To conquer ignorance: Sidney, like whom endite
> Even Plato would, as Jove (they say) like Plato write.

His literary squib gave Carew amusement amid the

growing burdens of family and public life, something to think about among his country recreations and hobbies, storing up folklore, riding about alternating with his passionate addiction to fishing. It is in keeping that next year, 1599, he should have written his piece 'Of the Antiquity, Variety, and Etymology of Measuring Land in Cornwall'. Cornish measurements, from a mile downwards, differed from the units that prevailed in England; so, too, with weights—even in my boyhood we weighed flour by the peck or quarter-peck: a quarter-peck weighed 8¾ lb. Immense variety existed, and there were local variations within Cornwall—in the making of butter, for instance: each farmer's wife had her own particular mould with its stamp upon the half-pound pat.

We must return briefly to Carew's public duties. In March 1595 the mayor, with Carew and George Cary of Cockington, sent up to the Council their estimate for finishing the fort at Plymouth: £800 had already been spent on the works. Sir Ferdinando Gorges was appointed to the command; they were to take up workmen for the speedy finishing of the job. That July there was an alarm upon the coast, when four Spanish galleys from Brittany landed a couple of hundred armed men, pikes and shot, in Mount's Bay. They burned for half a mile round, Newlyn, Penzance, Mousehole and the parish church of Paul. The inhabitants, unarmed, fled; until Sir Francis Godolphin arrived to give leadership and drive the Spaniards back to their ships. Carew wrote an account of the event into the *Survey* which he was now preparing.

The descent upon the coast gave point to the necessity for further fortification and the training of the county's armed bands—Carew's job as treasurer for the latter must have been exacting in itself. In October Godolphin and he, with Edgcumbe and Bevil, had trouble over the Muster Master, Captain Peyton, who had been sent down by the Council and Ralegh as Lord Lieutenant to train the bands. The impoverished county protested against being rated with his pension, while he could not train so large a multitude, now fifty companies, more than twice a year. They appealed to both Council and Sir Walter, yielding God thanks for Ralegh's safe return from Guiana.

Government was at its wit's end for money to carry on
the war on so many fronts—and now Ireland was to be added
to them. Early in 1597 it was reduced to the expedient of a
forced loan; Godolphin was given the ungrateful job of
rounding up the county. Meanwhile, at Plymouth Carew was
engaged, with the mayor, Gorges and Stalleng, the Admiralty
official, in sorting out the cargo of two prizes brought in.
Spaniards were to be sent up, French sent across Channel.
A complication ensued: one of the captures turned out to be
not lawful prize, and restitution was to be made to a French
merchant near St Jean de Luz.

In October Noel de Caron, agent for the States of Holland,
laid complaint that Captain Mohun and his accomplices had
unlawfully taken an Amsterdam ship, *The Flying Hart*, into
Fowey, laden with Spanish wools, ginger, etc. Here was the
teasing problem the English have encountered in every war—
when their allies and friends engage in trading with the
enemy. What to do? The Court of Admiralty ordered the
goods to be padlocked, Dutch and English to guard the cargo
for the owners.

After this chore Carew was on the road for London again,
to serve as member for Mitchell, in the Parliament called for
November to impose further taxation. The 1590s were a time
of distress. Plague for two years running, 1592 and 1593,
was quite exceptional; this was followed by dearth; 1594
was marked by appalling weather, with a succession of bad
harvests. The country was under great strain; yet the younger
generation, led by Essex and Ralegh, pressed for further
expensive campaigns—Cadiz in 1596, the Azores expedition
in 1597. Parliament in 1597–8 was concerned with taxation,
and social and economic legislation in regard to the prolifer-
ating poor; criticism was voiced against the monopolies,
which produced cash or rewarded service. It is not to be
supposed that Carew raised, or wasted, his voice. His son
and heir was now at his own old inn, Middle Temple, and
in 1598 was taken by his uncle George on his embassy to
Poland, upon which they had various adventures.

On Carew's return the necessities of the time are reflected
in his public duties. A ship of Emden, the *Fortune*, bound
for Rochelle with corn had been blown into Dartmouth. The
Privy Council gave order that, owing to the dearth and

scarcity of corn, the cargo might be sold there or at Plymouth
or Exeter to the best advantage. The mayor of Dartmouth
had sold it to certain rich men at a far lower price than it
was worth—to the owners' loss of £400. Satisfaction was to
be made, bonds taken of those who had bought the corn,
inquiry made at what price, and what quantity the mayor
kept for himself. They were to be made to pay the overplus.
Carew from Antony, and Edward Seymour from Berry
Pomeroy, were allotted the ungrateful job.

In November 1598 300 more soldiers from Cornwall were
levied as part of the army necessary to meet O'Neill's challenge in Ulster. Godolphin was at Scilly attending to its
defences—Star Castle had been built there; Carew was in
London. Christopher Harris reported that the men from
these two deputy-lieutenants' divisions, West and East
Cornwall ('my cousin Carew's') would be better embarked
from Fowey than from Padstow. Cornwall regularly counted
as no more than one-third part of Devon, yet it was now
charged almost equal.

In April 1599 Carew and Edgcumbe reported from
Cawsand that four ships had taken five fishing boats and
most of the men, and were still before the harbour—probably
a raid from the Spanish forces in Brittany, as four years
before upon Mount's Bay. In August the deputy-lieutenants
were at Pendennis Castle with the governor, Sir Nicholas
Parker, to discuss the redistribution of the defence-force of
1000 men and their places of rendez-vous. As the shire is
long—70 miles—a provost-marshal was needed, since so
many offenders (and deserters) escaped unpunished. Owing
to these alarms the county had been ordered to raise larger
forces of horse and foot. The clergy remained at their
previous rate, lower than the laity. A new rate of arms was
suggested from the clergy throughout the county. We see the
strain they were all under.

In December 1600 Dunkirkers—privateers prowling the
Channel from that port—were off the Lizard, so that the
victualling ships for the army in Ireland dared not put out.
The Council ordered Carew to certify the price of wheat and
whether 1200 quarters might be delivered at Plymouth and
Fowey at 6d the gallon.

His young son John was fighting abroad in the Low Countries, where attention was concentrated on the Spaniards' siege of the key fortress of Ostend. The ding-dong struggle around the entrenchments lasted for three years, July 1601 to September 1604, by which time England had made peace with Spain. Early in the struggle John Carew had his hand blown off by a cannon-ball. The Cornish folklore is that he brought it back and threw it on the table, with 'This is the hand that cut the pudding at dinner'. The event has made orthopaedic history, for the manipulative iron hand that was made for him is the earliest to survive.[6] It came down in the family of the Tremaynes of Heligan, into which his daughter Mary married. John married a Devon girl at St Thomas' Exeter in 1616, and had a family of daughters who married into old Cornish families, Tremayne, Hoblyn, Trevanion. From his apprenticeship to war he retired to farm Penwarne, near Mevagissey, where something of his house remains.

The same year the father had provided for the continuance of the family by pressing forward a marriage for his son and heir. After following in his father's footsteps at Oxford in Broadgates Hall and at Middle Temple, and returning safely from Poland and Sweden, young Richard accompanied another family connexion, Sir Henry Neville, on his embassy to France. Carew was not rich, and this was a less expensive way of providing acquaintance with the Continent for his son. On his return, as young Richard wrote in his autobiography, 'my father, himself having been a ward, was desirous to see me married before I was twenty-one; fearing by reason of his often sickness he should have died before I was of full age. Albeit I wanted not a quarter of a year when, by the motion of our friends and consent of our parents, I married Mistress Bridget Chudleigh of Ashton in the county of Devon'. This was in January 1601; she brought a convenient dowry of £1500, while Richard senior settled £60 a year on his son to set up his family. The young wife died in 1611, after ten years of too frequent child-bearing. Among her children were Alexander, beheaded on Tower Hill 1644, and John hanged as a regicide at Charing Cross in 1660— unimaginable fates for sober, quiet Richard's progeny! It may be that the Chudleigh marriage brought in an unquiet strain, for the family had a restless changing record in the Civil War.

Back to public chores. In January of this year 1601 we have a brief note of coat and conduct money, £9.10.8, paid to a servant of Carew's for twenty soldiers levied in Cornwall for Lough Foyle. In October Spanish forces arrived in Munster to aid Ulster's resistance from the south: this proved the critical turning point of the war in Ireland. With resources strained to breaking point, Crown lands having to be sold, the government asked the country gentry throughout the West to help by providing and equipping one light horse each. Mountjoy's decisive victory at Kinsale rewarded the government's efforts; henceforth O'Neill's resistance was gradually rolled back.

It was in these last years at the turn of the century that Carew took up again his manuscript about Cornwall and its antiquities, and brought it to the point of publication as the *Survey* of 1602. At some time during his visits to London he had been welcomed as a member of the informal society of antiquaries grouped around the master they acknowledged in William Camden, and meeting conveniently in Sir Robert Cotton's house in Westminster. Camden's *Britannia* of 1586 (in Latin) had set a model of antiquarian scholarship and placed Britain on the map of Renaissance Europe, historically speaking. Camden, like the headmaster he was, inspired the work of all the circle, but he also made use of their special knowledge of their localities for his general picture.

Thus in an enlarged edition of his *Britannia* in 1594 Camden paid tribute to Carew's help, as well as to his devotion to Antony and the improvements he had made there. Carew says that he had intended only a few manuscript copies to be circulated among his friends, 'but since that time Master Camden's often mentioning this work, and my friends' persuasions, have caused my determination to alter. Besides, the state of our country [i.e. county] hath undergone so many alterations since I first began these scribblings' that it was necessary to revise the original account. This had been 'long since begun, a great while discontinued, lately reviewed, and now hastily finished'. We may take this as an exact account of how the book came to be: it is borne out by the text, some of the hundreds briefly sketched and left incomplete.

The book was 'printed by S.S. for John Jaggard . . . to be

sold near Temple Bar, at the sign of the Hand and Star.
1602'. For the first and only time Carew declared himself
author by name on the title page, and in the dedication 'by
your lordship's poor kinsman' to Ralegh as Lord Lieutenant.
'Your ears and mouth have ever been open to hear and deliver
our grievances, and your feet and hands ready to go and
work their redress, and that not only always as a magistrate
of yourself but also very often as a suitor and solicitor to
others of the highest place'.

The *Survey* lives not only as a portrait of Cornwall in
Elizabethan days but by the personality of its author, kindly
and humorous, observant and scholarly, above all human,
eye and ear always open to what is characteristic, odd or
quaint. No point in traversing the book here, Elizabethan
classic as it is: it is there for all to read. It remains for us only
to pick out some points of personal interest. His instructive
account of Cornwall's tin industry, in which the little land
led Europe, he owed to his friend Godolphin, its leader. The
equally informative account of the fishing industry is his
own, with which we have seen him officially concerned. But
fishing was his personal passion, to which he could always
resort for recreation from family griefs, or provision for the
household. For he constructed upon the river below his
house an ingenious tidal pool by which he caught fish in
large number and variety. Thus he could write, among the
verses with which his prose is sprinkled:

> I wait not at the lawyers' gates,
> Ne shoulder climbers down the stairs;
> I vaunt not manhood by debates,
> I envy not the miser's fears;
>   But mean in state, and calm in sprite,
>   My fish-full pond is my delight . . .

It is obvious how much he loved Antony—and what
wonder when one knows that exquisite place with its outlook
upon woods and waters? A set of verses again describes its
descent to him:

> which down to me
> By four descents hath run:
> All which and all their wives expressed

A turtle's single love,
And never did th'adventrous change
Of double wedding prove.

Though this was an Elizabethan commonplace, I think we may see in it a reference to Shakespeare's poem, 'The Phoenix and the Turtle', which had come out in the volume in celebration of married love, *Love's Martyr*, only the year before.

The author presents us with a nice mixture of facts—social and economic, historical and antiquarian—and folklore: he has a good ear for a story, an eye to oddity, open-mindedness about dreams and what the Cornish call 'presentiments', with less credulity than most Elizabethans. In spite of, or because of, the war the increasing prosperity of the age is evident: of the sea-coast and coastal towns, shipping and fishing, the export of tin, slate, coarse woollens and mats made of bents, even corn in years of good harvests—while Devon and Somerset men pastured their cattle on the wide spaces of the northern moors. He gives us vivid accounts of Cornish specialities and peculiarities: the two kinds of the game of hurling, the out-of-door performances of the miracle plays, wrestling, bowsening—the throwing of mad folk into ponds to shock them into their senses, the healing properties of holy wells, as to which Carew was sceptical.

His outlook was naturally that of a man of his class and time: no illusions about the people, any more than Shakespeare had. He appreciated the hardships of the tinners' toil, but—'there let us leave them, since their own will doth bring them thither'. The Cornish preferred the hazard and gamble of tin mining to the steady toil of tilling the soil. For the horticultural improvements of the time, the growing of fruits, 'though the meaner sort come short, the gentlemen step not far behind those of other parts'. He has the gentry's attitude towards self-important small townsmen, jumped-up mayors and recorders—of whom there were too many—with 'their large exemptions and jurisdictions: a garment, in divers men's opinions, over-rich and wide for many of their wearish [shrunken] and ill disposed bodies'. He was saddened by the sight of decayed antiquity—romantic vestiges of the past, like Tintagel and Restormel castles.

His affections were for his friends, his admiration for their achievements. And first of them, Sir Francis Godolphin, 'whose zeal in religion, uprightness in government and plentiful housekeeping have won him a very great and reverend reputation in his country'. This was no more than just: 'by his labours and inventions in tin matters the whole country hath felt a general benefit'. He kept some 300 people continually at work; his own works yielded at least £1000 a year to the Crown, while the increase in the customs on tin amounted to more than £10,000.

He could not omit a tribute to the most famous Cornishman of the day, Sir Richard Grenville, who 'after following the wars under the Emperor Maximilian against the great Turk and his undertaking to people Virginia and Ireland, made so glorious a conclusion in her Majesty's ship, the *Revenge*'. Carew knew him from early meetings at Bokelly and Penheale; he was hardly a friend, however: Carew may not have approved of such a fire-eater, though forced to pay tribute to his end, as a hero of the age. More to his taste would have been William Treffry of Fowey, with whom he shared antiquarian interests: 'a gentleman that hath vowed his rare gifts of learning, wisdom and courage to the good of his country [county], and to whose judicious corrections these my notes have been not a little beholden'.

Nor was it only to the gentry that Carew directed his admiration: he valued a man for his achievement. There was old Veale of Bodmin for mechanical sciences: carpenter, joiner, mill-wright, free-mason, clock-maker, carver, metalfounder, architect, 'and quid non? yea, a surgeon, physician, alchemist'. And what about the excellent medical amateur, the rector of St Ewe, who mostly 'prescribeth milk, and very often milk and apples, a course deeply subject to the exception of the best esteemed practitioners'—and wrought so many cures? His success is hardly to be wondered at, when the professionals were liable to kill one.

Carew's book received little acclaim in its own time, though he himself was generally respected; it was not reprinted, though his translation of Huarte was printed four times. But it is the antiquarian work that has survived. An historian today has justly commented that, where so many of the grander historians of the past are hardly read at all, the county historians remain indispensable. There can be few days when their works 'are not consulted by somebody, somewhere. Every subsequent generation has been indebted to these men'[7]—and each succeeding century has seen a republication of the *Survey of Cornwall*.

With the Jacobean peace with Spain in 1604 the stress of war-time duties ceased; Carew could breathe a freer air, though now his health was not good. At New Year 1605 we find him writing to Cecil, now Lord Cranborne, about the education of two boys whose wardship Lord Burghley had committed to him. These were his sister's eldest son, Richard Erisey, of that delightful old house lost in lanes towards the Lizard, and Richard Grenville, younger son of his old acquaintance, George Grenville of Penheale, who had died in 1595. 'These twain, with a younger son of mine own—all of them between fourteen and sixteen years of age—I desire to place at the university of Leyden, where I hear they may profit in learning the arts and languages and other fit qualities'. It was necessary to procure a licence to pass beyond the seas; Carew appealed to Cecil, whom he knew, for warrant to proceed.

In April he was writing to Sir Robert Cotton a letter which gives us information as to the Elizabethan Society of Antiquaries, about which little is known. Carew expressed his 'grief that my so remote dwelling depriveth me of your sweet and respected antiquarian Society, into which your kindness towards me, and grace with them, made me an entrance—and unto which, notwithstanding so long discontinuance, my longing desire layeth a continual claim'. This would seem to put its beginnings, and his earlier attendance, back into the glorious 1580s when everything began: the new poetry, the new drama, the madrigals, the challenge to Spain.

As an educated man and a writer, Carew was conscious of England's backwardness and how much leeway there was to catch up. 'It imports no little disgrace to our nation that others have so many academies, and we none at all, especially seeing we want not choice wits every way matchable with theirs, both for number and sufficiency'. This is a judgment to which Carew would return in his well-known last writing, 'The Excellency of the English Tongue'. But it was only in

the last two decades that this had become so—with Sidney
and Spenser, Marlowe, Shakespeare, Drayton and Ben
Jonson; and with some of these Carew had had some
acquaintance. Sidney he had known; Drayton was indebted
to Carew's work in his *Polyolbion*; Carew admired Shakespeare, while Ben Jonson admired *him*, speaking of a work
of his own,

> Wherein was oil, beside the succour spent,
> Which noble Carew, Cotton, Selden lent.

Camden had given a new lead to historical writing: he was
Ben Jonson's headmaster at Westminster, and Carew's
friend. Besides the writers and dramatists were the great
composers, the new beginnings in science, the intellectual
expansion adumbrated by the young Francis Bacon, whom
Carew would have heard speaking in Parliament, a new
member with himself. It is significant to observe Carew,
quite well aware, on the margin of all this.

Such was the extraordinary promise of the 1580s when,
Carew had heard, the antiquarian Society was 'likely to have
received an establishment and extraordinary favour from
sundry great personages'. We do not know who these were,
but Burghley would certainly have been sympathetic: his
interests of mind were antiquarian and he had personally
supported Christopher Saxton's enterprise in producing his
beautiful series of maps of the counties of England. The
burdens and demands of the long war had pushed these hopes
aside; now, with the peace, and 'under so learned a king,
this plant should grow to his full height than quail in the
spring'. Carew hoped that Cotton—whose famous library at
Westminster was open to scholars—would push forward the
project with the King. Unfortunately, James's learning was
largely theological, his enthusiasm for the dreary wastes of
Calvinist theology. So far from encouraging the antiquaries,
James was positively discouraging to their Society, and it
shrunk in consequence. The impulse continued with individual scholars and in their works.

One of these came out this year, 1605, Camden's *Remains
. . . concerning Britain*, fragments from the great *Britannia*,
to which he continued to add from the work of his fellow

scholars, like Carew, to whom he paid further tribute. Carew was keen that Camden should carry his studies in etymology a further stage, to a systematic enlightment as to the origins of the English language. 'It may perhaps seem a barren and distasteful subject, but surely it will prove profitable in learning the true meaning of most words by the derivation from their originals'. The Elizabethans stood at the beginning of these things; writers were becoming self-conscious about the language, its character and potentialities. Carew was aware of this, but it was not his subject: he was uncertain as to the etymologies of words, and wished Camden to 'prosecute this beginning to a thorough accomplishment'.

From his eyrie by neighbouring Plymouth he was well placed to watch the voyages now making for the New World. Meanwhile, at home the language itself was undergoing comparable expansion. 'Through teaching how—by the warrant of precedents and the rule of congruity—we may still enrich our language with others [words] of like garb . . . where yet some are directly fetched from the Latin, some by way of the French, some carry a diverse sense from that in their fountain, and on some we build others not expressible in their mother tongue'.

Carew's essay on the subject, which Camden published in the next edition of the *Remains*, in 1614, has usually been regarded as an addition to the slender stock of Elizabethan literary criticism. It is, rather, as its title shows, an essay on the language and its potentialities. Meanwhile, in his rustication, he could not but envy Camden at the centre of things: 'I must confess that I am tainted with a spark of envy, or rather applaud to his good fortune which—*beyond mine*—hath assisted his industry with the sight and use of so many antiquities and antiquarians'.

We observe the disadvantage under which he lay, in his letter to Camden next year. 'I make bold to use my thanks for your kind remembering me by Sir Anthony Rouse, as a shoeing-horn to draw on a request'. The Rouses lived not far away at Halton, a few miles up the Tamar. Sir Anthony was John Pym's step-father, with whom the future Parliamentary leader was brought up. Carew had heard that Sir John Doddridge, the Solicitor-General, had written an account of the Duchy of Cornwall as an institution: 'this I much long to see, and heartily pray by your means to obtain a copy thereof'. Carew wanted it for a second edition of his *Survey*; in the first the printer had not observed the proper order of the heraldic arms, 'suitable to your direction . . . I imagine that I may cull out of Master Solicitor's garden many flowers to adorn this other edition; and, if I wist where to find Mr Norden, I would also fain have his map of our shire, for perfecting of which he took a journey into these parts'. Alas, nothing came of the projected second edition; it was too discouraging, and Carew's sight was failing.

In 1614 appeared the Epistle on 'The Excellency of the English Tongue' to W.C., i.e. Camden. In it Carew wished to sum up the qualities of the language, as Etienne had done for French. He proceeded under four headings: Significancy, Easiness, Copiousness, and Sweetness. We need not traverse the argument; but the fact that 'we read a very short grammar'—for Elizabethan English had already lost most of its medieval inflexions—in itself indicated something of its future utility as a world language: it was simple and direct in construction. But it was rich in expression: Carew cited the appropriateness of many words to their objects; 'for example, in *moldwarp* [mole], we express the nature of that beast; in *handkercher*, the thing and his use; in *upright*, that virtue by a metaphor; in *wisdom* and *domesday*, so many sentences as words'.

He went into the richness of the language as the result of the diverse origins of its vocabulary. 'Seeing then we borrow from the Dutch [i.e. German], the Briton, the Roman, the Dane, the French, the Italian and Spaniard, how can our stock be other than exceeding plentiful?' It is curious that Camden was rather more aware of Celtic origins than Carew, who was so much closer to them in Cornwall. He was, of course, aware of the dialectical diversity of English, probably greater than in any such small extent of territory: 'we have Court and we have country English'. Even Court grandees spoke the dialect of their native area: it was said of Ralegh that 'he spake broad Devonshire to his dying day'.

Once more it is curious that Carew did not use his opportunity to master the Cornish language—in which he was very defective. In the *Survey* he had written; 'the principal love and knowledge of this language lived in Dr Kenall the civilian [i.e. civil lawyer], and with him lieth buried'. Dr Kenall had been archdeacon of Oxford, and was evidently *unus ex istibus*, one of those who haven't the strength of mind or character to write down what they know—and so it is lost. 'For the English speech doth still encroach upon it and hath driven the same into the uttermost skirts of the shire'. Perhaps, if Carew had lived in West Cornwall, he would have done better for it. As it is, his treatment shows that his conversation was naturally with his fellow country gentry; and, as a cultivated Elizabethan, it was more important to know Italian, as indeed it was.

He concludes, with a burst of Elizabethan patriotism, on the different particularities in which English is superior. He says nothing about the playwrights who were to prove the chief glory of the age and to add most to the language. He did, however, make comparisons—like Francis Meres some years before (it was a mere commonplace to do so). 'Will you read Virgil? take the Earl of Surrey. Catullus? Shakespeare, and Marlowe's fragment. Ovid? Daniel. Lucan? Spenser. Martial? Sir John Davis and others. Will you have all in all for prose and verse? take the miracle of our age, Sir Philip Sidney'.

From next year, 1615, we have a last letter (in Latin) dictated by him, to a young Scottish writer, John Dunbar, whose friendship he had made while he was stopping at Plymouth under the wing of Sir Ferdinando Gorges. Dunbar was a writer of Latin epigrams, as was Charles Fitz-Geoffrey, parson of neighbouring St Dominick, both of whom wrote the usual flowery epigrams on Carew. Young Dunbar had done Carew the kindness of introducing him to Sir Henry Spelman, whom he did not know, though both were members of the antiquarian Society—perhaps we should describe it as a circle rather than a society. In 1613 Spelman had published his scholarly book on the complicated subject of tithes. He now wished to have Carew's information on the subject, for the customs in Cornwall would have some divergences and add their own interest. Carew thereupon forwarded the tract he had written on the subject, which would be complementary to Spelman's treatise, rather than contradictory. 'We are both striving with one heart and mind to reach the goal of truth, albeit by different paths. It would

be inconsistent with the politeness of letters if a difference
of opinion produced an alienation of hearts'.

It is very appropriate that this should have been the last
expression of Carew's spirit.

For some time he had been blind; then suddenly, in this
year, he recovered his sight. His son wrote: 'God restored
him his sight again—the light appeared with such a glory,
for the day was fair and the sun shined bright'. But his health
had gone; he had indeed never been strong, subject to a
continual cough during life, and latterly the stone.
Considering this, it is surprising how much he
accomplished—evidently by careful discipline and self-
control, the regular life, for all the burdens of duty he undertook, of an achieved spirit.

One can see something of that in the portrait of him that
was painted in 1586, when he was thirty-two. There are the
fine intelligent eyes—intelligent but kind; oval face with
noble forehead, auburn hair beginning to recede; sparse beard
and moustaches. He wears a high but simple ruff, the four-
fold gold chain of a gentleman over his sober doublet. He
holds a book, with the inscription, *Invita morte vita* (he lives
in spite of death); in the upper corner the personal motto he
chose always to use, the Italian, *Chi verace durera* (he who
tells true will endure). It is characteristic, too, that he thought
of this as an anagram of his name.

His son has a corroborative character sketch of him: with
Richard Carew everything holds together, no contradictions.
'His wisdom doth well appear in his writings, his conversation so full of sweetness as was able to gain everybody's
affection; and as sure a keeper by his constant loving honesty
as an assured getter by his ever ready courtesy, it being
always his greatest desire to do good, and his greatest joy
when he could do it'.

His last days were in keeping. He told his son that he
'would willingly be sick a little before he died, that he might
learn thereby the better to leave the world'. On his last day,
6 November 1620, he went up into his study to pray, and
there they found him, knees folded under him, in his pocket
a last copy of verses—in the making of which he had often
found solace:

Full thirteen fives of years I, toiling, have o'erpassed
And in the fourteenth, weary, entered am at last.

Notes

1. Cf. my *Eminent Elizabethans, op. cit.*, 'Elizabeth I's Godson: Sir John Harrington'.
2. See 'The Elizabethan Plymouth Fishery', in my *The Little Land of Cornwall* (Alan Sutton, 1986).
3. This refers to the Plymouth Fishery dispute.
4. Cf. 'Bess of Hardwick', in my *Eminent Elizabethans, op. cit.*
5. In the West Country a mixture of earth and cow dung made stout warm walls for barns, cottages, etc—cob-walls.
6. I owe this information to my friend and surgeon, Mr R. H. C. Robins.
7. *English County Historians*, edited by Jack Simmons (EP Publishing, 1978), p. 20.

Sources

Calendar of State Papers Domestic
Acts of the Privy Council
Historical Manuscripts Commission, *Salisbury Manuscripts.*
Carew's Survey of Cornwall, with Notes by Thomas Tonkin, published by Lord de Dunstanville (1811)—fullest edn.
Richard Carew of Antony, The Survey of Cornwall etc., ed. with an Introduction by F. E. Halliday (Andrew Melrose, 1953; Adams & Dart, 1969).
G. C. Boase and W. P. Courtney, *Bibliotheca Cornubiensis*, 3 Vols. (Longmans & Co., 1874).
F. E. Halliday, *A Cornish Chronicle: the Carews of Antony from Armada to Civil War* (David & Charles, 1967).
P. L. *Hull*, 'Richard Carew's Discourse about the Duchy Suit, 1594', *Journal of the Royal Institution of Cornwall*, Part 2 (1962).
A. L. Rowse, *Tudor Cornwall, op. cit.*
—— 'The Dispute concerning the Plymouth Pilchard Fishery, 1584–91', *Economic History* (January 1932).
N. J. G. Pounds, 'William Carnsew of Bokelly and his Diary, 1576–7', *Journal of the R.I.C.*, Part 1 (1978).
J. E. Neale, *Elizabeth I and her Parliaments, 1584–1601* (Cape, 1957).

8

Sir Richard Hawkins, Last of a Dynasty

Sir Richard Hawkins wrote the best and most delightful of Elizabethan seafaring books.[1] He was also the last member of the remarkable dynasty that made Plymouth what it became in the sixteenth century: the leading port for oceanic voyages—of trade, discovery, war, privateering—into the Atlantic and beyond. In the medieval period Plymouth had a history on a par with Dartmouth, Poole or Fowey, confined mostly to cross-Channel activities and around the bay of Biscay, the western approaches. In voyages of discovery to the New World, with which the modern age begins, Bristol first took premier place. In a few decades this shifted around to the coast further west, jutting out more conveniently into the Atlantic; and in this process of putting Plymouth ahead, both in trade and in voyages of discovery, the lead was taken by the remarkable Hawkins family.

At Plymouth the popular memories—in so far as there are any today—are all of Sir Francis Drake: understandable enough, the first seaman in our history (along with Nelson), with a touch of genius and a personality to annihilate the centuries between. But he was a poor relation of the Hawkins family, who gave him his first leg-up, the opportunity of which he knew how to take fullest advantage.

Of the Hawkins family three generations produced men of mark. 'Old' William Hawkins, who flourished in the reign of Henry VIII, began it all with the first English voyages into the South Atlantic, to Guinea and Brazil—where Portuguese and Spaniards were pioneers with such historic achievements to their credit. The English were slow in starting but quick in catching up. Of 'Old' William's sons the elder, another William, carried on the family business, developing trade and the port, made remarkable voyages of his own, was mayor of Plymouth in Armada year, and so on.

The younger, Sir John, was the man to whom Elizabeth's navy owed most: he built the ships that defeated the Armada. This was his finest achievement.

> It is remarkable that in the nineteen years of the Spanish war not a single Queen's ship was lost by leakage or unsoundness of hull or gear. A very different record is provided, for example, by the War of American Independence, when several great vessels, from the *Royal George* downwards, perished from these causes, and thousands of lives were sacrificed by corruption in the dockyards.[2]

In the popular mind Sir John Hawkins is celebrated for his three slaving voyages between Guinea and the Spanish West Indies. It is important to talk sense about this. There have always been slavery and slave-trading in some part of the world. The slave trade to Spanish America had been in existence for half a century before Hawkins tried to share in it. All human societies have enslaved others; we are all descended from slaves at some time or other—my own Cornish ancestors to the invading Anglo-Saxons, as recently as the ninth or tenth century, I dare say.

Sir Richard Hawkins was the son of famous Sir John— whom he greatly admired, and rightly—and his first wife, Katherine Gonson, daughter of the previous Treasurer of the navy from whom he took over. All the Hawkinses were fervent Protestants, like Drake, and rather religious. That worldly woman, Elizabeth I, did not appreciate this side to them much; she said once, on Sir John's return from a voyage: 'God's wounds! This fellow went out a soldier and is come back a divine'. The Puritans, their fellows, she called 'the brethren in Christ'.

Richard Hawkins was born in 1560, and first appears in his uncle William's successful voyage of 1582, which returned with rich booty from Spanish captures: sugar and hides, pearls and some treasure. This was a return for the Spanish treachery in the harbour of Vera Cruz (then San Juan de Ulloa) which had overthrown his brother's third voyage and inflicted immense losses upon all who had invested in it, including the Queen. It marked a turning point. None of

the Elizabethan seamen ever forgot San Juan de Ulloa, the
hundreds of men handed over to the Inquisition, the burning
of the second-in-command, Robert Barrett of Saltash, in the
market-place at Seville (to which I have made pilgrimage to
remember him).

The West Country seamen went on and on getting their
own back. But in 1585—with the Spanish attempt to throttle
the Netherlands nearly succeeding—war with Spain opened
up in Europe too. Drake had intended to follow up his
Voyage round the World with a voyage to the East Indies,
where the spices were, but was diverted to his thundering
campaign of 1585, destroying defences and fortifications in
the West Indies and along the Spanish Main, bringing back
a vast haul of cannon. Young Hawkins commanded the little
galliot, the *Duck*. Against the Armada he was put in
command of *The Swallow*, a Queen's ship of 350 tons; two
of the small fireships, which frightened the Spanish fleet off
Calais into cutting their cables and breaking formation to get
away, were young Hawkins' property.

He was already an experienced seaman when he put in
hand the building of a ship of some 350 tons, expressly for
a voyage into the Pacific, of which the Spaniards claimed,
and enjoyed, the monopoly. Richard had it in mind to follow
in Drake's path—now a figure of world-wide fame—and
make a fortune for himself. Richard's religious mother christened the ship, *Repentance*. He tells us that,

> the *Repentance* being put in perfection and riding at Deptford, the
> Queen's Majesty passing by her to her palace of Greenwich, commanded
> her bargemen to row round about her. And, viewing her from post to
> stem, disliked nothing but her name and said she would christen her
> anew: thenceforth she should be called the *Dainty*, which name she
> brooked as well for her proportion and grace as for the many happy
> voyages she made in her Majesty's services.

Richard recounted them, and then added, 'to us, she never
brought but cost, trouble, and care'.

The Pacific project was postponed for a few years, while
the *Dainty*, serving under Frobisher, captured a big Biscayan
of 500 tons. Then Richard served under his father in 1590
keeping the seas towards the Azores and watching for the
treasure-fleet from the Indies, which escaped them. In 1592

the *Dainty* played a chief part in the capture of the *Madre de Dios*, richest of East India carracks to be taken; but of this the chief share—what was left over from the spoil and pillage of the cargo—came to the Queen.

Next year, 1593, Richard was free to renew his Pacific project, and made preparations for his expedition. Other venturers were involved, for we know that the rich London merchant, Thomas Myddleton—much engaged in privateering ventures on his own—invested £150 in Richard's enterprise. There must have been a number of others, almost certainly his father, his uncle and Drake with whom he discussed the plan and from whom he got much information and advice.

Elizabethan seafaring was not all heroics: the seamy side to it was much more to the fore. Hawkins is more informative on this than Hakluyt in the accounts he edited for his epic of achievement. It took Richard a couple of days at Plymouth to gather his company together, with the aid of his friends and two J.P.s, searching

> all lodgings, taverns, and ale-houses. For some would ever be taking their leave and never depart, some drink themselves so drunk that, except they were carried aboard, they of themselves were not able to go one step; others, knowing the necessity of the time, feigned themselves sick; others to be indebted to their hosts and forced me to ransom them—one, his chest; another, his sword; another, his shirts; another, his card and instruments for sea. And others, to benefit themselves of the imprest [advance] given them, absented themselves, making a lewd living in deceiving all whose money they could lay hold of.

Thomas Cavendish—second of English circumnavigators of the globe—told Hawkins that, when he was ready to sail, fellows who had taken their pay in advance and then deserted cost him £1500: 'these varlets within a few days after his departure I saw walking in the streets of Plymouth'. They went unpunished: '*Impunitas peccandi illecebra*'—impunity is an incitement to wrongdoing. (It is the same with delinquents at any time.)

This is an aspect of Elizabethan life familiar to those who are versed in the State Papers, which are full of it. Ordinary folk, or a large margin of them, are pretty poor stuff: this is

only a part of the difficulties persons of initiative have to put
up with from them. Hawkins mentions others;

> the ambition of many which covet the command of fleets and places
> of government—not knowing their compass, nor how, nor what to
> command—do purchase to themselves shame, and loss to them that
> employ them; being required in a commander at sea, a sharp wit [i.e. a
> clear head], a good understanding, experience in shipping, practice in
> management of sea-business, knowledge in navigation and in command.
> I hold it much better to deserve it, and not to have it, than to have it
> not deserving it.

Nothing is known of Hawkins' education, but we see from
his familiarity with Latin that, like many Elizabethans, he
had had a good schooling.

Having gathered most of his company aboard and set sail,
12 June 1593,

> I luffed near the shore to give my farewell to all the inhabitants of the
> town, whereof the most part were gathered together upon the Hoe, to
> show their grateful correspondency to the love and zeal which I, my
> father and predecessors have ever borne to that place as to our natural
> and mother town. And first with my noise of trumpets, after with my
> waits and then with my other music, and lastly with the artillery of my
> ships, I made the best signification I could of a kind farewell. This they
> answered with the waits of the town and the ordnance on the shore,
> and with shouting of voices—which the fair evening and silence of the
> night were heard a great distance off.

So they disappeared from view, over the horizon, making
south-west out into the Atlantic. There were five ships in
company: the *Dainty* herself, the *Fancy* under Captain
Tharlton, a tender which was a store-ship, and a couple of
pinnaces. Tharlton's desertion with the *Fancy*, in a storm off
the River Plate, was a prime factor in the defeat inflicted
upon Hawkins later and the overthrow of the voyage.

No account of an Elizabethan voyage is more vivid or more
readable than Hawkins', for he had a gift for writing, as we
can already discern. He seems to have written his book about
1600–2 while in prison in Spain, and was preparing it for
publication in the year of his death, twenty years later, in
1622. A full-length book, it is yet only the first half of what
he intended. He concludes thus: 'What succeeded to me and

to the rest during our imprisonment, with the rarities and particularities of Peru and Tierra firma, my voyage to Spain and the success [sequel], with the time I spent in prison in Peru, in Terceira, in Seville and Madrid, with the accidents which befell me in them, I leave for a second part of this discourse, if God give life and convenient place and rest'. What a pity it was that, when he got back to England, he devoted himself to business rather than writing! For we have thus lost what would have made an even more informative Elizabethan book.

The Observations of Sir Richard Hawkins is, however, unique as we have it, giving us not only an account of the voyage but 'a fuller picture of life at sea than is to be found in any other Elizabethan work'. Besides that it is a prime document of Elizabethan seamanship, based on practical experience, full of sailing directions for both the Atlantic and the Pacific, written to instruct others as to what to do and what to avoid—for Hawkins was exceptionally candid about his own mishaps and mistakes. Its language is fresh and Elizabethan, full of sea-lore and sea-terms, and some fascinating words that have gone out. The word 'fenoed',[3] for instance, means mouldy, as applied to meal or bread. That word remains in West Country dialect in the form 'vinny'; I recall it from my childhood.

We begin with descriptions of the Atlantic islands, their geography, climate, people, products and fruits. Everything is fresh-minted and new. Here is the Elizabethan sailor's happy encounter with bananas—one can imagine with what satisfaction after a diet of salt meat, hard tack and fenoed meal.

In the top of the tree is his fruit, which groweth in a great bunch in the form of puddings. They are of divers proportions, some round, some square, some triangle; most ordinarily of a span long, with a thick skin that peeleth easily from the meat, which is either white or yellow, and very tender like butter. No conserve is better, nor of a more pleasing taste; for I never have seen any man to whom they have bred mislike, or done hurt with eating much of them, as of other fruits.

Elizabethans were very experimental in what they ate on these voyages, and men died from eating poisonous fruits.

Hawkins gives the commonsense direction that what beasts and birds will eat will commonly be harmless to men.

Coconuts: 'the shells of these nuts are much esteemed for drinking cups; much cost and labour is bestowed upon them in carving, graving and garnishing them with silver, gold and precious stones'. Many of these objects still remain from the Renaissance, garnished with silver or mother of pearl, rimmed with gold, stems of silver-gilt, patterned and enchased. 'In these islands are civet-cats, esteemed for the civet they yield and carry about them in a cod in their hinder parts, which is taken from them by force'. The musky smell of civet was immensely estimated in the Renaissance world, with all the strong smells about them. 'The courtier's hands are perfumed with civet', Shakespeare tells us; or, 'Give me an ounce of civet, good apothecary, to sweeten my imagination'.

One gets a glimpse of the Elizabethan mentality from what mariners would do to sharks. Hawkins has various bits of information, not otherwise recorded, about Sir Richard Grenville, whom he would have known. 'In the *Tiger*, when Sir Richard Grenville went to people Virginia, a shark cut off the leg of one of the company sitting in the chains [i.e. out over the ship's side] and washing himself'. Sailors hated sharks and, to revenge themselves,

> at the tail of one they tied a great log of wood, at another an empty *batizia* [jar] well stopped; one they yoked like a hog; from another they plucked out his eyes and so threw him into the sea. In catching two together they bound them tail to tail, and so set them a-swimming; another with his belly slit and his bowels hanging out, which his fellows would have every one a snatch at: with other infinite inventions to entertain the time and to avenge themselves.

All life preys upon all other life: Elizabethans had no liberal illusions.

Hawkins had no illusions about sailors either. 'Mariners are like to a stiff-necked horse which, taking the bridle betwixt his teeth, forceth his rider to what him list: so they, having once concluded and resolved, are with great difficulty brought to yield to the reins of reason'. Ships were as much endangered by careless workmanship. In the *Dainty* 'the calkers had left a seam uncalked which, being filled up with pitch only, the sea labouring that out, had been sufficient to have sunk her in short space, if it had not been discovered in time'. The big Queen's ship, the *Ark Royal*, had been put in danger at her first going to sea 'by a trivet-hole left open in the post and covered only with pitch'.

Pitch evidently covered a multitude of sins, for one fool on board, heating pitch in the cook-room, set the ship on fire; 'as the pitch began to run so the fire to enlarge itself that in a moment a great part of the ship was on a light fire'. It was with difficulty extinguished; 'let all men take example by us, not to suffer in any case pitch to be heated in the ship . . . nor to permit fire to be kindled but upon mere necessity, for the inconvenience thereof is, for the most part, remedi-less'. Addiction to drink we still have with us, as seamen's vocational disease; but northerners were apt 'in coming to fight, to drink themselves drunk. Yea, some are so mad that they mingle powder with wine to give it the greater force, imagining that it giveth spirit, strength, and courage, and taketh away all fear and doubt. The latter is for the most part true, but the former is false and beastly, and altogether against reason'.

One advantage the Spaniards had was in their temperance; another was in their better discipline. English individualism meant that the men were headstrong and many voyages were overthrown by the ships' companies insisting on turning back, or threatening mutiny. Hawkins had difficulty in persuading his men to hold on course: several times they tried to get him to turn back. He was evidently good at persuading them, himself determined not to give up; but it was at the cost of a certain forbearance, kindliness in his nature, which made him a friendly commander, less effective than the previous generation. He had not the toughness of his austere father, nor the magic touch of Drake with his men. (A Spanish prisoner of Drake's said that they all adored him.)

The desertion of the *Fancy* off the river Plate was a serious blow: her presence at the sea-fight in the bay of Atacames would certainly have tipped the balance. Hawkins blamed himself for putting Tharlton in command: 'I was worthy to be deceived that trusted my ship in the hands of an hypocrite, which had left his General before in the like occasion and in

the self-same place'. Here was another of the hazards of
Elizabethan voyaging—and not only Elizabethan, witness
Anson's Voyage[4] or the mutiny of the *Bounty*. Both Magellan
and Drake had had to execute a man who would have overthrown the voyage rather than attempt the Straits and out
into the unknown.

Hawkins' account of the Straits of Magellan—with their
twists and turns like a river, broadening then narrowing, the
few people they sighted, the relics of the Spanish posts that
had been placed there to keep interlopers out—is the most
readable I know. The first half of the navigation, a south-
westerly and due southerly course, was less hazardous,
except that it was uncharted and unknown. Then the channel
turned north-west, the Long Reach narrowing, mountainous
cliffs on either side. At one point the *Dainty* stuck on a
sunken rock: 'had not the wind just failed she would have
gone to pieces, leaving the survivors to the fate of Sarmiento's
Spaniards'. They lightened the ship of the wood they had
gathered; when the tide rose, she floated free without a
leak. But it had been a narrow escape; Richard invoked
Providence, but 'old John Hawkins knew how to build ships
as well as any man in England, and we may guess that the
skill lavished on the fleet that conquered the Armada had not
been spared in turning out the *Dainty* for his son'.[5]

The season in which it was possible to pass through the
Straits was a short one; the greatest difficulty of all was
getting out at the western end, for the wind mostly came
from the west and blew ships back within sight of the outlet.
Drake, as usual, had been exceptionally lucky, and made the
shortest passage of a century—in sixteen days. John Davis,
an equally skilled navigator, was held up for three months,
and just cleared the entrance when the wind blew him straight
back: he never made it. Hawkins was held up for over a
month going to and fro, then the wind suddenly favoured
him and he slipped out.

He was in the Spanish preserve of the Pacific, the vast
South Sea, with its unknown lands and a suspected continent,
Terra Australis, from all of which Spain was determined to
keep everybody out. The English were not going to sit down
under this sentence of exclusion; to the Spaniards they were
all pirates. They were not: this was wartime: they were priva-

teers, with a perfectly good right to exact retribution for
losses inflicted on them—for example, the immense losses
inflicted on Hawkins' father at San Juan de Ulloa. Neither
he nor Drake ever forgot it; and both sailed with the Queen's
commission to recoup themselves. Richard Hawkins has a
proper passage making clear the distinction between privateers and mere pirates, too often neglected today by mere
academics who wish to downgrade Elizabethan achievements. This is no reason why we should accept the enemy's
nomenclature for our seamen.

Hawkins pays proper tribute to Spanish achievements,
especially in the navigational improvements they had made
in their Pacific shipping, adapting it to the wind-system off
the coast of South America so that their ships could sail close
to the wind—in effect, the weatherliness and speed of these
ships, as he found to his cost: largely made since Drake's
pioneer intrusion into that sphere.

Drake had had the supreme advantage of surprise: this was
thrown away for Hawkins by the insistence of his ship's
company on immediate pillage.

> I purposed not to discover myself upon this coast till we were past
> Lima; but my company urged me so far that—except I should seem in
> all things to overbear them, in not condescending to that which in the
> opinion of all but myself seemed profitable and best—I could not but
> yield unto, though it carried a false colour [excuse], as the end proved.
> For it was our perdition. This all my company knoweth to be true,
> whereof some are yet living, and can give testimony.

Hawkins adds the moral to be drawn, for the benefit of
others: 'but the mariner is ordinarily so carried away with
the desire of pillage as sometimes, for very appearances of
small moment, he loseth his voyage and many times himself'.

This was what happened now; for their attacks on shipping
before they got clear of the port of Lima (Callao), advertised
their presence on the coast. In one big ship coming from
Concepcion they took a good quantity of gold, and in a first
encounter with the ships sent out to stop them they had the
best of it and managed to get away. The Spanish were alerted
to put everything into rounding them up—as the British
Admiralty put everything into rounding up the *Bismarck*. A
small armada was got together, sufficient to deal with the

Dainty. When it was sighted the crew were sure that it was the treasure-fleet, wrongly of course: 'the common sort of seamen, apprehending a conceit in their imaginations [i.e. getting an idea into their heads], neither experience, knowledge, examples, reasons nor authority can alter or remove them from their conceited [fixed] opinions'. Of course, they were full of fight, and carried the usual Elizabethan cargo of boastfulness.

'The Gunner, for his part assured me that, with the first tier of shot, he would lay the one of them in the sods; and our pinnace, that she would take the other to task. One promised that he would cut down the mainyard, another that he would take their flag'. They insisted on fighting—against overwhelming odds, for they were now down to some seventy-five men against several hundred in the Spanish ships. The sheer fighting spirit of English seamen has always been their chief asset—in the eighteenth century, for example, often against superior French ships. When it came to battle the men gave a good account of themselves. 'Our Master, Hugh Cornish—who was a most sufficient man for government and valour, and well saw the errors of the multitude— used his office as became him, and so did all those of best understanding'.

When they closed for action, it was found that the master gunner had let them down: 'our stern pieces were unprimed, and so were all those which we had to leeward, save half one in the quarter, which discharge wrought that effect in our contraries [opponents] as that they had five or six foot water in hold before they suspected it'. The master gunner had assured Hawkins that he had five hundred cartridges in readiness; when, 'within one hour's fight we were forced to occupy three persons only in making and filling cartridges. . . . Few of our pieces were clear when we came to use them, and some had the shot first put in after the powder'. Hawkins rightly takes the blame home to himself for this negligence, for one can never wholly trust inferiors: they may get it right, or they may not—one has to see to it oneself. One cannot imagine Drake or Hawkins' father being so easy-going and not seeing to things themselves.

All the same, when it came to fighting, especially hand to hand, the men fought like devils; but, though the contest went on for three days, Hawkins could never get clear from the ships that hemmed him in. 'The third day, our sails being torn, our masts all perished, our pumps rent and shot to pieces, our ship with fourteen shot under water and seven or eight foot of water in hold; many of our men being slain . . . the enemy offering still to receive us *a buena guerra* and to give us life and liberty and embarkation for our country' . . . There was nothing for it but surrender, before the ship sank. Hawkins himself was wounded, nineteen of his men killed, nearly forty wounded—only a handful remained unhurt. The terms of surrender were good: life and liberty, return to England; for the Spaniards were much taken with the *Dainty*: they reported their capture, 'a ship of 400 tons, most beautiful in all her parts'.

Hawkins was carried aboard the Spanish flagship, to be received by a noble gentleman, Don Beltran de Castro 'with great courtesy and compassion, even with tears in his eyes, and commanded me to be accommodated in his own cabin, where he sought to cure and comfort me the best he could. The like he used with all our hurt men, six and thirty at least'. Don Beltran gave his word of honour that Hawkins should be returned, and all the ransom he would exact would be a couple of greyhounds for himself and another for his brother, the Conde de Lemes. Thirty of the Englishmen were sent to Spain, and held prisoners for some time, though most got back to England. Two of them escaped, and reached Plymouth with their ill news. But the higher authorities would not allow Don Beltran to honour his word: Hawkins knew too much and, a young man of thirty-three, might well lead another expedition into their South Sea, the more dangerous for having learned from experience. He was held prisoner for nearly ten years.

It broke his life in half.

For the first three or four letters Hawkins was held captive in Peru—so that he is able to tell us a good deal about conditions in South America, the undying hatred of the Arancanian Indians of Chile for the Spaniards, for example. He gives us new information about the first and most promising English venture across the Isthmus to the Pacific, that of John Oxenham, and how it was destroyed by the folly of his infatuation for a Spanish lady whom he captured. (Neither of the Hawkinses, nor Drake, would have been undone that way.)

In 1597 Hawkins was sent back to Spain—and had a narrow escape from rescue. For Essex was at sea with a large fleet, the Azores expedition on the look-out for the treasure-fleet. He just missed it, and the treasure ships were able to take shelter under the guns of impregnable Terceira. Hawkins managed to smuggle a letter away to the Earl in England in October, in which he said politely, 'well do I know that if you had been amongst the fifteen ships which had us in the midst of them . . . I had been your prisoner, with 12 millions that came in six ships of 250 and 300 tons apiece'. These were fast gallezebras, specially built for a quick Atlantic crossing. Hawkins says, 'but God delivered them, otherwise see I not how it was possible for them to have escaped'. This fiasco does not say much for Essex's seamanship or capacity for command: one cannot think that Drake would have let them slip through.

Hawkins besought Essex to get the Queen to intervene for his deliverance, and was not to cease to besiege Queen, Privy Council, Essex, Robert Cecil, with letters for the next five years. Though the Spaniards honoured the terms of submission for everyone else of his company, they were not letting go of him: he was much too valuable. 'Till my imprisonment I had whereof to sustain my estate, and to give and lend to others, and therefore could not frame myself to beg of her Majesty'. Yet his services, 'performed with continual toil and hazard of my life' were 'without penny pay or recompense in any of them'. Their poor relation, Drake, had made a fortune; the well-to-do Hawkinses lost, on the whole, by their services to the Crown. This would be the signature tune of many a letter indited by Richard from his various prisons. He closed from Terceira, 'I write not more largely, for not being able. This I have done by stealth and in continual fear, and am forced abruptly to end'.

He was taken to the prison of the Contratacion, the grand depôt for the Indies, at Seville. The next we hear from him is a fascinating account of his attempted escape, which he smuggled out to Essex in August next year. It reads like something out of Le Sage's picaresque novel, *Gil Blas*, and has never been cited.[6] We may recall, what Hawkins tells us elsewhere, that his father—who had been a servant of King Philip during Queen Mary's reign—had been taken prisoner in their French war. At the treaty of peace the prisoners were overlooked and no terms made for them. The French demanded a ransom of 10,000 crowns for John Hawkins, which would have ruined him, had he not broken prison and escaped. Richard was once more trying to take a leaf out of his father's book—who had set aside £3000 in his will for his son's ransom in case he should be captured.

> A few days past, being desperate of my liberty by justice due unto me, I contrived with one Captain Borgen, my fellow prisoner, to break prison. We were to go out at the roof of the prison at midnight, and then to strike ourselves down by a rope, which was such as we could get and so small, and the prison so high, that in sliding down I fell more than four fathoms. Wherewith Captain Borgen, being dismayed, durst not follow me, thinking me to be dead in the street. . . . Though I lay without feeling a good space, at length I recovered breathing, and after feeling my legs to be sound, I began first to go [i.e. walk] and after to run, as your lordship may imagine, never looking behind me till I was outside the gates of the city, guided by a servant of mine which waited for me in the street.

A gentleman of well-known name and status, Hawkins always had a servant of one sort or another to wait on him, by whom he managed to get messages or letters out of the country.

The two of them took the Lisbon road; but shortly 'the hue-and-cry, which they call the Hermandad, was made after me, the city and country in an uproar, and large reward promised to him that could discover me'. Two leagues out of the city they hid in a vineyard, 'minding not to stir in many days but in the owl light. But at noon came the keepers, or owners, of the vineyard and found us sleeping. Who, fatigating us with interrogatories, put me in jealousy [fear] to be discovered'. Hawkins was in sailor's garments and evidently spoke Spanish well by this time. He decided to cross the highway and make up into the country.

Crossing the highway they ran into four men, Moriscos or mulattos, who were unarmed. They asked if the couple were those who had broken prison, for four men on horseback were coming along the road searching for them. If

they were those who had escaped, they should hide at once.
Hawkins was afraid to give himself away by doing so, until
they were out of sight; when two horsemen caught up with
them, who gave the alarm, 'Here they be'. They once more
took cover among vineyards and olive gardens, till they had
run out of breath. Hawkins concealed himself up in an olive
tree, his servant in a bramblebush. Till sunset the whole force
searched the area, men several times passing under Richard's
tree without discovering him (like Charles II in his oak tree
after the battle of Worcester), until by chance they happened
upon the servant, whom they beat up. He, 'being a white-
livered fellow, brought them to the tree where I was'; they
levelled their pieces at him to force him down. 'In fine, I fell
again into the hands of thieves, for they took from me all
that I had but the clothes on my back and—what grieved me
most—a rapier and dagger dedicated to your lordship many
months before'.

Hawkins was haled back to prison, but now to a dungeon
in the common jail, put in irons day and night, 'and in that
necessity and misery which words cannot paint. . . . In four
years and more they never gave me one rial to sustain me,
and now they have not only taken from me the money which,
by friendship, I had procured—to be repaid by my wife upon
exchange, but my apparel, and what I had, saving the clothes
on my back'. And now, instead of Don Beltran's
greyhounds, they required for ransom nine cannon of those
Essex had from Cadiz, i.e. 35,000 ducats worth, and 'except
I free them they say I shall never have my liberty. I have no
hope of freedom but in the Queen and yourself'. He did not
forget to put in a word also for 'the rest of your servitors
here in prison, who make daily prayers for you'.

Meanwhile, both Drake and Richard's father had died on
their last unlucky expedition to the West Indies, and been
buried at sea. Sir John Hawkins left a widow, his second
wife, who was co-executrix of his will along with Richard.
Richard's wife took up the cudgels on his behalf, for his step-
mother dragged her feet in paying over the £3000 Sir John
had provided in case of need for his son. Letters passed
to and fro, with all the delays imposed by Sir Richard's
imprisonment. From these we learn that Sir John had left
only some £10,000, after founding and providing for his

hospital for decayed seamen at Chatham. Lady Hawkins said that he had set up Richard with lands worth £140 a year, while she had paid out £1250 towards payment of the soldiers and sailors in the voyage upon which Sir John died.[7]

More surprising than the numbers who were killed, or died of disease, or were eaten by sharks, are those that returned after such adventures from the other side of the world. In 1599 a returned prisoner from Hawkins' company got back via Spain, from which he reported that he could give information about Sir William Stanley—the traitor who had betrayed Deventer to the Spaniards—and other converts. A servant of Hawkins came out of Spain to St Jean de Luz, got passage in a French boat which was driven by storm into Le Croisic, whence he went overland to St Malo, bearing letters for the Privy Council, Lady Hawkins and others. At New Year 1600 we hear of another servant, of the common West Country name of Tucker, who had been familiar with one Walpole, tailor to the English College at Seville. Next Year Thomas Myddelton reports that a man of Hawkins' company had come from the South Sea, via Spain, with letters forwarded by a kindly friar; Myddelton would send him down to Richard's disconsolate wife at Plymouth.

Richard had married a West Country girl, Judith Hele, and had one child before he left. Here was the burden of his petition to the Queen in 1599, from the common prison at Madrid to which he had been moved: eight years of separation from wife and child, seven of these in prison. He knew that exchanges of prisoners were being made, and negotiations for peace discussed; he was afraid of being forgotten. No likelihood of that, it was rather that he, a Hawkins, was a special case.

Information as to Flemings who had followed in his path to the coast of Peru came back from Thomas Gray, who had been captured with him and was repatriated from Spain. No hope for Hawkins, though various prisoners in England put themselves forward for exchange: Hortensio Spinola for one, a Spanish friar named Cardinas for another. They were not on his level: he would have to pay the full ransom expected. In 1600 he was writing to Thomas Edmonds, Secretary to the Queen for the French tongue, citing his father's case at the peace with France and hoping that he would not be

overlooked in any peace negotiations. Similarly he pleaded
his case with Sir Henry Neville, the ambassador in Paris. He
had surrendered on the General's promise of liberty—after
most of his men had been slain or hurt, and himself received
several wounds. Most of his people had been freed long ago:
he was kept prisoner lest he returned to that coast. Would
the ambassador make representations to the Queen through
some person of Antonio Pérez' house? This was Philip II's
ex-Secretary of State, a familiar at Essex House and to all
that circle.[8]

Hawkins was kept in the common jail at Madrid, a
dungeon 14 feet wide, with four or five common fellows—
not like the courtesy Spanish prisoners of status received in
England. In 1600 he heard that Cecil was appointed to treat
for peace; he thanked him for the efforts already made on
his behalf. At last, as peace drew nearer, a member of the
Spanish government took up his case on the ground that it
was contrary to Spain's honour to detain him, when he
had surrendered on the promise of being given his liberty.
Meanwhile, at Plymouth his employees were making away
with his goods; his house was used by the corporation to
keep Spanish prisoners in.

We learn from the town archives in 1602 that he returned
'the week before Christ-tide'—we note the Puritan inflexion
of the phrase. Puritanism had made strides in the towns in
the last decade. A few references to the years before he left
remain in the documents—as I remember going through them
in the basement below the old Guildhall, totally destroyed
in the German *Blitz* on Plymouth in 1941. In the year before
the Armada the Corporation had paid him £12 for a silver
cup given to Sir Walter Ralegh, Lord Warden of the Stannaries (i.e. the tin jurisdictions) of Devon and Cornwall. In
1590–1 Richard Hawkins and James Bagge had been fined
6s 8d for coming late to the mayor-choosing on St Lambert's
day. In Hawkins' long absence of nearly ten years James
Bagge had advanced mightily. A newcomer, he put that right
by marrying a Fortescue and, full of energy and ambition,
was on the way to becoming 'the bottomless Bagge' of West
Country folklore: Sir James Bagge of Saltram, able to challenge the primacy the Hawkins family had enjoyed in
Plymouth for three generations.

It was a rather different Richard Hawkins who returned to Plymouth after a decade: no longer the youth and forward-looking promise with which he had set out in Drake's foot-steps in 1593. Moreover, his circumstances had changed: from being a rather well-off young man, he was now a rather poor middle-aged one. In addition to the total loss of his voyage and the very large ransom, heavy expenses had piled up during his imprisonment, with nothing coming in. He would need to be a sharp man to recover ground, if at all; and understandably, he had developed the habit of complaining.

He put in a petition for his losses to be considered in the peace negotiations in hand: he rated his father's at San Juan de Ulloa at a round £100,000, his own at £30,000. Even since the arrival of the Spanish ambassador, Myddelton and Hawkins, partners in a trading voyage to San Domingo, had had a loss of £1500. They had sent out a pinnace with a cargo of goods; their men had been invited on land to trade, then set upon, men killed, their goods made away with. His estate impoverished, he was unable to live as his forefathers had lived.

At first all looked well enough. A Hawkins was back again in the town to take the lead; he was chosen mayor for 1603–4, and one of its members for the Parliament of that year. While in London he was one of several hundreds knighted by King James in the garden at Whitehall—clearly inflation was setting in for such things. For his services in Parliament the Corporation paid him for eighty-seven days at 6s 8d a day, £29. (His fellow M.P., James Bagge received £40.) His wife, Judith, involved him in a spot of trouble. The new mayor and his wife had been employees of the Hawkinses. 'Lady Hawkins, disdaining to sit below one that had been her maid, endeavoured to keep the upper hand—which the other attempting, the Lady gave her a box on the ear'. Then the fat was in the fire. We find Sir Richard involved in a suit against the town, and having to give it a house in Market Street for satisfaction. The family moved out of town to live on their country manor at Slapton. Things were not on such a neighbourly footing as of old. James Bagge remained on the spot.

Hawkins resumed his office as Vice-Admiral for Devon, but when he had a servant of the Lord Admiral's arrested for piracy, Bagge, mayor in 1606, reported that the man was known to be no pirate; Hawkins was doing his lordship dishonour in the West Country. Bagge hoped that this latest indiscretion would result in his removal, and 'cause him to lay down his patent at your lordship's feet'. Obviously Bagge wanted his job.

There were other signs of trouble. One of the Plymouth Parkers made dissension between Hawkins and Sir Ferdinando Gorges, an Essex follower who had now—after burning but his fingers in the Essex rebellion—been allowed to return as governor of the fort at Plymouth. Hawkins did not forget his old companions in distress: he wrote up a testimonial to Captain Luff: 'I was an eye-witness and partner in his calamity'.

From 1605 we have a quantity of long detailed letters to Cecil, now Lord Salisbury, Lord Admiral Nottingham, and the Privy Council about naval matters and privateering in the Channel. Hawkins had been urged to make representations against 'the hard intreaty which our countrymen receive generally in the Spanish dominions, contrary to that was expected and far worse than when, for the same, we took occasion to war against them'. Peace had been made, but this did not mean peace in the Channel. The declared war between the Dutch States and Spain continued, the Channel was alive with Dunkirkers, privateers from that port.

> There rides at this instant [1 February 1605] in Cawsand Bay a rich prize, which was taken about Portsmouth laden with Spaniards' goods . . . I beseech you that some direction may be given that all the country may take knowledge what they are to do in such case. For it has been alledged unto me that the Spaniard has no open war with the States, and we, being friend to both, ought to be indifferent [i.e. impartial]. And how can we be indifferent if we take either of their goods and deliver it to their enemy?

Prize-law and custom left wide margins for error—and taking the law into one's own hands for profit in those times. We cannot go into these matters in detail, but we can see that Hawkins would get challenged either for arresting ship or man for piracy, or for not pursuing the matter and letting them off—for a consideration. He was delated by Bagge to the Lord Admiral for the former. Perhaps that made him

more remiss in his duty; but it was the latter that eventually
got him into serious trouble. He was accused by one Bouillon
of Jersey of 'my neglect of justice in apprehending such as
had piratically robbed him, and for privity to the escape of
a prisoner. At all times when he has come to me, either
myself in person or my officers have gone, ridden, laboured
and written for him, without one penny charge unto him.
By my means he has recovered a great part of his goods'. . . .
Then comes the gramophone record: 'I have served this
Crown and your honours [the Privy Council] twenty-two
years in command by sea and land, during all which time
this most honourable senate never had any just complaint
against me'. May be, hitherto; Richard could always write
plausibly, but complaints began to accumulate after his return
from Spain. Bouillon said that he had received only £200
worth of his goods, a small portion of the whole; the rest
had been made away with. Tenaciously he pursued his case
and hung on to Hawkins' heels.

At Plymouth Hawkins had an inveterate enemy in Bagge,
who laid informations against him to the Lord Admiral. In
reply Sir Richard procured a testimonial from the mayor
and aldermen. Bagge had his supporters, who complained of
Hawkins' conduct not only of his business as Vice-Admiral
but of 'his general miscarriage towards all in the place where
he lives . . . whereby the gentleman, we hear, is drawn into
great troubles and likely to be undone'. On the contrary, his
supporters testified: 'We know his carriage here where he
lives to be so well deserving of us, we cannot charge him to
have deserved the least ill of us, unless in standing too much
upon the Lord Admiral's jurisdictions here amongst us'. We
might gather from that reflection that Plymouth folk rather
favoured more laxity in the conduct of his office—and we
should not be far wide of the mark. West Country people
expect to enjoy some advantage from their proximity to the
sea and do not appreciate too rigorous an application of the
law to their doings, whether in regard to smuggling or
winking an eye at where goods may come from. Sir Richard
would naturally share their point of view; the testimonial
itself might be held to encourage him to go easy on
delinquents.

His next report to the Privy Council—enormously long,

almost a booklet in itself—gives us an insight into the difficulties of administering his office and the disputes and quarrels to which it led. He had arrested a chest of sugar from a pirate ship riding at Cawsand, 'purposing to proceed with the parties according to justice. I had scarce entered my house in Plymouth when I was certified that James Bagge, late Mayor, had assembled a multitude to consult how they might repossess themselves of the sugar'. They broke open the cellar where it was stored, while Bagge's men made formal proclamation: 'Know all men, and we require you in the King's name and my Lord Admiral's, that you take notice that Sir Richard Hawkins is not Vice-Admiral, but that Mr Christopher Harris and Mr James Bagge of Plymouth be vice-admirals'.

When Hawkins repossessed himself of the sugar, on landing from his boat he was met by the mayor and Bagge at the head of a crowd, and the renewed proclamation: 'Oyez! Mr Mayor and you, Mr Justice Bagge, vice-admiral, I require you in the King's name and the Lord Admiral's that you apprehend Sir Richard Hawkins and all his company!' There were now two parties in Plymouth: Hawkins had 'the better sort of the shire' with him, while the popular party in the town aimed at forcing him out of his office. So also did the Lord Admiral's agent, one Jobson (suitably named) who 'has caused me to be sifted upon my oath in the Court of Admiralty and continues suit against me only to force me to surrender my place'.

Evidently Jobson had secured Hawkins' temporary sequestration from office, for Sir Richard stated that Jobson had 'gathered into his hands of that which belongs to me more than I have received in all the time of my vice-admiralty'. This was a tell-tale admission: it gave colour to the complaints that he was hand in glove with the piratical persons who used the roadstead at Cawsand—on the Cornish coast at the western entrance to Plymouth Bay, a convenient smuggling resort through the centuries. He concluded with an appeal which also told its own tale: 'my poverty and weak means cannot bear the indignation of a peer in so great authority'. He had lost the favour of the Lord Admiral.

To all this was now added a further complaint to that of Bouillon, which was proceeding on its tangled way through the Court of Admiralty, letters, protests, replications on the part of Hawkins. One Guérin, another French merchant, had a similar case to put—of Hawkins having failed to bring the depredators upon his goods to book, in order to share in the spoil. These were not the good old days of war-time, when all was free for the taking. These were the years of the Jacobean peace—and Hawkins, like Ralegh, was a belated Elizabethan. Ralegh was in the Tower, and in a year or two Sir Richard would be laid by the heels. For the French ambassador weighed in heavily on behalf of the injured merchants and—in spite of Sir Richard's offer of large resti-tution, which bespoke his guilt—he once more found himself in prison.

For a couple of years he had tried to brave it out, and stave off retribution, in the contemporary manner. He protested to Lord Salisbury at having to dance continual attendance upon the Council to support his reputation, another expense in itself. Indeed he protested too much; in the end he had to confess his error, pay a fine and submit to a spell in prison. This did not seem to damage his reputation. Elizabethan persons were accustomed to such *contretemps*; many of the best people saw the inside of a prison once, if not more, in their lives. Had not Queen Elizabeth herself been put in the Tower? Nor did Hawkins think himself particularly guilty in the matter; he confessed to his 'error'. What was more important was the incidence of a fine, in his circumstances no longer prosperous. In a final letter to his old patron Salisbury, in 1610, he admits only as much as to say, 'what I once thought justifiable myself do now condemn for error, and in all humbleness fly to the seat of mercy. If my fault have not clean blotted out the merit of my former well-deserving, and so deprived me the hope of any recompense, let it and my inability to satisfy the fine imposed upon me, my estate being almost spent in the service of the commonwealth . . .'. It is likely that his fine was remitted; he was soon out of prison, and continued as Vice-Admiral of Devon.

There are no notices of further troubles, but of further employment, and hopes for command, at sea. As late as 1614 a project was put foward for another voyage through the Straits of Magellan and across the Pacific, and Hawkins was still willing to go. This came from the East India Company, which was a sequel to Drake's original attempt to open up the spice trade with the East Indies to the English. The voyage was to make across the Pacific to the Solomon Islands, which mesmerised the minds of Spaniards and English alike, for they were thought to be abounding in gold. Hawkins was designated leader of the expedition, as a man 'held to be of courage, art and knowledge' for the enterprise. He offered to raise £20,000 from himself and his friends; negotiations continued for some six months, and then the project was dropped.

Three years later his name was again proposed as commander of the Company's next fleet to the Indies. He was growing old for so long and taxing on assignment; a younger man was appointed in his stead. Three years later again he was not too old to go as Vice-Admiral of a fleet to subdue the Algerine pirates who were now preying upon commerce not only in the Bay of Biscay and the Atlantic, but even in the Channel. The long Jacobean peace had allowed the navy to decay and the menace to grow. Hawkins was at sea again in the last year of his life, but the expedition failed of its purpose: the navy was now 'incapable of dealing with the pirate ports as Drake and Howard had dealt with Cadiz of old'.[9]

In the spring of 1622 Hawkins was back in England, once more frustrated; in April he died, a newsletter remarked, 'of vexation'. On the 16th April Sir Richard made his will, 'being sick and weak of body, but of perfect mind and memory'. He was no longer a rich man, after the losses he had endured. Only the manor of Poole at Slapton and a certain amount of house property in Plymouth remained. This was to go to his widow Judith for life—she died seven years later—afterwards to the eldest son John. The three daughters received modest dowries: two of them £120 each; the eldest Margaret, called after her grandmother, £100—since the old lady had previously bequeathed her £100 and a jewel worth £20. The family property did not continue in its possession for long. Son John parted with what he had in Plymouth before the Civil War; the manor out at Slapton was lost to the family after that upheaval.

Though the name and descendants continued, Sir Richard

was effectively the end of the eminent dynasty that had done so much to make Plymouth—apart even from what his father had achieved in building the Elizabethan navy.

Sir Richard himself lives for us, a more real and sympathetic figure of a man, by his book, *The Observations*, which he was preparing for publication at the time of his death; it had to be seen through the press by another hand. The book received a singular transformation in the Victorian age: it became the basis upon which Charles Kingsley built his *Westward Ho!* 'The good ship *Rose* of Amyas Leigh is in effect the *Dainty* of Sir Richard Hawkins, and the *Rose*'s fight with the *Madre Dolorosa* is conducted as Sir Richard would have wished his own battle to have been, had all things not gone wrong'.[10] Kingsley adapted his Elizabethan seamanship and sea-warfare from the *Observations*; names and characters reappear, but how much transmogrified!

Historical novels raise an awkward problem for the historian: if he is immersed in his period, he is apt to find the novelist's view of it unsatisfactory, anachronistic or downright false to the period and the people. As an uncritical schoolboy, early in this century, I swallowed *Westward Ho!* with zest. As a critical historian I find Kingsley's view of the Elizabethan age through Victorian spectacles distasteful, and his Victorian moralism intolerable, quite out of key with the age, which had its own, tougher morality, without many illusions. In reformed old age, in the later twentieth century, I would far rather read *The Observations of Sir Richard Hawkins* than read *Westward Ho!* again.

Notes

1. *The Observations of Sir Richard Hawkins*, ed. J. A. Williamson (Argonaut Press, 1933).
2. *Ibid.*, p. xliii.
3. Elizabethans would have pronounced it 'fennied', or 'vennied'.
4. Cf. my *The Byrons and Trevanions* (Weidenfeld and Nicolson, 1978) Ch. 8.
5. Williamson, *op. cit.*, p. lxv.
6. *Salisbury Mss.*, VIII. 289ff.
7. In her letters Lady Hawkins regularly refers to Sir John as 'Mr Hawkins'; cf. Thomas Thorp's dedication of Shakespeare's Sonnets to 'Mr W. H.', i.e. Sir William Harvey.

5353333333

302   Court and Country

8. He is caricatured as Don Adriano de Armado in *Love's Labour's Lost*.
9. Williamson, *op. cit.*, pp. lxxxvii–lxxxviii.
10. *Ibid.*, p. xc.

Sources

Calendars of State Papers Domestic.
Historical Manuscripts Commission, *Salisbury Manuscripts.*
Acts of the Privy Council.
R. N. Worth, ed., *Plymouth Municipal Records*
C. W. Bracken, *A History of Plymouth*
J. A. Williamson, ed., *The Observations of Sir Richard Hawkins, op. cit.*
K. R. Andrews, ed., *English Privateering Voyages to the West Indies* (Hakluyt Society, 1959).

Index